365 Days of Yes

365 Days of Yes

Daily Prayers and Readings for a Missional People

Church Mission Society

www.cms-uk.org

CANTERBURY PRESS

Norwich

© Church Mission Society 2012

First published in 2012 by the Canterbury Press Norwich
Editorial office
3rd floor Invicta House
108-114 Golden Lane
London ECIY OTG

Canterbury Press is an imprint of Hymns Ancient & Modern Ltd
(a registered charity)
13A Hellesdon Park Road, Norwich,
Norfolk, NR6 5DR, UK

http://www.canterburypress.co.uk/

British Library Cataloguing in Publication data

A catalogue record for this book is available
from the British Library

978-1-84825-060-4

Printed and bound in Great Britain by
CPI Group (UK) Ltd, Croydon CRO 4YY

CONTENTS

A TABLE OF THE MOVEABLE FEASTS

for one hundred and seven years according to the foregoing calendar

The Year of our Lord	Sundays after Epiphany	The First Day of Lent	Easter Day	Ascension Day	Pentecost	Sundays after Trinity	Trinity 1	Advent Sunday
2012	4	February 22	April 8	May 17	May 27	25	Proper 5	December 2
2013	2	February 13	March 31	May 9	May 19	26	Proper 4	December 1
2014	5	March 5	April 20	May 29	June 8	23	Proper 7	November 30
2015	3	February 18	April 5	May 14	May 24	25	Proper 5	November 29
2016	2	February 10	March 27	May 5	May 15	26	Proper 4	November 27
2017	5	March 1	April 16	May 25	June 4	24	Proper 6	December 3
2018	3	February 14	April 1	May 10	May 20	26	Proper 4	December 2
2019	5	March 6	April 21	May 30	June 9	23	Proper 7	December 1
2020	4	February 26	April 12	May 21	May 31	24	Proper 6	November 29
2021	3	February 17	April 4	May 13	May 23	25	Proper 5	November 28
2022	5	March 2	April 17	May 26	June 5	23	Proper 7	November 27
2023	4	February 22	April 9	May 18	May 28	25	Proper 5	December 3
2024	3	February 14	March 31	May 9	May 19	26	Proper 4	December 1
2025	5	March 5	April 20	May 29	June 8	23	Proper 7	November 30

FOREWORD

There is a very close connection in scripture between prayer and prophecy. If God's people are to live prophetically – as signs of God's coming world breaking into this present world – and if we are to speak words of prophecy to our world pointing to God's way of living, then we have to be deeply rooted in prayer, *daily prayer, 365 day prayer*.

Prayer in the Christian Tradition, emerging as it did from Jewish patterns of prayer, has always been surrounded by scripture and the saints. From the earliest days Christians have placed their prayer in the setting of scripture, so that our speaking to God responds to God's word to us. Christians have also – right from the time the Lord taught us to pray *'Our Father'* – sought to pray together, physically with others or in the clear consciousness of our spiritual communion with the community of believers, the saints of God.

365 Days of Yes is an important step along the way to community life in the Church Mission Society (CMS). It will be another way of binding members of the community together in a common life of mission flowing from prayer. It is also a gift of this community of mission to other Christians, perhaps especially to those who are looking for ways to relate their daily prayer to two fundamental dimensions of Christian existence: the reality of being part of Jesus' world-wide family and the responsibility to make him known in every part of the world, including that part which is closest to us.

In this daily diet of prayer and devotion you will find yourself taken to a passage of scripture, given a short reflection and then led into prayer. The movement of the daily prayers will carry you through the cycle of the Christian year with the different hues and shades of the seasons beginning with Advent, that great time of prophetic hope. Throughout the 365 days of the year you will not only be praying with members of the Church Mission Society, you will be given a sense of the amazing span of the Church across the centuries and the continents. The reflections and prayers travel the world and listen in on the thoughts of many of the great figures of Christian history. The passion that binds all this variety together is the desire to be so grounded in the God of grace that we will grow daily into our calling to live in the grace of God and draw other people to Jesus Christ, so that they may say their *yes* to Jesus and to his way that leads to life.

Christopher Cocksworth
Bishop of Coventry and Episcopal Visitor of CMS

HOW TO USE THIS BOOK

365 Days of Yes offers a Bible reading, a reflection on an aspect of mission, and a prayer focus for each day of the year. Many of the reflections come from members of the CMS Mission Community – people engaging in mission in diverse ways in many different contexts throughout the world, not least here in the UK. The year begins on Advent Sunday, and at the top right hand of each page you will find a box with the date of the reading in 2011 – 2014. This allows for the moveable date of Easter in different years.

The book is designed to enable individuals to explore what the call to mission means and how we might respond. We suggest setting aside a period of time each day to reflect on the material and having a Bible, notebook and a pen to hand. There are pauses for reflection, where you are invited to prayerfully consider the questions raised – and determine what you can say 'yes' to in your own life and calling.

Although the book is primarily designed for use by individuals, it may also be used with another person or perhaps a small group. An important part of the ethos of the CMS community is a commitment to support and learn from one another as we seek to be more intentionally mission-focused in our local churches and our daily lives.

Our prayer is that you will find this book both practical and inspirational, and that we will all sense a fresh call to say 'yes' – perhaps for the first time, perhaps as a recommitment – to living a mission lifestyle and sharing the good news of Jesus Christ for all creation.

Please feel free to contact CMS (01865 787400, communitymember@ cms-uk.org, www.cms-uk.org) if you'd like to know more about the CMS Community.

ADVENT – DAY 1
WAKE UP, O SLEEPER . . .

Ephesians 5.8–16

A preaching that awakens, a preaching that enlightens – as when a light turned on awakens and of course annoys a sleeper – that is the preaching of Christ, calling, 'Wake up! Be converted!' this is the Church's authentic preaching. Naturally, such preaching must meet conflict, must spoil what is miscalled prestige, must disturb, must be persecuted. It cannot get along with the powers of darkness and sin.

Oscar Romero (1917–80), 22 January 1978

In what ways is Christ calling us as individuals to wake up and be converted afresh? How can we challenge the world around us with the wake-up call of Christ?

> O You who are our great Chief, light a candle in my heart,
> that I may see all that is within,
> and sweep the rubbish from your dwelling place.

An African Schoolgirl's Prayer

> Make us, we beseech thee, O Lord our God, watchful
> in awaiting the coming of thy Son, Jesus Christ our Lord;
> that when he shall come and knock, he may find us not
>   sleeping in sin,
> but awake, and rejoicing in his praises;
> through the same Jesus Christ our Lord.

South India

ADVENT – DAY 2
TRUSTING GOD'S PLANS

Luke 1.5–25

My plan was to leave Kisiizi in July, but I have had a growing conviction that this may not be God's will. Another doctor, Josephine, will return to Kisiizi next summer as a paediatrician. I have been asking for someone to fill the gap between when I leave and when she returns. The children's ward will manage fine, but I'm not sure about the special care baby unit. I think that God has been telling me that I should be the one to fill that gap. Perhaps baby Kakye illustrates why. He weighed only 800 grams (1.7 pounds) at birth. When I was called to see him I thought that he was too small and that I would not be able to do anything for him, but when I saw him, he opened his eyes and cried. As I write this he shows every sign of continuing in life.

Ann Moore, a paediatric nurse and CMS mission partner working at
Kisiizi hospital in south-west Uganda

God our Father, we acknowledge that what we know of your great plans is only ever partial. We, like Zechariah, struggle to receive the bigger picture of what you are doing in our lives and in the world we are called to serve. Help us to trust in your provision for our future and to respond to your plans for our lives with hope and imagination.

Lord God,
when all we see are the problems we face,
help us to discover the opportunities that lie within.
When we have more questions than answers,
help us to respond in faith and not in fear.
Where we are crippled by doubt and indecision,
shine your light into our lives and illuminate our thinking.
Where we struggle to see the path ahead,
help us to learn to follow one step at a time.

When we feel weary and discouraged,
remind us of your call to follow.
When we fear what the future might hold,
help us to trust in your love. Amen.

ADVENT – DAY 3
ANNOUNCING GOOD NEWS

Luke 1.26–38

*Mary's great gift was the willingness to believe the good news in faith –
'I am the Lord's servant,' Mary answered. 'May it be to me as you have
said' (Luke 1.38). Sometimes we see the good news of Jesus unfold before
our eyes. Sometimes we have to believe in it by faith, trusting God to
bring it about.*

One of the people we trained, Pastor Bishnu, and I recently went to a
prison cell to hold a baptism for about 40 prisoners who had accepted
Jesus Christ as their Lord and Saviour as a result of Bishnu's prison ministry. The prison warden and deputy chief district officer were also present.
After 15 minutes of praise and worship, the deputy chief district officer
gave a short talk on how he considered religion a good thing because it
encouraged people – and society – to live in a godly, harmonious way.

Following this, Pastor Bishnu gave a short message on baptism. We
then went down to the prison yard, where 11 buckets of water had been
prepared. Inside the prison walls there is no such thing as a pond or a
tank that could be used to immerse those being baptized. The men stood
quietly as I prayed for each one and poured a bucket of water on them.
One by one, as each man was baptized, they praised the Lord and shared
a feeling of freedom in their hearts even though they had been behind
bars for several years.

Ram Prasad Shrestha, a Nepalese CMS co-mission partner, who has trained
hundreds of Christian leaders in Nepal

O Holy Spirit,
bearer of the good news of Jesus,
help us to trust in your saving work,
even when that work is hidden in secret places,
even when we find that good news hard to receive,
even when we fail to fully understand,
and even when you choose us to be the messenger. Amen.

ADVENT – DAY 4
COMING ALONGSIDE

Luke 1.39–56

Two women were brought together by the hopes and threats of their shared circumstances. Sharing in the unfolding work of the good news of Jesus brings us into partnerships with those who hold a similar hope and vision. We need that support. A burden shared is a burden halved.

I feel that my role is more to help people see for themselves what needs to be done for children. When we teach child rights, we take a strong line on the responsibilities that each child has as well. We do not advocate rights without responsibility. If we are able to help our children to understand this, we are helping them to grow into good members of the community. The community workers I have worked with have been very proactive on behalf of children. As a community they have decided that all children should be going to school, and parents who choose to keep their children away are fined. There has also been a problem with children and alcohol, but now adults are not allowing the children to drink, and parents are taking a more proactive approach in knowing where their children are, and preventing them from going to unhelpful places. The community workers are also making house calls in order to see how they can help people. We are excited, because I didn't prompt them to do this – they took the training and applied it to their own setting.

Ruth Radley, CMS mission partner

What have you given and received from others as you have shared in mission?

Lord God,
thank you for those who come alongside us for our support
   and encouragement.
May we know how to receive their encouragement and vision,
as we learn how to encourage and envision others.
Help us to cultivate friendships that nourish us.
Help us to bear friendships that drain us.
And help us to make friends more easily. Amen.

In love and in friendship,
in sharing common goals and common fears,
in being part of the same extended family,
in admitting that we are so alike,
in recognizing that we are so very different,
in finding a kindred spirit,
in accepting the insights of others,
may we hold in common the things that unite us,
may we hold together the calling we share,
may we know that we are stronger together than divided,
this day and for evermore. Amen.

ADVENT – DAY 5
SIGNS OF THE KINGDOM

Luke 1.57–80

The birth of John heralded the coming of the kingdom of God to a people struggling with adversity yet gripped by a spirit of expectation. The arrival of John reassures us that God is not absent and powerless, but rather working in small ways to build the big picture of what his coming kingdom is like.

Jill Ball is a CMS mission partner in Ecuador working with disabled children. She is also about to start a home for abused women. She says:

> Two professionals from a charity that works with abused women came to give a group of us two days of intensive training. Many of the invited group have themselves escaped from abusive relationships. We were shown a film of wealthy women in the United States who had suffered abusive marriages, and there was hardly a dry eye in the house. In June, we will learn more about how to counsel abused women and how to deal with the all-important legal issues. Thanks be to the Lord that we have been given the free use of a very suitable building to use as a respite centre. It is a huge blessing for this work, and we are immensely grateful to the persons who have decided to lend it to us.

Where can you see the signs of God's kingdom – however small – in your context?

God, our Father, your servant John proclaimed the coming
    of your kingdom.
He called people to repent and baptized them in the river
    Jordan to wash away their sins.
Bless all who are involved in reconciliation between nations,
    communities and families, that they may bring hope out of despair
    and joy out of sorrow.
Help us who have been baptized in Christ
to live in the joyful hope that his coming has meant for the world.
We ask this through Jesus Christ, the Prince of Peace. Amen.

In the preaching of your message of forgiveness – let your
    kingdom come.
In our fresh starts and new beginnings – let your kingdom come.
In repentance and the willingness to change – let your kingdom come.
In lives transformed by your call to follow – let your kingdom come.
In the symbolism of baptism – let your kingdom come.
In the cost of discipleship and opposition – let your kingdom come.
In a life offered to you in the service of others – let your
    kingdom come.

ADVENT – DAY 6
SHARING THE LIGHT

Isaiah 42.5–7

Last year, our church took part in the CMS Share the Light Advent mission resource. Everyone in our congregation agreed to give a candle to a friend or neighbour. We all prayed together about who to give them to, and we gave ours to a couple who are building a house for themselves at the end of our road. We offered it as a token of peace for Christmas and as a way of saying welcome to the village. They were really touched by the gift and we have kept in contact since. We're looking forward to them moving in when the house is ready at the end of this month.

Mike and Jan from the Church of the Good Shepherd,
Widmer End, Buckinghamshire

As Christmas approaches, how might we reach out in practical ways to share Christ's light with our friends and neighbours? Who might God be placing on your heart to share Christ's light with today?

> O Christ, the light of the world,
> we thank you that your light shines among us.
> Draw us ever closer to you,
> so that free from sin
> we may show forth the light of your glory in the world.

Torres Straits, Australia: commemoration of the arrival of the first Christian missionaries

The CMS Share the Light Advent mission resource involves giving a candle to someone you know, praying for them and perhaps inviting them to a Share the Light service at your church/community. Share the Light service materials and candles are available at www.cms-uk.org/advent

ADVENT – DAY 7
THE VIEW FROM THE ROAD

Luke 24.13–16

The missiologist David Bosch once said that we are called to live a spirituality of the road, not of the balcony.

A spirituality of the road evokes images of movement, change, journeys, new places, discovery, and crossing borders. It can also suggest feelings of weariness and disorientation. But the idea is that we grow more as participants than as observers. I personally found this to be true; it was during my time in Uganda that I began to understand more fully the goodness of God.

When it comes to a spirituality of the road, we must ask a couple of questions. One, at what pace should we travel? Should we rush from point A to point B, ignoring the scenery along the way? Or should we travel at the speed of love, as Kosuke Koyama suggests in *Three Mile an Hour God*?

Koyama writes:

Love has its speed. It is an inner speed. It is a spiritual speed. It is a different kind of speed from the technological speed to which we are accustomed. It is 'slow' yet it is lord over all other speeds since it is the speed of love. It goes on in the depth of our life, whether we notice or not, whether we are currently hit by storm or not, at three miles an hour. It is the speed we walk and therefore it is the speed the love of God walks.

Koyama says that Jesus' pace was not rapid; it was more like this speed of love. Think of the journey along the Emmaus road and what riches those followers of Jesus (and all of us since) would have missed out on had they rushed past Jesus and ignored him. What is our pace? Are we so busy engaging in mission that the scenery and relationships pass us by? Are we so caught up in achieving and doing that we do not pause to engage with the stranger and listen to the promptings of the Holy Spirit? If so, we may as well be in the balcony.

Cathy Ross

Lord, help us to walk at the speed of love.
Help us not to rush by, intent on achieving our aims,
  however empty they may be.
Help us to stop.
Help us to listen.
Help us to see. Amen.

ADVENT – DAY 8
THE SPIRITUALITY OF THE COMMONPLACE

Luke 10.38–42

A second, related, question to ask is, in our rush to do more 'important things', are we missing out on what David Bosch calls the spirituality of the commonplace? It's easy to be captivated by the spectacular, by a wonderful meeting and powerful ministry – we sing about 'more love, more power'– but is that really what God calls us to? Is that really the experience of most people?

People underestimate how challenging, yet rewarding, it is to discover spirituality in daily life. Yet, kingdom life is ordinary life lived in the real world: in things like earning a living, bringing up a family, having fun, enjoying parties, building cities, mourning loved ones, healing sickness, making music, playing sport, studying and travelling. It's all about doing these things to the glory of our Creator and Redeemer, and resting in who we are meant to be in Christ.

As we engage in mission wherever we are, I suggest some characteristics or disciplines that we might observe in order to develop our spirituality of the road. They're disciplines because they take some effort.

Cathy Ross

Reflect on your own life – relationships, work, leisure. Do you engage in them to the glory of God?

Prayer when opening a door
I pray thee, Lord, to open the door of my heart to receive thee within my heart.

Prayer when washing clothes
I pray thee, Lord, to wash my heart, making me white as snow.

When sweeping floors
I pray thee, Lord, to sweep away my heart's uncleanness, that my heart may always be pure.

When posting a letter
I pray thee, Lord, to add to me faith upon faith, that I may always have communication with thee.

When lighting lamps
I pray thee, Lord, to make my deeds excellent like lamps before others, and more, to place thy true light within my heart.

When boiling water for tea
I pray thee, Lord, to send down spiritual fire to burn away the coldness of my heart and that I may always be hot-hearted in serving thee.

Prayers for Chinese Christian women, adapted

ADVENT – DAY 9
A LEARNING POSTURE

Luke 2.41–50

We are called to be both inquirers and learners.

Inquirer
Ask questions about every facet of life – the political, the economic, the industrial, the social, the spiritual.

Learner
We need to learn the culture and subcultures of where we are. In learning from others, we begin to learn more about ourselves, what makes us function, how we can grow and develop. As we learn, let us maintain a self-awareness and practise humility under God.

Cathy Ross

Are we open to asking questions with humility and self-awareness? Are we ready to listen to the answers?

Jesus, you sat among the learned,
listening, and asking them questions.
Inspire all who teach and all who learn.

Central Africa: Ukaristia

Almighty God,
you have brought us together in this place.
We have asked each other many questions
and heard many answers.
Help us to live with the questions,
that have no ready answers,
save in the love of Jesus Christ our Lord.

Prayer on a visit to East Germany, 1980

ADVENT – DAY 10
LEARNING TO LISTEN

John 4.7–20

Listener
We must listen to the assumptions behind the words and world views of others and learn to hear Jesus speaking through them. This will challenge our own understanding of how God works in the world, which will in turn deepen our spiritual life.

Cathy Ross

Jesus encounters people and hears the 'words behind the words' – the things that aren't said, the unspoken pain, the assumptions that shape their world view. How can we learn to listen better so that we can more fully understand people's hopes, fears and needs – and learn from them?

Father,
Let my existence be ruled by a great silence.
Let my soul be listening, be given to the needs of others.
Let me be silent in my innermost being, not asserting myself.
Let my soul be detached, not grasping at anything in this world.
And thus overcome in my life the power of habit, daily routine,
    dullness, fatigue and fear.
Let me create within myself a carefree tranquillity, a place for
    every encounter, unreserved receptivity, and unhurried disposition.
Extinguish within me the feelings of self-importance and the last
    stirrings of my ego,
and make me gentle.
Let me answer thoughts and situations rather than words.
Through Jesus Christ our Lord,
Who taught us to be holy as you are holy. Amen.

Hassan Dehqani-Tafti, one-time Bishop of Iran, in exile

ADVENT – DAY 11
THE SPEED OF LOVE

John 8.3–11

Lover
As we learn to love others with patience and gentleness, we will find our
hearts being opened out and softened. As we grow in Christ-like love, our
spiritual life will be enhanced. Ask yourself, 'How can I live at the speed
of love? What will that look like in my life?'

Cathy Ross

*How might I live at the speed of love today? What will I need to do or
change to enable that to happen?*

Lord, give me grace for today
and help me to love as you love. Amen.

ADVENT – DAY 12
NO LONGER AT EASE

Jeremiah 1.4–10

Disturber

What does it mean to be a disturber? I think it means questioning the status quo, and engaging with people who may have very different ideas to ours. We are inviting others to see Jesus and live in relationship with him, so this will likely disturb their lifestyles, relationships and futures. As T. S. Eliot expressed in 'Journey of the Magi', the three kings, those enigmatic wise men, returned to where they had come from 'no longer at ease here, in the old dispensation, with an alien people clutching their gods'. Once they had seen Jesus, they knew. They knew this baby, this King of the Jews, was one to adore. They knew that somehow Jesus changed their lives. As followers of Jesus, we must allow people to see another way of living and being.

This will have profound implications for our spiritual lives. We may indeed be out of synch with the world in which we live, we may be uncomfortable, and this will force us to rely on God more.

Cathy Ross

Lord – help us to live prophetically,
by our actions as well as our words.
Where we have become complacent,
disturb us
and help us to live a different way.
Give us courage to speak out in your name,
trusting in your mercy alone. Amen.

ADVENT – DAY 13
VISIBLE SIGNS

Mark 1.4–8

Sign of the end
We are to live as visible signs of hope that God's kingdom is reality, that we are living on the frontier of a new heaven and a new earth, and that will have profound implications for our spiritual life.

Cathy Ross

In Kibera, a vast slum in Nairobi, Colin Smith trains Christian leaders. They start seed projects in the name of Jesus that witness to God's love in practical ways and change people's lives. Here are some of them:

- new home-grown industries, such as soap-making, urban vegetable gardens, breeding rabbits and creating a cyber cafe
- schemes where members can learn to save and access capital to develop and grow businesses
- HIV/AIDS programmes to help young people change their behaviour and pre-schools to care for those who are orphaned.

How can we live as visible signs of the kingdom in our own context?

Lord, may we live in such a way,
that when people encounter us, they may say
'The kingdom of God is among us.' Amen.

ADVENT – DAY 14
NOT 'HOW TO' BUT 'WHERE TO'

Galatians 2.20

You may be surprised that I haven't yet spoken of reading the Bible and prayer. Yes, we do need God's word to nourish us and we need to develop a deep and ongoing life of prayer, as John V. Taylor explained in *The Go-Between God*:

> To live in prayer, therefore, is to live in the Spirit; and to live in the Spirit is to live in Christ . . . Prayer is not something you do; it is a style of living.

Prayer is both our privilege and our responsibility as we engage in the *missio Dei*.

A spirituality of the road embraces prayer as an integral part of the journey. It is not all about living a life of relentless activism (though this may be part of it); the end to which we strive ultimately is, as Roland Allen has expressed it so beautifully, 'the unfolding of a Person' – the revelation of Christ. The heart of mission is communion with Christ – daily, constant, ongoing – through the enabling of the Holy Spirit.

Further, a spirituality of the road realizes that models and 'how tos' only get us so far. There is no blueprint, or map or sat nav that contains every turn, bump or unexpected circumstance. We will have our challenges and disappointments, our dark nights of the soul. We will have our feelings of betrayal, and thoughts that God has left us to struggle on this road alone. Are we willing to face that? Is our spiritual life robust enough to face the heartache and brutalities of a broken world? As we give up our seats in the balcony and step out along this road, committed to a long obedience in the same direction, maybe some of the above qualities can help us live life in all the fullness to which Jesus has called us.

Cathy Ross

Father, may we live in prayer,
live in the Spirit,
live in Christ –
that we may remain steadfast in the twists and turns
of daily life
and daily be transformed into your likeness.
In the name of Jesus, who journeyed in prayer. Amen.

ADVENT – DAY 15
RAISING THE BAR

1 Corinthians 9.24–27

How can we help people raise the bar of discipleship to become more missional? The first step is to help people discern their calling. We encourage people to compose what we call a 'personal calling statement'. Then we encourage them to work in small groups to help each other reimagine and free up time for daily Scripture reading and prayer, free up time to build relationships and free up a couple of hours a week for witness and service as the opportunity presents itself.

Tom Sine

Reflect on the balance of your life at present. How might you free up time and energy to engage more wholeheartedly with mission?

Look upon us, Lord.
Hear and enlighten us.
Show us your very self.
Take pity on our efforts and strivings towards you.
For we have no strength without you.
Teach me to seek you,
And when I seek you show yourself to me,
for I cannot seek unless you teach me.
Nor can I find you unless you show yourself to me.
Let me seek you in desiring you,

and desire you in seeking you.
Let me find you by loving you,
and love you in finding you. Amen.

Anselm of Canterbury (1033–1109)

ADVENT – DAY 16
IN AT THE DEEP END

Matthew 5.1–12

Most of all we're taking our leap in the dark because we've belatedly realized that the Sermon on the Mount might actually be a manifesto for life, rather than a few nice ideals to take out for a spin on a Sunday morning. We've come to believe in the survival of the weakest, not just the fittest. William Vanstone once came out with the great line that the Church is like a swimming pool: all the noise is at the shallow end. We felt called to the deep end, to the place where it's more quiet, more dangerous maybe, more radical.

Tobias Jones, author of Utopian Dreams, cited
in the Guardian, 17 November 2009

How does the Sermon on the Mount speak into, challenge or confirm your mission lifestyle? How does it challenge us as a Christian community? What does it mean to be called to the deep end?

Father, may we be a community of mission at the 'deep end',
a community committed to transformation and hope,
a community of Christ. Amen.

ADVENT – DAY 17
GOOD NEWS FOR ALL NATIONS

Isaiah 60.1–3

It was just a year ago that we moved intentionally from a relatively quiet garden suburb of Bristol to the inner city. Convinced of God's plan to draw all the nations in worship of him, we were following a deep sense of calling that God has given to us to share Jesus with the increasing number of people who have come to settle in Easton from a variety of (mainly Muslim) nations.

Jan teaches English for speakers of other languages part-time in local community venues and schools and so has been able to make contacts with many women in the area. On bonfire night we welcomed these women and their children (Somali, Bengali, Sudanese and Turkish) to our home for an evening of fireworks. Pancake Day was similarly celebrated. We've also had a 'cook-in' where recipes were swapped, and the end of summer saw some of us enjoying a picnic in a local park.

More opportunities to meet people came when friends of ours from the Middle East invited us to a party to celebrate the birth of their child. It was particularly interesting for Derek to observe the men at prayer together. Part of what we want to do is just to have fun with people of other faiths, since fun is a great route to friendship. Moreover, it's often as a result of sharing in such times that people feel free to raise questions of faith or personal struggle.

Our constant prayer is for spiritual discernment so that we may begin to recognize which of our contacts are seeking God. We have had some encouraging encounters and have been able to share prayer and the word of God with three of our friends.

Derek and Jan Pike, Bristol

Father of all peoples and all nations,
Help us to build relationships of friendship and trust
with our neighbours,
so that boundaries may be crossed,
lives shared

and hospitality given and received
with generosity and grace. Amen.

ADVENT – DAY 18
MISSION IN ALL PLACES

Luke 4.16–24

'Can someone from Kibera [the vast informal settlement outside Nairobi] be ordained in the Anglican Church?' I posed this question to a class of students from an ecumenical university who were studying at our Centre for Urban Mission, based in Kibera. It wasn't a very original question. Forty years ago, our vicar in Bermondsey had asked something similar about dockers in London's East End. Thousands of years ago, Nathanael asked regarding Jesus: 'Can anything good come from Nazareth?' 'No!' my class replied. Whether the students were being pessimistic about Kibera residents or the Anglican Church, I'm not sure. Either way, they were proved wrong. On 26 October the Archbishop ordained three Centre for Urban Mission graduates. Lillian had lived in Kibera virtually all her life until she had to flee the post-election violence a year ago. Her classmates, Zadock and Barrack, helped her get out of Kibera with the few belongings she could carry. Seeing all three of them ordained was a wonderful affirmation of the gifts, calling and experiences that people from Kibera and other 'slums' can bring to the rest of the Church. I don't know whether they were the first people from Kibera to be ordained, but three in one day – that must be a first!

Anita and Colin Smith, Kenya

Where do you see mission flourishing in your local context? Is God stirring up a new call to mission in surprising people or places you know? Is God stirring up a surprising new call to mission within your own life?

Lord, grant us eyes to see your presence and peace
in strange places and unlikely people,
even in ourselves. Amen.

From the USA

ADVENT – DAY 19
GO TO YOUR OWN PEOPLE

Mark 5.18–20

I thought there would be far-off scenes the challenge of lost souls; till thou didst show in seas of sameness ordinary folk I passed in blind familiarity – more lost than those whom distance still enhances.

Ruth Spinnanger, www.cmf.org.uk

How often do we look far away when we consider the call to mission and miss the needs and opportunities under our noses? Why is it sometimes easier to do that? How might we engage both globally and locally as we respond to God's call to mission?

O God, you have made of one blood all the peoples of the earth
  and sent your blessed son to preach peace to those who are far off
  and to those who are near.
Grant that people everywhere may seek after you and find you.
Bring the nations into your fold.
Pour out your spirit upon all flesh,
and hasten the coming of your kingdom through Jesus Christ
  our Lord,
who lives and reigns with you and the Holy Spirit,
one God, now and forever. Amen.

ADVENT – DAY 20
FAITH IN ACTION

James 2.14–17

In the winter months, the homeless suffer greatly, particularly in countries where weather is severe: warmth and sustenance are equally hard to come by. A charity in Toronto, Canada, has devised a novel solution: it gives baked potatoes in socks to homeless people to keep them warm and, when the warmth wears off, to feed them. In Toronto, temperatures fall as low as minus 40 degrees, and 15 people die yearly from exposure. Ve'ahavta, the organization behind the Potato Tikun Olam program, says the potato-sock keeps sleeping bags warm for five hours and pockets for about three. The potatoes then provide a good source of fibre, potassium, and energy.

From *500 Ways to Change the World*

Reflect on your own local community and the particular needs and challenges it faces. How might you demonstrate Christ's love in action? How are you doing that at the moment?

Lord God, so often it's the simplest actions that offer hope and love.
Yet so often, we make it all too complicated
and end up doing nothing.
Teach us, we pray, to put our faith into action,
action that speaks louder than words. Amen.

ADVENT – DAY 21
YOU DID IT FOR ME

Matthew 25.31–40

For I was hungry and you volunteered for Crisis at Christmas, read with a teenager who constantly disrupted the class because he starved for attention, regularly took a single mum – off her tether looking after three young children – to the supermarket.

I was thirsty and you supported projects removing arsenic from water supplies in Bangladesh and gave generously to support the mission partners doing this work.

I needed clothes; you culled your wardrobe, mended and dry cleaned, and added new socks and underwear for a local clothing appeal. You made friends with the women's shelter and ran a whip-round when they said they needed toiletries. You gave your spare coat to a homeless man.

I was new, a stranger; you introduced me to people in the neighbourhood. You walked me and my children to the school gate on the first day of term. You told me the best places to shop, where to find the dentist and how to sign up for the doctor's surgery.

I was sick with swine flu and you brought in hot food, did my washing and took my children to school.

I was in prison and you joined the support group for prisoners' families. I was in a prison because I spoke little English; you gave of your time so I could practise English conversation.

I tell you the truth, whatever you did for one of the least of these brothers and sisters of mine, you did it for me.

Paraphrased by John Martin

Almighty God, whose Son our Saviour Jesus Christ taught us that to serve the least of his brethren is to serve him; we give you thanks that Simon from Africa was there to help Jesus our Lord carry his cross, and we beseech you to grant us compassion like his and a ready willingness to serve the weak and helpless as though we were serving Jesus. Amen.

From the Middle East

ADVENT – DAY 22
EVERYTHING IN TURN TO ALL

1 Corinthians 9.19–23

Janet had been a Reader and church leader for many years and also ran a cell group. Much of her life was devoted to church ministry, but she also had a passion for making cards. Once she began to share that passion, she gathered together a nucleus of 40 or so local people who all wanted to learn the craft and find community too. As a good cell leader, she also wanted to make a connection between her craft friends and Christian friends, so she extended many invitations to her cell group, all of which were politely declined. One day, we began to apply the 'what we might have in common' principle and dream of what the church might look like in the setting of her card group, and where it might begin. The natural starting point came with the seasons. As Christmas approached, they started to make Advent cards and Janet gave a little introduction on the meaning of Advent. She did it briefly and tentatively, asking whether people minded as she moved around the tables after her little talk. To her surprise, they were not only enthusiastic but the explanation opened up the most natural conversations about what was happening in lives and where God and faith fitted in.

Phil Potter

Are there ways that you could make connections between your passions and interests and your Christian faith to enable you to share your faith creatively with others? How might we become 'everything in turn to all, so that in one way or another we can save some'?

O God, help me to walk in the boots of the miner,
the shoes of the trader,
the moccasins of the trapper,
and in the sandals of Jesus Christ the Master
and to see others as he would see them. Amen.

Canada: an Indian prayer from the far north

ADVENT – DAY 23
INCARNATION

John 1.14

As we write, Christmas is almost upon us and, having tried to walk through the anticipation and waiting of Advent while hurtling through the gamut of extra Christmas events added to our already packed workload, we are more than ready to stop and reflect and celebrate.

Two thousand (plus) years ago God's people had moved so far from God, into their own mess, that it became difficult for them to see how God related to any of their troubles. We love to remember at this time the wonderful way in which *love* chose to come close, to take on flesh and blood and come tangibly to show us the way back into a right relationship with God, with each other and with the world.

Christmas is in fact part of our work through the whole year, as we try to pattern our work on the incarnation – God coming among us, becoming known to us in our own context. Or as *The Message* puts it: 'He took on flesh and blood and moved into the neighbourhood.' Here in Hull, in the midst of a community that struggles to see that God might be interested, we are trying to be the flesh and blood of the gospel. We can celebrate Christmas because we know that he is.

Chris and Anna Hembury, Hull

In the coming Advent and Christmas season, as we again seek to grasp the wonder of the Word made flesh, our prayer is that the Church, both here and at home, will be increasingly the living expression in our communities of the Lord whose name we bear.

Allan and Anne Lacey, Uganda

ADVENT – DAY 24
MAKING IT REAL

John 1.1–8

'Light of the World' became so real for us this Christmas as it is a significant symbol here in identifying Christians. As Christmas approached we began to see lights and star-shaped paper lanterns going up to decorate homes. It was beautiful to see lanes lit up with various lights. And quite challenging for us as before Christmas there had been threats made to Christians, and yet this did not stop the celebrations.

Not only was there a display of lights but also real joy in celebrating the birth of Christ. In our area of the city, where many Christians live, we had frequent visits from 'carollers' which included lots of music, dancing and drums. Their enthusiasm, joy and energy were great to see. They visited most buildings in the area spreading their excitement.

David and Sarah Hall, Bangladesh

Pray for Christians all over the world who will face persecution this Christmas-time, that they may know the joy and peace of Christ in the face of danger. Pray that all of us, wherever we are, may find real joy in celebrating the birth of Christ afresh.

> May the same Jesus Christ
> who came to Bethlehem 2,000 years ago
> find room in our hearts and celebrations today,
> not just in a small corner on the side but as the highest Lord
> of honour and our closest friend.

Alison Gibblett, Ukraine

ADVENT – DAY 25
EMMANUEL

Matthew 1.22–23

We call Mary's child 'Emmanuel', because we see in him the God who has always been with us, always in the midst. There is no need for him to intervene as a stranger from the outside world. He is already here.

John V. Taylor

God of God . . .
Only the sound of an infant
Crying in the night.
A familiar, homely, human sound
Like the sound of hooves on flagstones,
Like the rattle of chains tethering cattle,
Like the crunch of straw in the mouths of oxen,
Like the rustle of hay tossed in a manger.

Light of light . . .
Only the light of a star
Falling on an infant in a crib
Like the light in a shepherd's lantern
Like the light in the eyes of a mother
Like the light in the learning of the wise men
Like the light that lightens each dawn.

Very God of very God . . .
Only a pillow of straw
And an infant in rags and tatters
Like the weather-torn blankets of shepherds
Like dusty, travel-stained garments of travellers
Like old cloths thrown to a beggar
Like cloths stuffed in a stable window
To keep the draught out and the cattle warm.

God is with us,
Terribly, simply with us.
And the shadows of men and women
With arms outstretched to take him
Fall across the manger
In the form of a cross.

From India

ADVENT – DAY 26

CROSSING BOUNDARIES

Philippians 2.5–7

The theme of the fortnight-long confirmation class was that Jesus was born poor and humble and shares our life; and the question was: Why? The women present were all poor. None had much formal education. Most were migrants from rural areas. All knew real hardship. They could easily identify with a poor family on the move whose baby had been born in harsh circumstances. Indeed, a one-minute reading of Luke's account of the nativity provoked a one-hour discussion of the injustices, humiliations, and hardships that the mothers themselves had experienced.

They discussed the terrible health services available in the area and how a local woman's baby had been born, while she was waiting in a queue to see the doctor. (The baby died.) They exchanged accounts of having to wait in shops while better-dressed people were served first, and how, as domestic servants, they were treated without respect by their mistresses. They spoke of the high price of food in the local shops.

After an hour of such talk, the catechist put the question: 'Why did Jesus choose to be born poor and humble?' 'Maybe,' said one woman, a mother of ten of whom three had died and only two were working, 'it was to show those rich people that we are important too.'

A ripple of excitement passed through the room. Was God really making such a clear statement about their humanity? About their rights as people? The discussion progressed, but with an electric charge in the air. Half an hour after a young woman said, 'I think we still haven't got the right answer to the first question!' A complete hush. 'I think,' she went on, 'I think God chose his son to be born like us so that we can realize that we are important.'

An account of an experience in a confirmation class
on the outskirts of Sao Paulo, Brazil

Jesus breaks down the boundaries that divide and calls us to do the same. The Christmas story crosses many boundaries as it challenges us. As we hear about the shepherds, we are reminded of the importance of mission in our local vicinity and that it is the poorest who encounter Christ first; as we read of the wise men travelling from afar to worship and returning home with a story to share, we are challenged by the task of mission to the ends of the earth.

All the people who encounter the Christ child have one thing in common – however they choose to respond, their lives can never be quite the same again. And for us, as we hear the story again and look to the New Year, the question is – having encountered Christ, how will we respond?

ADVENT – DAY 27
BELIEVING IN PEOPLE – BELIEVING IN JESUS

John 10.10

One person I will never forget is one of our young boys called David (not his real name). He was 13 years old, when he came to the project. David was a gang member and the gangs were after him and wanted to kill him. I never found out what he had done but it was something very serious, because he spent ten months with us (at our safe house) until he ran away and when the gangs caught up with him, they shot him in the shoulder. Thankfully he survived. When he was in hospital, another project leader and I would visit him. I remember paying for him and his uncle to live with his grandmother far away from the gangs to be safe. David was doing really well until his mother, who had psychological problems, became jealous of her mother having custody of her son. So she went and got David from his grandma's house and brought him back to the city. On Christmas Eve 2008, the gang shot David in the head five times and killed him.

The Bible says that the devil comes to kill, destroy and steal and that is something he tries to do all over the world – but perhaps it is most apparent here in Olinda. At Christmas-time, I always remember David because the last thing he said to me was 'You and Rose and the rest of the guys at the project are the only ones who ever believed in me.' We weren't able to save David physically, but I am sure that we got through to him spiritually. We believe in David, because we believe in Jesus. Amen.

Andy Roberts, Brazil

O God, grant that we may not seek the child Jesus
in the pretty figures of our Christmas cribs;
but rather look for him
among the undernourished children,
who have gone to bed tonight with nothing to eat;
among the poor newsboys, who will sleep
covered with newspapers in doorways. Amen.

El Salvador, based on some words of Oscar Romero (1917–80)

CHRISTMAS EVE
UNWRAP OUR DARKNESS

Isaiah 9.2–7

We can scarcely believe it, God,
this story of your birth in the world.
We rationalize and reason,
we read the headlines and we doubt,
and still, we hope, desperately,
that it just might be true.
If we have lost faith in the promise of change,
unwrap our doubt to make a space for love.
If we only know despair over your church,
unwrap our grief to make a space for joy.
If we've been angry with your people,
unwrap our resentment to make a space for peace.
If we've looked back on the past nostalgically
unwrap our sentimentality to make a space for life.
If we're looking forward cynically,
unwrap our scepticism to make a space for hope.
God, if we have lost the faith to believe that you are
making your world and your church new,
unwrap our darkness to make a space for light.

Cheryl Lawrie www.holdthisspace.org.au

My prayer for you, as I wish you every blessing of Christmas and the New Year, would be that in this season, and in the coming year, all your comings and goings, your work and relationships, would be lit by the light of Christ. As John, Jesus' closest friend, puts it: 'The true light which enlightens everyone, was coming into the world . . . The Word became flesh and lived among us, and we have seen his glory, the glory as of a father's only son, full of grace and truth' (John 1.9,14).

Robbie Langford, Sudan

CHRISTMAS DAY
BE BORN IN US

Luke 2.1–7

What good is it to me,
if Mary gave birth
to the Son of God,
and I do not also give birth to him
in my time and culture?

Meister Eckhart (1260–1327)

Jesus of Bethlehem and Nazareth and Calvary
We celebrate your birth
Come and be born in us
Jesus of the manger and the inn
Jesus of the workshop and the temple
Jesus of the lakeside and the city
Jesus of the fireside and the roadside
We celebrate your life
Come and be born in us
Jesus of Mary and Joseph
Jesus of shepherds and angels
Jesus of children and animals
Jesus of fishermen and priests
Jesus of women and men
Jesus of tax collectors and prostitutes
Jesus of all who will receive you
We celebrate your resurrection
Come and be born in us. Amen.

Doug Gay

CHRISTMAS – DAY 2
LIGHT OF THE WORLD

John 1.9–13

Light in Loy Krathong

Around this time of year, Thais celebrate a festival known as Loy Krathong, which is said to have drawn its origins from India and the Hindu Deepavali festival, but was later adapted to become a Buddhist tradition. *Loy*, means to float and *krathong* are dinner-plate-sized rafts ornately decorated with banana leaves and flowers, with a candle placed in the centre. Come the full moon, folk will take their *krathong*, light the candle and set it afloat on a river or into the sea. The act is symbolic, the idea being that, as the *krathong* is released, you send all your bad deeds, anger and unforgiveness with it. Some people even include hair and nail clippings in the *krathong* to represent this. In some parts of the country, huge lanterns called *khom fai* are released into the night sky – also symbolic of a 'letting go' of whatever in the past you may feel bad about or ashamed of.

I always find this a poignant reminder of the reason Jesus, the true light, came into the world, to offer us a final answer to the problem of sin and to bring us ultimate forgiveness and release. One Thai man once told me that this real possibility of ultimate forgiveness was what, to use his words, he most 'envied' in the Christian faith. Of course, the wonderful news is that Jesus offers this gift to all.

Gail Phillip, CMS mission partner in Thailand

Pray for people known to us who are struggling with guilt and sin, who need to experience Christ's light afresh or for the first time this Christmas season. Pray for the parts of our own lives where we need Christ's light to shine and to bring healing, forgiveness and peace.

Dear Master,
May thy Light
Shine on me now
As once it shone

Upon the shepherds
As they kept their flocks
By night.

Ozaki, a Japanese leprosy patient

CHRISTMAS – DAY 3
CHRISTMAS STORY – OUR STORY

Psalm 33.20–22

It's easy to forget, of course, why we celebrate Christmas. Why we do all this stuff. Why we engage in this blur of consuming credit, making merry and pursuing peace. What really is the point? What has changed to inspire this activity?

Perhaps one starting point in the exploration of Christmas is to be found in the turning of the seasons. Most of us have forgotten what our ancestors knew instinctively – that human life is very dependent on the seasons. And that the turning of the seasons needs to be respected, marked and celebrated. The timing of the festival of Christmas in December reminds those of us in the relatively dark and cold north that, in God's good care, the seasons will change. That light will come. That crops will grow. That we will once again be able to sit in the sun. And, if we wish, even walk barefoot in the grass. At the darkest time of the year Christmas enables us to mark the passing into deep winter with hope of a new season. This is helpful and good. But there may be something even deeper going on.

The Nativity is not just a convenient marker in the calendar. What is it about this event that so grabs our imagination? What is the hidden strength of the Christmas story that has enabled it to survive attempts to ban it, exploit it, corrupt it, belittle it, or damn it with cheap decorations? Why does it continue to work away at us?

Perhaps it is because the Nativity understands and shines light on the human story – on each of our stories – and gives us the possibility of a new way to live with hope, adventure and generosity whatever the state of the world and however we are feeling. Christmas has the capacity to change us for good. And if it changes us, it can change the communities to which we belong, and then even begin to shape the whole world for better.

Ian Adams

Jesus
Holy child
Light of the World,
Thank you for coming to be with us,
one of us, alongside us.
Thank you for coming in such humility,
as a small child, in a forgotten place.
Help me to see the holy possibility
in the small, the hidden, the unspectacular.
Even in me.
Help me I pray
Jesus
Holy child
Light of the World. Amen.

Ian Adams

CHRISTMAS – DAY 4
HOLY INNOCENTS

Matthew 2.13–18

These verses are about a stone statue of the Blessed Virgin Mary holding the child. The child's head had been broken off. People had suggested that a new head should be carved. 'No' was the answer. And so the Archbishop addresses the Virgin Mary in the words of this prayer:

I meet him every moment
Your Son and our Brother Christ,
Hunger causes physical, mental and moral damage.
When I see the children of my people,
the Silent World, wasted away, stomach distended

heads enormous and often very empty,
retarded as if it were missing,
it is Christ that I see.
Mother, we understand each other so well
that I have no need to explain or ask you anything.
I shall keep your statue with the deformed child
as in life, as in our world
in which egoism breeds monsters.
Even when the Third World gains a head and a voice,
the Child will continue to be headless
as a remembrance of the days of sorrow
that will belong for ever in the past.

Archbishop Helder Camara of Brazil

Pray for people around the world suffering injustice, persecution and famine. Pray for those who are refugees and victims at the hands of dictators and unjust governments. Pray for ourselves – that we may never forget the plight of so many people throughout the world today.

Lord, take our voices and speak through us.
Speak words of truth, words of compassion.
Take our hands and help us work for justice.
Take our hearts, our lives – all that we are.
May we weep with those who weep
and work tirelessly for the coming of your kingdom.
We pray this in the name of Jesus,
who was born in poverty and forced to flee into Egypt. Amen.

CHRISTMAS – DAY 5
HOLY AND SACRED

2 Corinthians 2.15

Christmas, Christmas!
Well, Christmas has again come, reminding us of the holy child born on that holy night – making all those who truly believe in him and who do

his will holy and sacred. In the Orthodox Church there is the belief that a holy Christian makes the other people around them, and the nature around them, holy, bringing holiness to all the world, a world that has been created holy and that will again return in its primary condition to its creator. So let us not think that holiness is something that a Christian achieves after his departure from this life – holiness is now and here in our devotion and deeds and urge to perfection. Let us continue to strengthen and enlighten our heart and mind in Jesus Christ and he will be faithful to keep in us the holiness we acquire through our faith and deeds in order to spread this holiness to others and to nature.

Valentin and Daniela Kozhuarov, Bulgaria

2 Corinthians 2.15: 'For we are the aroma of Christ to God among those who are being saved and among those who are perishing.' How do our lives spread holiness – the fragrance of Christ to the world around us?

As we look to a new year, pray that God would make us and Christians throughout the world holy, that we may be the fragrance of Christ, that through this holiness all creation will be transformed and made holy, that even when we feel defeated by the challenges and suffering of this earthly life, we may trust God's promise that all creation will be made holy as we are made new in Christ.

CHRISTMAS – DAY 6
A LIFE-CHANGING STORY

Luke 2.8–20

Matt's story
I was brought up on a sprawling council estate on the edge of the Peak District in Derbyshire. By the time I was in my later teens, I was in with a gang of older lads. They were a pretty bad crowd, into all kinds of drugs and all kinds of crime. I was driving my parents round the bend, ending up in police cells. I was doing lots of drugs.

On Christmas Eve 1993, me and my mate had been getting drunk and we were sat under a bridge. He turned to me and said, 'It's Christmas, isn't it?' I said, 'Yeah,' and he said, 'We ought to say Happy Birthday to Jesus.' So there we were with a spliff saying Happy Birthday to Jesus and suddenly we heard church bells ringing. And we were like, 'Oh it's a sign, the church bells.' We followed the sound of these bells and half staggered into the back of a Midnight Mass. And there I had probably the most profound religious experience of my life. It was quite a formal service, but I had an incredible sense of God's presence. We sang 'What can I give him, poor as I am? If I were a shepherd, I would bring a lamb. What can I give him? Give him my heart.' As we sang, I knew everything had to change. For months, I counted the cost of letting go. I began to connect with a church in the city centre of Manchester, but it was difficult to extract myself from my old scene. Everything came to a head just after my twenty-first birthday. I thought, 'It's all got to go, everything's got to be surrendered.'

So, a week after my birthday, I walked into the church where I'd been going and tried to find the holiest person that I could, which was a guy with a bald head with the light shining off it, looking a bit like a halo. I went over to him and said something like, 'I want to give my life to Jesus right now.' He looked stunned, and he led me through a prayer, and I started blubbering. I hardly stopped crying for about a month.

And that was it. Some profound healing began to take place as well as a restoration in my family and other relationships. After that, I had a tremendous sense of how many other young people are going through the stuff I'd been through. I had this incredible compulsion to tell these teenage kids, 'What are you doing?' I felt that God was going to use the stuff I'd been through to redeem it and channel it for his good.

Pray for young people like Matt, who find themselves caught up in a cycle of hopelessness, and for those who work with them and bring the truth of the gospel to them where they are. Pray that God will use our experiences, painful and positive, to bring good news to all around us.

O God, who before all other didst call shepherds to the cradle of thy Son; grant that by the preaching of the gospel the poor, the humble and the forgotten may know that they are at home with thee; through Jesus Christ our Lord. Amen.

The Book of Common Worship, Church of South India

CHRISTMAS – DAY 7
WHERE NEXT?

Luke 2.33–40

It's the one great religious festival here in this land that is as marked in its climax in its secular dimension as for those who celebrate the mystery at its core. For weeks the commercial world has banged its drum ever faster; for weeks the rhythm of preparation in street and home has grown more frenetic. Then it reached its climax, for faithful and unbelievers alike – and now we live in its aftermath.

Tidying the crumpled wrapping paper, finding space for the unwrapped and exclaimed-over presents, waving goodbye to the departing Christmas guests, savouring the simplicity of plain fare at meal times, we pause at last to draw breath and contemplate the pilgrimage achieved.

Where have I travelled to, my Lord, over this festive season? What is reshaped within me – even if only a very little – by standing in the place I stood and seeing what I saw?

I stood in a place of achieved Love. Lord, I saw it and I thank you.

For what more potent sign of completely selfless unconditional love could you give, than that of divine power abandoning its royalty of command, to lie a helpless infant, wholly dependent on the will and care of others, and subject to their thoughtlessness and cruelty?

And so the Christmas work begun demands of me too, my infant Lord; not less than everything. Teach me, far beyond gifts and cards and Christmas hospitality, how to give when it costs; that with all who have glimpsed the astonishing mystery at the heart of Christmas I may take my part, today and into the future, in the Christmas work which has again this year, just begun, through the gift of God himself. Amen.

Ruth Etchells, adapted

Is it true?
Lord, if it is, it will cost me my all.
Help me – help us – at the start of a new year to recognize afresh our
    Own calling to mission,
Our calling to follow you, wherever and however you may lead us. Amen.

CHRISTMAS – DAY 8
WE ARE SAYING YES!

Joshua 24.14–15

Yes is a daring word, one that requires courage. To say Yes implies risk. It means moving forward. It reminds me of something that Dag Hammarsjkøld says in *Markings*: 'at some moment I did say Yes . . . and from that hour I was certain . . . that my life, in self-surrender, had a goal'. This is the Yes to Christ's call to discipleship.

I pray Yes at the start of every day, accepting what lies ahead, and hoping that I may, in all that happens, see and feel and know the presence of God.

I pray Yes at the end of every day as I hand all that has happened over to God and ask his blessing on it.

So that Yes that I say in prayer gradually becomes my Yes to the whole of life. The Yes that holds everything together; that brings everything into focus and gives it meaning.

You dare your Yes – and experience a meaning.
You repeat your Yes – and all things acquire a meaning.
When everything has a meaning how can you live by anything but
    a Yes?

Nor is it enough to say Yes just once. I have to say it time and time again, to repeat it and go on repeating it . . .

Esther de Waal

How is God calling you to say Yes to him in your discipleship?
How can we say Yes together as a community of mission service? What does it mean to say Yes to mission on a daily basis?

Take some time to think about the year ahead – your hopes and dreams, and resolutions for the months ahead. How is your commitment to sharing the gospel reflected in the plans and resolutions you might make? Offer the year ahead to God, asking him to use you to his glory.

CHRISTMAS – DAY 9
CHRISTMAS CHEER . . . WAY BEYOND CHRISTMAS

Genesis 11.1–9

Jesus House for all Nations, one of the parishes of the Redeemed Christian Church of God based in Brent Cross, London, engages in many charitable projects both in their local and their international communities. These projects are all facilitated by their Church Social Responsibility (CSR) team.

One of their signature projects in their local community is the Novo Centre, based on a council estate in Burnt Oak. This centre serves a particularly disadvantaged community providing various forms of help and support ranging from youth activities, community meetings, games and counselling.

Arguably the most popular initiatives that Jesus House is known for would be the 'Christmas lunch on Jesus' – the distribution of Christmas hampers to over 2,300 homes, 'Spreading Christmas Cheer' – the serving of tea, coffee and mince pies at all the underground stations around Brent Cross and the Manna Supermarket – a food distribution initiative for families who, as a result of their financial status, are unable to purchase food items. Abroad, among other projects, the church partners with 'Habitat for Humanity' to build homes for the poor in Romania, has been involved with projects to economically empower impoverished communities in Rwanda and has also built a shelter for children caught in the war in Northern Uganda. These projects have provided an opportunity for the church to bring the love of God to their community in a practical manner.

Sola Irukwu, who heads the CSR team, writes:

I never cease to be fascinated by what can be achieved when a group of passionate and committed people set their minds to achieving a goal. We have several examples through the ages, from the story of the tower of Babel in Genesis 11.1–9, where God himself had to rein in the people, to the construction of the over-50,000 km-long Great Wall of China, to the world's tallest building – the Burj Kahlifa in Dubai – opened in 2010, which stands at 2,717 feet.

What impact the Church would have if it, for example, put its resources to putting an end to the premature death of 25,000 young children every day from preventable diseases such as malnutrition, diarrhoea, and malaria. The statistics make dismal reading and often leave one wondering if anything one does can or will make a difference. The good news is that you can make a difference. It is God who is at work within us and through us to will us to do his good pleasure. He has given us the grace and ability to make this change, if we take the first step and do something (no matter how small). Small is always big in the Master's hands.

At the beginning of a new year, how might we take small steps and use our gifts to engage with our local communities – to make a difference and through this to share the good news?

Christ has no body but yours,
No hands, no feet on earth but yours,
Yours are the eyes with which he looks compassion on this world,
Yours are the feet with which he walks to do good,
Yours are the hands, with which he blesses all the world.
Yours are the hands, yours are the feet,
Yours are the eyes, you are his body.
Christ has no body now but yours,
No hands, no feet on earth but yours,
Yours are the eyes with which he looks compassion on this world.
Christ has no body now on earth but yours.

Teresa of Avila (1515–82)

CHRISTMAS – DAY 10
A STAR IS BORN

Matthew 2.1–2

The fact that God chose to speak to the magi in the language they could understand is one of the most wonderful aspects of these nativity stories.

It tells us something very important about God: he wishes to communicate the good news of his son Jesus to all people, regardless of their faith and beliefs. It is often assumed that the good news about Jesus is really only relevant to church people and that if God is going to speak about him, then only church people will understand the language. The story about the magi and Herod tells us that this is far from true. Herod, who is the one who should have heard the news about the Messiah, misses it completely, whereas the pagan magi hear it perfectly. For those of us who are churchgoing Christians, this is rather a disturbing story. It implies that we in the Church can quite easily miss what God is telling us about his son, whereas those outside the Church who have hearts that long for all that is good, peaceful and healing for this world may actually understand what we are too deaf to hear. But then, how many modern 'magi' do hear the good news, make a long journey to church to worship him, but find they are rejected because they don't fit in culturally?

One of the most influential books on mission in recent years has been Vincent J. Donovan's *Christianity Rediscovered*. In this book, the writer, working from his long experience with the Masai people, argues that true mission involves walking alongside people in their journey and becoming fellow explorers, working with the conviction that the Holy Spirit will be the guide. It's a risky journey, because Christians may well have to readjust some of their views as they listen to the other. In a preface to the second edition of his book, Donovan quotes a young person's reflection on his book:

In working with young people in America, do not try to call them back to where they were, and so not try to call them to where you are, as beautiful as that place might seem to you. You must have the courage to go with them to a place that neither you nor they have ever been before.

Michael Mitton

How can we learn to speak the gospel afresh, in a language that our own culture can understand and identify with? How might we go to new places in mission – places that neither we, nor the people to whom we reach out – have ever been before?

Lord, as you led the magi by a star,
lead us by your Spirit,
that we may travel with you to places we cannot yet dream of
    or imagine. Amen.

CHRISTMAS – DAY 11
GOLD, FRANKINCENSE AND MYRRH

Matthew 2.9–11

Holy God, accept our prayers today.
You asked for all of our being, our thoughts and actions,
our creativity and expression.
What do we give you?
We think back two millennia to when the Christ child was born.
What would we give the baby?
What does a baby need?
What does the baby ask of us?
What gifts did the baby receive?

Gold – a gift for a king
A metal so precious that we have died and killed for it.
We treat your creation like it wasn't our home.
We've robbed the earth of its riches and left its wounds
open to infection.
Forgive us for not giving you the best of us.
What's the point of offering the religious bits,
if the rest is kept closely guarded?
Think of the best parts of your life.
Give them to God.

Frankincense – a gift for God.
The fragrance of worship, God's eau de cologne.
Worship giving God the honour that is due to him.
Forgive our efforts to worship you only when it is
convenient to do so
and with people that we choose, making outcasts of our
brothers and sisters.
Forgive us when our actions make our words of
worship meaningless.
Think of your worship.
Give it to God.

Myrrh – a gift for a mortal
The smell of a cover to hide death and decay,
But nothing is hidden from you.
Forgive us for denying the reality of pain, suffering and
struggle.
Do we get angry and shout at God?
Or do we bury our pain?

Mike Rose, Grace Pocket Liturgies

CHRISTMAS – DAY 12
GIFTS FOR A KING

1 Chronicles 29.11–14

O small Lord of the whole world.
to whom at your Epiphany,
came men, discerning,
offering gifts, frankincense, and myrrh;
India's gift came late, prevented,
rain-washed, flood-drenched,
sun-baked, dust-covered,
yet still on time.
If not for birth, at least for death;
spikenard by Mary of Magdala's hand,
reared and compounded on Himalayan hills,
and Joseph's gift – who also gave a tomb –
a winding sheet from hottest Sind
for that cool body.
Of birth (they say) this land knows more
than most,
of death, still more.
Its constant gathering place
the burial plot, as young
and old in Indian years
are laid to rest.

With Mary's outpoured balm
and Joseph's finest cloth
sent by this land,
accept the gift of this folk's fortitude,
and laying hold on these her gifts
touch also the giver and her monstrous dying
with the hope of the world's resurrection.

Prayer for Pakistan

Pray for many parts of the world devastated by human conflict and natural disasters. Pray that Jesus, the prince of peace, may bring peace and healing – the hope of the world's resurrection.

Thank God for the many different gifts we bring within the world-wide community of Christians.

Pray that we may know more fully the cost of following Christ – the Christ of the manger and of the cross.

EPIPHANY
RETURNING BY ANOTHER WAY

Matthew 2.12

The idea that we cannot go back the way we have come is an important spiritual metaphor: having encountered the Christ-child, we can never just go back. Even if we return to the same life, we find that it has somehow changed. This is by no means a new idea. Pope Leo the Great wrote that the change of plan in the magis' journey home was not only to baffle Herod's murderous plan, but also that 'it behoved them now that they believed in Christ not to walk in the paths of their old line of life, but having entered on a new way to keep away from the errors they had left'.

We never find out any more about the magi; we simply know that, having encountered Jesus they cannot return the same way. He continued to affect their lives after the moment of acknowledgement and worship; their lives changed direction because of this encounter. Similarly with Jesus' family: they found that this child, small and vulnerable though he was, and so early in his life, compelled them to make urgent and unplanned journeys to ensure their safety.

We see Jesus' family and the wise men being pushed out into new and unfamiliar surroundings, changed for ever by their encounter with this holy child. The nativity story does not have a neatly tied-up ending, but rather a dramatic exit into the unknown, the only certainty being that there will never be a return to business as usual.

Maggi Dawn, adapted

Two thousand years have slipped by
Like freshets in the Ganges
Since St Thomas came to our land.
Here, though the cross is lifted
Amidst the paddy fields and coconut palms
And white-clad Christians flock to the churches
When the bells call them to worship;
our wise men have not yet seen the star

and the manger of Bethlehem
is not yet the cradle of our land.
But Christian hope never dies
and the ends of the strands of destiny
are held safe in the hands of God.
Pass it on to the ends of the earth!
Christ is the answer – Ours! Yours!

Chandran Devanesen, India

Pray that the gospel may spread to the ends of the earth – beginning with
us, right here and now.

EPIPHANY – DAY 2
SETTING SAIL

Genesis 12.1–5

Pilgrim
    when your ship,
    long moored in harbour, gives the illusion
    of being a house;
    when your ship
    begins to put down roots
    in the stagnant water by the quay: put out to sea!
    save your boat's journeying soul and your own pilgrim soul,
    cost what it may.

Dom Helder Camara

*As you begin the New Year, make time to reflect on where you are in your
walk of faith; identify any parts of your life that are perhaps too-safe har-
bours or even stagnant waters, areas where God might be calling you on
to new things and fresh encounters with him and with others.*

Father, lead me deeper in my journey with you,
cost what it may.

By your grace, may I be prepared to put out to sea,
to leave the safety of the harbour
and to follow your call
cost what it may. Amen.

EPIPHANY – DAY 3

TAKE MY LIFE . . .

Matthew 4.18–22

Looking ahead though, to my imminent departure, my feelings are of excitement and some nerves – 'What have I let myself in for?' But at such times, I am taken back to my ordination retreat, pre-priesting, and once again find myself reflecting on the words of the hymn, 'Take my life and let it be, consecrated, Lord, to thee', written by Frances Havergal in 1874. She began writing verse at the age of seven and soon found her work being published in various religious journals. Whenever I sing these words, I am reminded too of the prayer of Saint Patrick, '. . . Christ in the heart of everyone who thinks of me, Christ in the mouth of everyone who speaks to me, Christ in every eye that sees me, Christ in every ear that hears me'. A reminder that despite my fears and anxiety about what is to come, by stepping out along the path of Christian discipleship and embracing the unknown I need not have any worries about the future. Indeed, it has been a truly liberating experience to be affirmed and encouraged in following this call to working overseas, and I rejoice in the company of all the saints, past and present, who have also uttered these words in their prayers: 'Take myself and I will be, ever, only, all for thee.'

Becky Mathew

> Christ be with me, Christ within me,
> Christ behind me, Christ before me,
> Christ beside me, Christ to win me,
> Christ to comfort and restore me.
> Christ beneath me, Christ above me,
> Christ in quiet, Christ in danger,

Christ in hearts of all that love me,
Christ in mouth of friend and stranger.

I bind unto myself the Name,
The strong Name of the Trinity,
By invocation of the same,
The Three in One and One in Three.
By whom all nature hath creation,
Eternal Father, Spirit, Word:
Praise to the Lord of my salvation,
Salvation is of Christ the Lord.

St Patrick's Breastplate

EPIPHANY – DAY 4
CALLED TO STAY

Ephesians 2.19–22

We spent 13 or so years on the outskirts of Bradford, in a wonderfully mixed community, where we grew close to people in a small church that felt like family. We learned many valuable lessons while we were there but particularly that when God called us to that church and community, he called us to get involved and to stay involved.

Our reflections are that often it's harder to stay involved than to get involved – to stay than to go. It was much harder to continue to keep it as our home when we'd been there a while, and things were harder work. We were tempted to look, and listen, for calls to elsewhere (and don't get us wrong, it's often right to look and ask) – but it became evident that hearing nothing was confirmation that we were in the right place!

We also learned something about what it is to be part of a community and to work at creating community – both 'secular' and 'sacred'. Maybe unsurprisingly, sacred and secular looked similar in lots of ways, although the sacred sometimes had an additional dimension. It also started to be apparent that people could, and would, try our church-based community once they'd become comfortable in our home-based 'community'.

Martin and Pam Lawson, Tunisia

The common life we share is not primarily for ourselves, but so that others might see Jesus and find fullness of life in him.

Lord Jesus Christ,
alive and at large in the world,
help me to follow and find you there today
in the places where I work,
meet people, spend money, and make plans.
Take me as a disciple of your kingdom
to see through your eyes
and hear the questions you are asking,
to welcome all with your trust and truth,
and to change the things that contradict God's love.
By the power of your cross
and the freedom of your Spirit. Amen.

EPIPHANY – DAY 5
VENN PRINCIPLES – FOLLOW GOD'S LEADING

Proverbs 16.1–9

During my internment, I served the Holy Liturgy every Sunday and Church holiday. At first, the guards insulted me and beat me to make me give it up. I held fast, and at last they left me alone. To their way of thinking I was crazy, but my craziness was the kind spoken of by St Paul: 'For the message about the cross is foolishness to those who are perishing, but to us who are being saved, it is the power of God. For it is written: "I will destroy the wisdom of the wise, and the discernment of the discerning I will thwart"' (1 Cor. 1.18–19).

It was Sunday, and I was isolated. It was one of the days without food, and I couldn't serve the Divine Liturgy, because I had no bread. On that Sunday, I asked the Lord to help me forget my sadness at the impossibility of serving the Holy Liturgy for lack of bread. Nevertheless, a thought came to me: to ask the guard for some bread. The evil guard was on duty, and I knew that my request would make him angry; he would insult me, and he would ruin the peace I had in my soul for that holy day. But the thought persisted and grew so strong that I knocked on the iron door of the cell. A few minutes later the door was violently opened, and the furious guard asked me what was the matter. I asked him for a piece of bread, no more than an ounce, for serving the Holy Liturgy.

My request seemed absurd to him; it was so unexpected that his mouth dropped open in amazement. He left slamming the door as violently as he had opened it. Many other hungry prisoners asked him for bread, but I was the first to ask for bread in order to serve the Divine Liturgy. I regretted my impulse.

Twenty minutes later, the door of my cell opened halfway, and quietly the guard gave me the ration for a whole day: four ounces of bread. He shut the door as quietly as he had opened it. And if I had not been holding the bread I would have thought that it was all an illusion.

This was the most profound and most sublime Holy Sacrament I have ever experienced. The service was two hours long, and the guard did not disturb or insult me as at other times; the entire duration of the isolation section was peaceful.

Later, after I had finished the Liturgy, and the fragrance of the prayer was still in my cell, the door opened quietly and the guard whispered: 'Father, don't tell anyone I gave you bread, or you'll ruin me.'

Fr Gheorghe Calciu, Romanian Orthodox Priest, imprisoned 21 years for speaking against Communism

Look upon us, Lord, hear and enlighten us. Show us your very self. Take pity on our efforts and strivings toward you, for we have no strength without you. Teach me to seek you, and when I seek you show yourself to me, for I cannot seek you unless you teach me, nor can I find you unless you show yourself to me. Let me seek you in desiring you and desire you in seeking you, let me find you by loving you, and love you in finding you.

Anselm of Canterbury (1033–1109)

EPIPHANY – DAY 6
A CALL TO MISSION

Ephesians 2.10

What is most satisfying about my calling to be a mission partner is that it is out of the ordinary. With my training and qualifications, I could be doing a job more lucrative and 'attractive'. I chose to become a mission partner more as a calling of God upon my life. When I was young, I saw and knew people in a similar vocation who became role models in my life. I have had no second thoughts about my choice.

I am sure of this direction in my life as I am convinced that this is God's direction for my life. I would not be more fulfilled in any other job. What I love about the job is the freedom to do a pioneering role, working cross-culturally in spite of its challenges, and the opportunity to equip and enable the Church/people of God.

Emil and Mano Chandran

Reflect on these words: 'For we are God's workmanship, created in Christ Jesus to do good works which God prepared in advance for us to do' (Eph. 2.10, NIV).

Lord, where are you calling me?
What are you asking me to do?
What are the 'good works' – the mission – that you call me to fulfil?
Like the first disciples,
may I hear your call afresh
and follow in faithfulness and trust. Amen.

EPIPHANY – DAY 7
IN THE FACE OF DANGER . . .

Psalm 27.1–6

In the face of danger . . .
Adam and Eve hid
Abraham stepped out
Jacob wrestled
Moses killed
Joshua marched
Jonah complained
Job endured
Noah built
Elijah fled
Ezra confessed
Nehemiah wept
David fought
Solomon dreamt
Hezekiah pleaded
Esther spoke out
Daniel trusted
Mary sang
Joseph believed
Peter walked
The disciples prayed
Paul praised
Jesus submitted to God.

SafeSpace, Telford

In the face of danger, how do you respond? Spend time reflecting with God on how you can trust him more.

EPIPHANY – DAY 8
UPS AND DOWNS

Matthew 8.23–27

Life is full of ups and downs but the joy is that the Lord is always there, often working his miracles behind our backs. What the Lord has done recently in terms of revealing weapons, saving his people, rescuing a kidnapped girl, encouraging and strengthening his Church – it is just amazing. May we never cease to give thanks.

Susan Essam, Nigeria

How do we respond when the storms of life buffet us? Do we believe that Christ is there in the midst?

Lord Jesus,
the storm is life and life is the storm
and there is no escaping it;
but what matters is that you are in the storm with us,
a Beacon and a Presence that is sure.

From Madagascar

EPIPHANY – DAY 9
PRAISING GOD AT ALL TIMES

Philippians 4.11–13

Praising God in the good times . . . and bad! Being on God's payroll is a wonderful but often puzzling thing! Most of the time, we seem to skim over the waters of poverty, never quite soaring into the air of riches but always, always, having what we need. Then, just as we get used to this kind of subsistence living, God throws us off balance, and we find ourselves spending a couple of nights in a luxury hotel or, in my case right now, in a first-class train carriage travelling down to Hong Kong. God is good, but sadly it seems that it often takes these extravagant blessings of God to make me realize how good he really is and how great his love is for me.

I know full well that the real measure of a person's faith is marked by their ability to praise and thank God in the bad times, as well as the good. It is something that I have been trying to learn and often takes a mighty act of willpower, to go against my feelings and outward circumstances and thus declare out loud: 'And yet I will praise the Lord!'

Once done though, these words have an amazing effect on the spiritual climate and on my own countenance. So, right now, as I sit in my first-class carriage, with an en-suite bathroom, enjoying some much needed rest and relaxation, I will still declare out loud: *'The Lord be praised! And blessed is the one who puts her trust in him.'*

Mike and Tracey Walmsley

Are we content to praise God whether we have little – or much?

The Lord be praised! And blessed are all who put their trust in him!

EPIPHANY – DAY 10
DIFFICULT DAYS AHEAD

1 Peter 1.5–7

Martin Luther King was born on 15 January 1929. This is an extract from his speech on the day before he was assassinated:

Well, I don't know what will happen now. We've got some difficult days ahead. But it doesn't matter with me now. Because I've been to the mountaintop. And I don't mind. Like anybody, I would like to live a long life. Longevity has its place. But I'm not concerned about that now. I just want to do God's will. And He's allowed me to go up to the mountain. And I've looked over. And I've seen the promised land. I may not get there with you. But I want you to know tonight, that we, as a people will get to the promised land. And I'm happy, tonight. I'm not worried about anything. I'm not fearing any man. Mine eyes have seen the glory of the coming of the Lord.

Many of us face will face trials in the coming days – some great, some small.

Are we prepared to put our faith in God and the vision of his kingdom he has shown us?

Lord, we put our faith and trust in you,
trusting that you will protect us in the time of trial,
trusting that you will save us.
Lord – test our faith
Refine us like gold in your fire
And renew in us the hope of your kingdom. Amen.

EPIPHANY – DAY 11
SEEING THE NEW THING

Isaiah 43.19–21

In considering what might be involved in Christian mission in the third millennium, John V. Taylor is a trustworthy guide, because his vision is never narrowly compartmentalized. Christian mission, as he understands it, embraces the whole of life, all the facts, all the beauty and all the pain. Only God is catholic, while we remain sectarian. We long for a catholicity that is yet to be revealed. John V. Taylor is one of those rare saints offering us glimpses of what such wholeness and completeness feels like. In a time when the Church is traumatized by decline and terribly anxious about the future, his all-embracing vision is wonderfully liberating, inviting us to trusting faith just as our fears overwhelm us.

John V. Taylor's significance for mission today, I would argue, lies in refusing to let us huddle together in the secure Christian ghetto, becoming ever more theologically conservative, building higher the walls of division, marking out more clearly who is saved and who is not, and shouting louder to make ourselves heard. He offers us a way forward that is at once thoroughly orthodox and marvellously sensitive and human. He does this by remaining absolutely true to scripture and Christian tradition on the one hand, while holding himself wide open to experience fully the new thing God is doing.

David Wood

Do we understand mission as encompassing 'the whole of life, all the facts, all the beauty and all the pain'? Do we find ourselves huddling in a Christian ghetto at times? Are we able to see the 'new thing' that God is doing among us?

Lord, when we are tempted to despair, renew our hope.
When we are tempted to hide, give us courage.
Help to us live a life of mission that embraces the whole of life –
all the facts, all the beauty, and all the pain –
and to trust that you are doing a new thing among us. Amen.

EPIPHANY – DAY 12
THE INNER LIGHT OF CHRIST

1 John 1.5–7

The Inner Light, the Inward Christ, is no mere doctrine belonging peculiarly to a small religious fellowship, to be accepted or rejected as mere belief. It is the living Centre of Reference for all Christian souls and Christian groups.

Thomas Kelly (1893–1941)

Spend time reflecting on the light of Christ that we share. Light a candle and pray that disunity between Christians throughout the world may be dispelled in the light of Christ.
God, we thank you
for the faith of our forebears,
and for the faith of the forebears of others.

Forgive us
if in pride or throughtlessness
we have disparaged the faith of fellow believers
because their faith is not precisely ours,
or ours but not expressed
as we would express it.
We all must seek you.
For your Spirit in our hearts prompts the quest.
Yet whatever in the end we know of you
is what you gave rather than what we sought,
what you revealed rather than what we found out.
Before in our need we sought you,
You in your son sought us,
Through him alone,
Seeking and being sought, finding and being found
We all come to you.

Jamie Wallace

EPIPHANY – DAY 13
UNITY IN CHRIST

John 17.22–24

What should our unity in Christ look like? Here are some thoughts:

- It should be interpersonal rather than organizational.
- It should be constantly co-operative.
- It should preserve intact the integrity of each party.
- It should build interdependence.
- It should consist of our pouring love into each other.

Geoff and Gill Kimber

What might the 'complete unity' Jesus describes in John 17 look like?
How can we 'pour love into each other' in practical and meaningful
ways?

We offer our thanks to thee
For sending thy only son to die for us all.
In a world suffocated with colour bars,
How sweet a thing it is to know
That in thee we all belong to one family.
There are times when we,
Underprivileged people,
Weep tears that are not loud but deep,
When we think of the suffering we experience.

We come to thee, our only hope and refuge.
Help us, O God, to refuse to be embittered
Against those who handle us with harshness.
We are grateful to thee
For the gift of laughter at all times.
Save us from hatred of those who oppress us.
May we follow the spirit of thy son Jesus Christ.

Prayer of an African pastor

EPIPHANY – DAY 14
WHERE TWO OR THREE ARE GATHERED . . .

Matthew 18.18–20

Christ is no less surely present, as he promised, where two or three are
gathered together in his name. We very easily assume, and quite wrongly,
that the promise is primarily related to meetings for prayer. But we need
not meet in his name only to pray. Every occasion and every activity
when Christians meet should be 'in his name'.

Missionaries tell me many stories of how vividly the presence of Christ is realized by Christians doing things together: a hospital with an African nursing sister bringing a nervous European patient the assuring 'presence' of Christ; an art class working together on a difficult task. From a women's training centre a missionary says, 'in every situation which arises out of our living together, Christ is met in someone involved'.

'Always present' – 'the continuing present' of the grammar book has found its equivalent in experience if there is to be valid testimony. That is the emphasis of the Revival Movement in East Africa, which has the disconcerting habit of taking seriously the words 'New every morning is the love' and to have something new to say about it every morning! That is an insight that our Christianity badly needs.

Incidentally, it suggests a dynamic approach to the study of theology. A staff member at an overseas theological college told me: 'I may come into the classroom to teach doctrine. I may speak of the cross, or of the history of the Church's teaching of the cross. I may illustrate by saying how the cross first became a living reality for me. But one more step remains. My students must know that they and I are experiencing still *today* the forgiveness and power of the cross.'

Max Warren

Father, may we know your presence with us
as we share together in mission,
as we share the love freely offered to us,
as we experience daily the forgiveness and power of the cross. Amen.

EPIPHANY – DAY 15
A PILGRIM FAITH

Colossians 3.2

We believe in one source and centre of our faith, Jesus Christ, risen from the tomb, face of God for our sight, word of God for our minds, food of God for our souls.

We praise God that he has come to us in Jesus, and confirmed us in faith by the Holy Spirit.

We hear God's call to follow the way of Jesus, so that the whole world may see the new creation where justice and peace live together.

We confess that as we follow Jesus we are fearful pilgrims, clinging to a small loyalty, afraid of great challenges, compromised for the sake of security and forgetting the promise beyond death.

We confess that as churches we are stumbling pilgrims, unable to accept each other as God accepts us, preferring our partial histories to the wholeness of creation, sometimes intolerant, often witnessing to a faded past and not the living Lord.

We travel on, asking forgiveness and renewal, confident that the God who called us into faith will hold us and heal us and make us one.

We believe God has great purposes for us.

As Jesus was a pilgrim through agony and death to be lifted up in glory, so we trust in him to draw us to himself, to unite us with him, no longer strangers to the promises of grace but pilgrims together on the road.

We believe that the living Christ speaks in word and sacrament, in saints and martyrs, in love and understanding, in the hungry, the weak, the homeless, and the lost.

We will listen to that voice.
We will make the Lord our guide:
We will learn his way of life.
To him be glory in the church throughout the world
for ever.

Bernard Thorogood

Lord God we thank you
For calling us into the company
Of those who trust in Christ
And seek to obey his will.
May your spirit guide and strengthen us
In mission and service to your world;
And may we be strangers no longer
But pilgrims together on the way to your kingdom. Amen.

EPIPHANY – DAY 16
REALLY PRESENT

Ephesians 4.3–6

We begin to think about mission, then, knowing that we are all in the same boat, that we all belong together, children of God together, gloriously made in the divine image but marred by human frailty and sin. This radical humility is our starting point, an honest recognition demanding of us grace, sensitivity, patience, gentleness and genuine openness to the leading of the Spirit.

For John V. Taylor, this starting point can hardly be stressed too much, and it all comes together when he talks about us being really present. His jokes about this underline the seriousness of what is at stake. The eucharistic action, the central act of Christian worship, is all about presence, the real presence of Christ in word and sacrament. We might imagine it follows naturally that Christians are well rehearsed in being really present to one another. The trouble, however, with professional Christians – as he wryly observes – is that often we are not all there! Being really present to one another is actually quite rare. Listening is an art form at which too few of us excel.

Mission, however, demands of us real presence. It is all about meeting and greeting. Mission is encounter, impossible apart from relationship. It happens, if it happens at all, face to face. I need to be here with you, not somewhere else, attentive to you, not distracted, really looking, listening, paying attention. Only so can we move closer together, only so do we begin to trust each other, and without trust nothing of any lasting value will pass between us.

Dialogue is, by definition, a sustained conversation between different people who are not saying the same thing. Dialogue is a conversation between people who are not saying the same thing, but who nevertheless go on talking. It happens whenever we recognize and respect the differences between us, the contradictions, the mutual exclusions between our various ways of thinking, yet refuse to abandon one another.

David Wood

Lord God, may we learn what it means truly to
  encounter one another.
May we be attentive to one another.
May we learn to truly listen in our differences
and refuse to abandon one another. Amen.

EPIPHANY – DAY 17
PEACE SHARED . . .

Luke 10.2–6

Simplicity, focus, peace shared, and peace received. Jesus' emphases seem to be both relevant to, and reflected in, the experience of many of the communities and projects that we are in contact with through CMS Small Missional Communities.

The call for simplicity and focus in Jesus' instructions are reflected in the experience of the Hopeweavers project in Southampton (www. hopeweavers.co.uk). Team member Jacqui Lea says, 'Your prayers for this new adventure together are most welcome. We are seeing some folks linking in from local estates – a "simple life" type of model – which is interesting. Lots of pondering about how to hold it all without getting swallowed up in some kind of structures-fest and forgetting that all we need is to be clustered around Christ.'

From its base in Rochester Cathedral, the Gathering (www.gathering. me.uk) is finding a peaceful welcome at a local pub where they are holding a regular 'pub theology' session. The leader of the community, Rob Ryan, says, 'The staff have been very supportive and have just offered to reserve tables for us.' In Bradford, the Roots Community and Joshua Project (www.joshuaproject.org.uk) are seeing some amazing examples of the kind of 'peace resting on' people experience that Jesus seemed to have in mind. Project leader Rich Jones says, 'Two young people from really tough backgrounds made a faith commitment around a month ago, and their journey has led them to wanting to be baptized. I continue to be excited as I see young people and their families connecting with God in a real way, because it has been made easy for them through the way we are church. Love it!'

Ian Adams

Risen Lord,
Give us a heart for simple things.
Love, laughter, bread, wine, and dreams.
Fill us with green growing hope.
Make us a people whose song is Alleluia,
whose sign is peace,
and whose name is love. Amen.

EPIPHANY – DAY 18
A 'MIXED ECONOMY'

Matthew 13.52

I love it when I come across traditional and evolving streams of church seeing each other as partners, diving into the flow of God's reshaping of the world in the way of Jesus. I am delighted to find them seeking wisdom from each other, practising generosity in spirit and in resources and honouring each other's distinctiveness.

My experience is that engagement in mission can be both a route into, and a result of, such mutual appreciation. When we focus on the bigger picture of mission, our differences can become creative, not destructive.

Ian Adams

How might we benefit from the treasures and insights of both 'old' and 'new' expressions of church?

Lord God, help us to understand the mystery which is your Church.
Open our eyes to see the meaning and relevance of the pictures and
    metaphors we find in your word.
Open our hearts to the needs of your Church in our place, in our time.
Receive our thanks for the gifts of the Spirit given to everybody in the
Church – those gifts of ministry which are so different from one another, yet which need each other – and which only together can form
your body.

Help us to rediscover the gifts you are giving us for our time –
and to recognize and use these gifts so that your Church may have
    new life,
for the sake of the world. Amen.

Scottish Churches Council

EPIPHANY – DAY 19
NO HALF MEASURES

Luke 9.57–62

Christ says, 'Give me all. I don't want so much of your time or so much
of your money or so much of your work: I want you. I have not come to
torment your natural self but to kill it. No half measures are any good.
I don't want to cut off a branch here and a branch there, I want to have
the whole tree down. Hand over the whole self, all the desire which you
think innocent as well as the one you think wicked – the whole outfit. I
will give you a new self instead: In fact I will give you Myself: my own
will shall become yours.'

C. S. Lewis (1898–1963)

*What do I need to hand over to God to enable him to use me more
effectively in mission?*

Open thou mine eyes and I shall see.
Incline my heart and I shall desire.
Order my steps and I shall walk,
in the ways of thy commandments.
O Lord God, be thou to me a God,
And beside thee let there be none else,
no other, nought else with thee.
Vouchsafe to me, to worship thee and
Serve thee, according to thy commandments
in truth of spirit,

in reverence of body,
in blessing of lips,
in private and in public.

Lancelot Andrewes (1555–1626)

EPIPHANY – DAY 20
MASAI CHRIST

Revelation 5.1–5

Take time to reflect on the image of Jesus below. Is it an image that appeals to you? Does it reflect the Jesus you read about in the Bible? How does it challenge you to think differently about Jesus?

Jesus, our brother, Lion of Judah,
Protect us we pray. Amen.

EPIPHANY – DAY 21
LAUGHING CHRIST

Matthew 11.16–19

Take time to reflect on the image of Jesus below. Is it an image that appeals to you? Does it reflect the Jesus you read about in the Bible? How does it challenge you to think differently about Jesus?

We praise you, Lord God, for the many emotions you bless us with. Help us to be fully alive – to embrace pain and joy, laughter and tears. May we be people who truly share in the fullness of life you offer. Amen.

EPIPHANY – DAY 22
ANGRY CHRIST

Mark 11.15–17

Take time to reflect on the image of Jesus below. Does it reflect the Jesus you read about in the Bible? How does it challenge you to think differently about Jesus? What 'tables' might Jesus want to overturn in our churches today?

Lord God, there are so many things in our world that make us angry –
  injustice, greed, complacency, hypocrisy . . . the list goes on.
Lord, break our hearts with the things that break your heart and give
  us courage to take a stand.
In the name of Jesus Christ we pray. Amen.

EPIPHANY – DAY 23
GOD'S BOX

Mark 2.23–28

When
the box that I've built
to define the things of God
breaks
it feels like
I've lost God.

But I haven't lost God.

Just the box.

Jane Upchurch

Do we put God in a box?

Lord, give us grace
to see beyond the box,
to see beyond the limitations and rules we create,
to be surprised,
to be challenged,
and to trust. Amen.

EPIPHANY – DAY 24
CLAIMING OUR BIRTHRIGHT

Genesis 25.27–34

Do I believe that I am God's child, whom God wants to bless and use abundantly? Do I have confidence in who I am in Christ?

Hebrews 12.16 (NIV) says: 'See to it that no one is godless like Esau, who for a single meal sold his inheritance rights as the oldest son.' Are there ways in which we 'sell our birthright' as God's children for the immediate satisfactions that the world offers rather than living for the blessings that God yearns to pour upon us?

Lord God, give us, your children,
the grace to recognize your calling,
to live as your children,
beloved, blessed and free,
and to be confident in our identity in you. Amen.

EPIPHANY – DAY 25
RECOGNIZING OUR UNIQUENESS

Psalm 139.13–16

Leonardo da Vinci painted one Mona Lisa, Beethoven created one Fifth Symphony, and God made one version of you. You're it!

You're the only you there is. And if we don't get you, we don't get you. You're the only shot we have at you. You can do something no one else can do in a fashion that no one else can do it. You are more than just a coincidence of chromosomes and heredity, more than just an assemblage of somebody else's lineage. You are uniquely made . . .

Can you be anything you want to be? I don't think so. But can you be everything God wants you to be? I do think so.

And you become that by discovering your uniqueness.

Max Lucado

Take some time to think about how God has created you with a particular set of skills, abilities, and personality type. It may be helpful to note down a few of the gifts that you feel God has given to you, and how/where you are using them at present.

Spend some time thanking God that you are 'fearfully and wonderfully made', and praying that in the coming days you will discover a deepening awareness of how he wants to use you to share in mission.

EPIPHANY – DAY 26
REFLECTING ON EXPERIENCE

Genesis 50.19–20

People go abroad to wonder at the heights of mountains, at the huge waves of the sea, at the long courses of rivers, at the vast compass of the ocean, at the circular motion of the stars, and they pass by themselves without wondering.

Augustine of Hippo (354–430)

How often do we allow ourselves to stop, and, like Joseph, to reflect on our life experiences, and see God's hand within our lives – both in good times and bad, in painful experiences and in times of joy? How might God want to use our experiences, both good and bad, to help bring new life to others as we share in mission?

'What if the essence of who you are is enough? . . . pay attention and wait . . . then just let go and dance.'

Oriah Mountain Dreamer, *The Dance*

Lord, we bring all that we are before you
we wait on you . . .
teach us to let go
teach us to dance. Amen.

EPIPHANY – DAY 27
SHAPED BY CHRIST FOR MISSION

Acts 20.24

God has given each of us a unique emotional heartbeat that races when we think about the subjects, activities or circumstances that interest us. We instinctively care about some things and not about others.

These are clues to where you should be serving . . . Repeatedly the Bible says to 'serve the Lord with all your heart'. God wants you to serve him passionately, not dutifully. People rarely excel at tasks they don't enjoy doing or feel passionate about. God wants to use your natural interests to serve him and others. Listening for inner promptings can point to the ministry God intends for you to have.

Rick Warren

The same breath is blown into the flute, cornet and bagpipe, but different music is produced according to the different instruments. In the same way, the one Spirit works in us, God's children, but different results are produced, and God is glorified through them according to one's temperament and personality.

Sadhu Sundar Singh (1898–1929)

Come Holy Spirit
Breathe upon me.
Fill me with your life.
Be glorified in me. Amen.

EPIPHANY – DAY 28
CHERISHING AND CELEBRATING

Luke 2.25–32

For many years there had been a long-held dream of St Paul's church in Kandy to build a home for the elderly. In Sri Lanka it has been traditional for children to look after their parents. This has changed for many reasons, especially increasing living costs. As a result, some elderly men and women are urgently looking for somewhere to live. During the last couple of years, since our arrival we have been praying and holding fundraising events here in Sri Lanka and in the UK, so that we might care for the needs of these most vulnerable people. Then in 2007 a lovely couple sold us a large, beautiful house for this purpose at a bargain price. This past November, we welcomed our first residents to the Eventide home for the elderly! It was wonderful to see the gratitude on their faces as we interviewed them and found out about their lives and their desire to move into the home. By Easter we will have at least 11 residents. At Eventide, the love of Jesus is shared in word and deed with people from all faiths and communities.

Paul and Ina Watson, Sri Lanka

Sister Constance, a 105-year-old sister of the Sisterhood of St John the Divine in Canada, says this: 'The latter years of our lives are given us by God to give him thanks, to use our maturity, to use our manifold gifts because there's no one more varied than the elderly person. These years are not just ours to salt away; they are ours to help leaven society.'

IAFN Newsletter

A recent prayer request from a Christian couple in retirement said: 'We live in a community of retired clergy and their wives. Please pray that we may regain our sense of mission!' Another said: 'Please pray that I may be more effective as an evangelist (I shall be 90 next February).'

Father, there are those among us who like Simeon
have worked all their lives in your service.
Thank you for all they have taught us

and demonstrated to us of your kingdom.
Keep them fresh in their faith
and a continued inspiration to the young.
Make us sensitive to their growing physical needs
and give us a generous spirit in serving them. Amen.

From Pakistan

EPIPHANY – DAY 29
BEGIN ON A SMALL SCALE (VENN PRINCIPLES)

Matthew 13.33

Rong Tao Tang has lived and worked in Guizhou, one of China's poorest provinces, all his life. Situated in mountainous south-west China, Guizhou, like many of the interior provinces, has been neglected in terms of both church development and resources. Tang's solution has been remarkable. Through sheer hard work and aptitude he informally trained himself not just in Chinese medicine but also in Western medicine. So successful was his practice that in spite of his lack of formal qualifications he was recognized by the authorities and licensed to work and practise as a doctor.

Tang ploughed the proceeds from his medical practice into mission work. His priority is to train rural people in biblical literacy, church ministry and leadership skills. These aims have been met in the near derelict rooms of his Guizhou Bible class. As well as the theological and pastoral studies, Pastor Tang also gives the students a general education and ensures that they get some basic medical training too. Over the years he has been able to bring in young men and women from the far reaches of the province. Most of the trainees are from minority tribes, especially the Miao people. Many of these young people come from farming communities in which literacy levels are low. Normally, such people would not even get to go to school. Guizhou has been battling against poor academic standards due to its isolation. A lack of well-trained teachers means that there have been few well-educated pupils. It is a vicious circle. Nevertheless, with his little money and despite having to work against many handicaps, Pastor Tang has successfully trained over 300 men and women. A handful of his best students have gone on to higher academic study while the others have been sent home, where they are equipped to minister in village contexts. In this way, 250–300 villages and communities have obtained pastors.

In autumn 2005, 2,000 people – many from remote villages – gathered in Guizhou, to celebrate the opening of their new Bible school, the largest Christian building the province has ever seen. Pastor Tang can now continue to live out his love of God by continuing to build up thousands of people.

> Dear Lord God
> we thank you for mustard seed
> and for the wonders of yeast
> and for how these things teach us about your love.
> Lord – plant your seed into our lives
> help us work your yeast into our hearts
> that wonderful things may happen;
> we ask it in Jesus' name. Amen.

Richard J. Fairchild – *Spirit Networks* (2002–6)

EPIPHANY – DAY 30
HEART'S DESIRE

Psalm 37.3–4

One Sunday I was introduced at church to Krishna (an alias), a Nepalese student who had been living on the streets in Woking for two days. His situation was desperate and similar to the parable of the prodigal son. When we met he smelled of the streets and alcohol. As we talked, he broke down and cried; he wanted to return to Nepal but also mentioned that he wanted to see the sea before he died. I took this as a sign from

God as I was taking my Nepalese housemate to the sea the next day. Krishna stayed for the service, before a church member took him into his home. At first he was unsure, but soon he was visibly moved by the worship songs, which spoke of God taking care of the weak and the unworthy. By the end of the evening, he was singing too! He thoroughly enjoyed the trip to the sea also.

Michael Green, Jordan

How might we be open to recognize the dreams that people have – even for the simplest things? How can we respond and enable them to encounter the One who alone can fulfil the deepest desires of our hearts?

Pray for people like Krishna, far away from home, that they may discover their true and lasting home in Christ. Pray for those working with the homeless on the streets. Pray that we may discover afresh that our deepest desires and longings are fulfilled only in Christ.

EPIPHANY – DAY 31
MUSTARD SEED MISSION

Mark 4.30–32

Do you know what's in a bottle of washing-up liquid? At a training day in an urban church in Asunción, Paraguay, we saw the following ingredients being added: water, caustic soda, sulphuric acid, Trietanaloamina – an ingredient that softens and/or lubricates the skin, scent, colouring.

The government programme DEAG, a bit like the UK Department of Environment, Food and Rural Affairs, uses every opportunity to share their trained knowledge to improve people's lives or economic situations. We had sewing in the morning and detergent making in the afternoon. The day was a hit with everybody. Our prayer is that lots of people take initiative and start mixing, bottling and selling. Everyone uses detergent and the supermarket quality is often not as good as homemade. People can boost their incomes very easily by selling door to door.

Caroline Gilmour-White

Reflect on how God can use even small things to bring transformation to people and societies. Are there creative ways that you can make a difference, even with very limited means?

> Lord, great things grow from small beginnings.
> Trees from tiny seeds.
> New quality of life from a small business venture.
> Faith in Christ from a word shared or kindness performed.
> The kingdom of God from shoots of faith.
> Lord, please – give us vision and give us faith. Amen.

EPIPHANY – DAY 32
THE LESSON OF PATIENCE

Hebrews 6.11–12

The past year has not been a flaming success; there haven't been mass conversions by the thousands. Yet it has been a fulfilling one where I could make a difference in small ways – from lending a listening ear to my younger sisters in church to building up the confidence of the newer musicians in the worship team. Although there were days when I felt really discouraged at the standstill in my language skills, because I haven't had any lessons since last November, I'm learning the lesson of patience – taking a step at a time and to be less of a perfectionist.

Jane Lee, Thailand

Do we trust that God is always at work, even when we can't see instant results? Are we prepared to keep focused and wait patiently?

> O Lord our Joy
> May we love you more and more
> Share in your caring for all
> And lead some to your feet.

Midday prayer of the Women's Order of Sisters and
Companions for North India

EPIPHANY – DAY 33
PLACES OF HEALING

Psalm 103.2–4

A local Sikh woman, who suffered from depression through a stressful work situation, joined our food-growing project to seek physical and mental healing. She has since found a new vocation and built friendships and confidence. Now, as the food-growing project has grown so large, she is planning to start her own community allotment with friends, family and neighbours; she has also regained confidence to go back to work after almost six months of uncertainty.

A Kurdish refugee woman had been involved in a terrible car accident in which several close family members died. She came to the allotment with her family, seeking to deal with her grief through digging and growing food. Through the community food-growing project, she and her children have begun to form friendships, share food, and learn about growing healthy food.

We're very grateful to God for placing us in a position to support and help people such as these, in times of need, apart from our environmental activities.

Kim and Khailean Khongsai, Southall

How can we offer 'touching places' where those in need of healing can come and discover new life and hope?

Thank God for projects that give people a place to come and encounter the healing of Christ.

Lord God,
we praise you for your healing love,
and we acknowledge our own need for healing and new life.
May we come in humility and touch the edge of your garment,
and, receiving your healing afresh, provide places of hope for others.
In faith we pray. Amen.

EPIPHANY – DAY 34
WHERE CAN WE START?

Ephesians 1.17–19

A parish church in a fairly well-off town in Hertfordshire struggled to find ways to reach out to their community. Then someone said: 'Let's look for things that are ugly and find ways to bring the beauty of the gospel to them.' It didn't take long to make a start. The churchyard was a favoured loitering place for homeless people who left cans and bottles strewn about. The parish started a drop-in centre for these people. Later they invited them to the annual carol service. That's the simple beauty of the gospel at work.

Story told at a CMS members' meeting

> We ask the God of our master, Jesus Christ,
> that we will be good apprentices in our manner of life;
> in our direction, faith, and steadiness;
> in our love and patience;
> in troubles and in sufferings.
> And as the scriptures train God's servants
> to do all kinds of good deeds,
> we ask the glorious Father to give us his spirit,
> to make us intelligent and discerning in knowing him personally
> and knowing how to serve. Amen.

EPIPHANY – DAY 35
SOWING SEEDS

Matthew 13.1–9

This year we have also been able to share the good news of Jesus with many people we have got to know, which has been really good. At

Christmas, Amrita (our home help) and I baked ginger biscuit men, some with smiley faces and some with sad faces and, together with Jason and Ruby, visited all the shopkeepers we have become friends with, as well as the one restaurant in town, to give them out. Then, while Jason prayed, Amrita and I talked about the faces on the biscuits and why you're happy if you know Jesus and sad if you don't! It was such a good afternoon and for Amrita was the first time she had ever shared her testimony so publicly. We all really enjoyed it, and it was nice to be able to give something and talk more closely with the people we have been living alongside for the past three years. We pray that good seeds will have been sown.

Tracy Day, Nepal

Sometimes seeds are sown in the simplest way. How can you sow seeds of the gospel?

Lord, help us to be sowers of your good news and help us to entrust the results to you. Amen.

EPIPHANY – DAY 36
ONE SQUARE MILE

Acts 3.6

A Baptist church in Bangor, Maine, USA realized it didn't know its neighbours. So they ran a bonfire picnic in the churchyard and invited everyone in. Next it offered some of its space around the church building for a community garden. This kind of project is beginning to catch on in many other parts of the USA. In the UK the Evangelical Alliance has encouraged churches to think in similar ways with One Square Mile projects, setting up simple mission initiatives aimed at people living within one square mile of where they are located.

Tom Sine

What could my local church do within one square mile?

Lord, help us to offer what we can,
even if what we can offer seems paltry at times.
Give us hearts to love and serve our neighbours
for the glory of your kingdom. Amen.

EPIPHANY – DAY 37
MISSION AND INTEGRITY

Matthew 25.14–23

Ruth Coggan, daughter of Donald Coggan, a former Archbishop of Canterbury, spent nearly 30 years working as a CMS missionary doctor on the north-west frontier in the Afghan border region of Pakistan. One day, while travelling on a local bus, she suddenly realized she'd forgotten to pay the fare. Every eye followed as she got up from her seat and paid the driver. Her action set in motion a buzz of conversation. What the locals didn't know was that Ruth understood what they were saying: 'Look at the foreigner, how honest she is. Do you know she's a doctor at the Christian hospital? Do you know they never operate on anyone without praying to God first? . . . Do you know a lot more of their patients get better after their operations than in the government hospitals?' Ruth's eyes filled with tears. This was one of those moments when her decision to leave her family circle, a career path as a National Health Service surgeon and the material well-being of England made complete sense. About 150 years ago CMS built five missionary hospitals on the Afghan borders. It was a strategy that required great faith to sustain. But one thing's certain: the word that's got round about those five hospitals, and about the work of doctors like Ruth Coggan, is that Christians care. Who knows what all this could mean for Afghanistan . . . even yet?

John Martin

Be faithful in small things because it is in them that your strength lies.

Mother Teresa

O God, mindful of the presence of your son arraigned before his accusers yet maintaining absolute integrity; we ask that, in thought and in deed, in speech and in silence, at work or at leisure, in public and in private, our lives also may embody the perfect consistency of his life and death; to his glory. Amen.

EPIPHANY – DAY 38
TREADING THE FRONTIERS

Luke 22.24–30

First, strive to do another's will rather than your own.
Second, choose always to have less than more.
Third, seek the lower places in life, dying to the need to be
recognized or important.
Fourth, always and in everything desire that the will of God
may be completely fulfilled in you.
The person who tries this will be treading the frontiers of
peace and rest.

Thomas a Kempis (1380–1471)

Reflect on your life. Where do you cling to power and significance?

Lord – teach us what it means to do the will of another,
what it means to live with less, not more,
what it means to seek the lower place,
what it means to see your will fulfilled in us –
and teach us, too, to bear the cost.
In Jesus' name we pray. Amen.

EPIPHANY – DAY 39
DEEPLY ROOTED

Luke 22.31–34

Powerfully
I am drawn to that which has grown slowly
And driven its roots deeply
Which has permanence
And knows the pains of growth.

To grow is my wish
But am I prepared to receive the wounds of life?
To let any weather pass over me?
Am I ready to give shelter to many?
Yet to seek shelter only with you?

I want to be radiant from the inside
I want to stand firm and to mature
To grow into you
To draw my roots deeply
To live through you
But I know
That the price is high.

Ulrich Schaffer

Henceforth, let me burn out for God. Amen.

Henry Martyn (1781–1812)

EPIPHANY – DAY 40
THE POWER OF A SMILE

Nehemiah 8.8–10

Did you know that there are 13 different acknowledged types of Thai smiles? Here they are: 'I'm-so-happy-I-am-crying' smile/ the polite smile for someone you barely know/the 'I-admire-you' smile/the stiff . . . 'I-should-laugh-at-the-joke-though-it's-not-funny' smile/the smile that masks something wicked in your mind/the teasing or 'I-told-you-so' smile/the 'I-know-things-look-pretty-bad-but-there's-no-point-in-crying-over-spilt-milk' smile/the sad smile/the dry 'I-know-I-owe-you-money-but-I-don't-have-it' smile/the 'I-disagree-with-you' smile, also known as the 'You-can-go-ahead-and-propose-it-but-your-idea's-no-good' smile/the 'I-am-the-winner' smile/the smile in the face of an impossible struggle/and the 'I'm-trying-to-smile-but-cannot'.

The authors [Holmes/Tangtongtavy in *Working with the Thais*] explain that smiles '. . . are intended to relieve tension, in an effort to preserve the relationship, social harmony on which people depend'. In each culture where I have lived, I have tried to assess whether or not a smile is appropriate. Here all types are! Are we not all guilty at times of wearing one outside when we feel the opposite inside?

Curiously enough, the word 'smile' is not in my concordance. Apparently in the European Middle Ages, Christians did not smile or laugh, as there is no scriptural reference to Christ doing either of these. Joy, encouragement and happiness are listed, but not how they were facially expressed! I am glad to be living in this era where the smiles of Jesus' followers should reflect genuine friendliness. More than one Buddhist monk has looked surprised when I smiled at them on the street.

The prophet Nehemiah says in 8.10: '. . . the joy of the Lord is my strength'. May this be true of us, and may we be aware of how our facial features are affecting others!

Shelagh Wynne, Thailand

Am I filled with joy, and ready to smile whenever I have opportunity?

Father,
today, as I go about my daily life,
may I know your joy welling up within me.
And even in the midst of difficulty and challenge,
may I bless others with a smile that speaks of your love. Amen.

EPIPHANY – DAY 41
A SCRIPTURAL FOUNDATION

John 2.1–11

Every spirituality needs to be rooted in scripture, and mission spirituality is no exception. One needs to ask the question, therefore, what passage(s), books, or themes of scripture are those that ground one's missionary life.

There may, of course, be some passages that figure large at certain times of one's missionary service. One may take strength and inspiration, for example, from some of the great vocation passages like Isaiah 6.1–8, Jeremiah 1.4–10, Matthew 4.18–22 (the call of Peter and Andrew, James and John), or Jesus' invitation to Andrew and Peter to 'come and see' in John 1.35–39. One may also be buoyed up in difficulty by Jeremiah's sufferings in Jeremiah 38, by Jesus' passion as a consequence of his own faithful missionary witness to the reign of God, or by Paul's being suspect by fellow Christians (Acts 9.23–30) or those whom he had tried to evangelize (for example, Acts 9.19b–25 or 13.50–52).

There may also be passages, however, that can provide basic guidance, inspiration and direction to one's work of crossing a culture, struggling with a language, being accepted by a people, bonding with the people among whom one works. Paul's passionate statement that he had become a slave to all so that he could win more of them to Christ – indeed, that he had become 'all things to all people', so that he might 'by all means save some' (see 1 Cor. 9.19–23) might serve as the anchor and beacon for missionaries in a very different culture from their own.

One of my own inspiring passages is that of John 10.10. The reason for my ministry, the reason for witnessing to and proclaiming Christ, is to bring, like Jesus, abundant life to the world. One missionary in a course on missionary spirituality, my colleague Larry Nemer relates, chose as a foundational passage the story of the wedding at Cana in the second chapter of John's Gospel: the missionary, this person explained, is like water, but at the word of Jesus and in his hands he or she can be transformed into rich, joy-giving wine. The movement of the Acts of the Apostles has always struck me as a marvellous story of missionary spirituality. It is the Spirit who challenges, calls, pushes the church beyond the boundaries of their understanding of the gospel to include all peoples and all cultures in the plan of salvation. It is precisely this move of the Spirit that calls the Jesus community to be church.

Steve Bevans

Which passages of scripture are the ground of your calling to mission?

Lord, we thank you for the inspiration and nourishment of
  your Word.
We pray that it may renew our call to mission –
Our call to follow,
our call to stand firm in suffering,
our call to bring fullness of life,
to be water which will be transformed, by your hands,
into rich, joy-giving wine. Amen.

EPIPHANY – DAY 42
MAKING SCRIPTURE LIVE

Romans 10.13–17

Along with other dioceses, Manchester promotes a shoe shine on Maundy Thursday as a modern take on foot washing. The cathedral clergy thought about this and decided to do it in the Arndale, which is Manchester's biggest city-centre shopping mall.

So in our red cassocks we went over to the centre and set up our stall in the Halle Square at the heart of the Arndale. We had four chairs, shoe shining equipment, and some leaflets explaining about Maundy Thursday and inviting people to church on Sunday. Despite the fact that it was a hot day and many were wearing sandals, we had a steady stream of 'customers', who were rather surprised by our free offer.

Shoe shining is a fairly intimate task and so you have five minutes to talk with your customer, explain about Maundy Thursday and Easter and listen to their story. One of my customers was a businessman who had come down from Glasgow; he shared how his sister had lost a baby at seven months the previous day; we were able to share in his pain and to offer our prayers and concern.

We had over 30 customers in the hour we had been allocated and had many conversations, even with those who didn't want their shoes shined.

The whole thing was possible because the dean of our cathedral spends time each week visiting the centre, being available for pastoral talks and building up relationships with the management there; his hard graft week by week now pays dividends in allowing us to be in the public square sharing our faith. And it was great fun!

Mark Ashcroft

How might we 'make scripture live'?

> Lord, give us creativity, we pray,
> as we read what Jesus did
> and seek to live it out today.
> May we make scripture live,
> so that faith may come through seeing and hearing. Amen.

EPIPHANY – DAY 43
WEEPING FOR THE WORLD

Jeremiah 3.21

We live in a broken world full of need, some of which we see around us, and some of which we experience ourselves. Find a newspaper and tear out images and stories about brokenness in the world that needs God's love and intervention. Try to find stories that connect with your own life, as well as huge global issues – brokenness in families, neighbourhood, church, country and the world.

What does God want to do about this brokenness? What has he done already? How might he intervene in these situations to bring healing to the world? Like Jesus, we are called to have compassion on – to weep for – the world around us. God works through his people – he calls us to be involved in his mission. Look particularly at the stories that are local, Christ calls us first of all to where we are.

Place the newspaper cuttings around you and spend time praying for God's intervention in these situations of pain and need.

EPIPHANY – DAY 44
NEW EVERY MORNING

Lamentations 3.22–24

Every morning, when I draw back the curtains, the first thing that I see is a fresh array of the beautiful blue flowers of the plant called 'morning glory' that climbs over our garden fence. Perhaps the struggle to get it to grow has made success feel even sweeter. The special feature of this creeper is the fact that by the end of the day all the flowers, which I will always associate with Uganda, have died and every morning fresh ones are blooming, nudging the first words of a hymn into my mind. I will only quote the first verse but the other verses are well worth reading.

Rosalind Arnold, Uganda

New every morning is the love
Our wakening and uprising prove;
Through sleep and darkness safely brought
Restored to life, and power, and thought.

John Keble (1792–1866)

Father God, it is hard to hope each morning, to look forward to new treasures and mercies, discovered when we are alive to your presence in all that we encounter.

Open our minds to the endless possibilities of life and power and thought.

Help us to meet you in our everyday life, in our anxieties and difficulties, for you are there with us in our pain and sorrow.

Lift us from despair to new hope. Restore and renew us each returning day, so that we may find joy in our journey with you. Amen.

From the Mozarabic Sacramentary (tenth century)

EPIPHANY – DAY 45
A MILLION MINOR MIRACLES

John 6.5–13

I'm standing at night in this subterranean place of prayer, and perhaps it's the coffee, or the music, or the Spirit, but the darkness doesn't seem too strong. I'm praying for miracles in the city where I live – for healings, and salvations, and justice, and revival, and all those usual kingdom kind of things. But tonight, as I do so, I find myself suddenly startled – like a boy blinking at fireworks – bewildered by how many miracles there already are.

It occurs to me that here in my city today, doctors dispensed healing – can you imagine anything more wonderful? Neighbours did favours. Dog-walkers in the park silently admired the shape of trees. Jokes were told in nursing homes. For a moment or two, thousands and thousands of people prayed, or wished, or merely unwittingly wanted what God wanted.

Chances are that somewhere today a young man and a young woman began to fall in love (although they don't yet know it). A teenager picked up trash she had not dropped. A single mother decided, just for once, to buy herself a slice of chocolate cake and to celebrate the moment in long, slow, mouthfuls of happiness. A painter-decorator stepped back from a wall he'd just painted the colour of claret, and maybe at that moment the sunlight broke through the window, and he saw that it was a good piece of work. A man resisted the temptation to click the link he wouldn't want his wife to see. Maybe he failed yesterday. Maybe he'll click it tomorrow. But today he overcame. In the hospital perhaps a surgeon pinned a broken arm with immaculate skill. Delicious food was prepared and cooked and served in thousands of homes joyously. A pastor's words, so carefully crafted, brought a little comfort to grieving relatives. People cried, but a check-out girl smiled at a lonely old lady. People died, of course, but babies were also born. From time to time today, I was born too. We all were. A million, minor miracles.

We do not pray *ex nihilo*. We pray for more of whatever it is we see. Nothing comes from nothing – certainly not faith like this. Tonight I'm blessing the evidence of miracles; the pre-existing goodness, the presence of Christ in these streets, these surgeries, these schools, these art galleries, these pubs, these homes, these wards. Witnessing so many minor miracles I applaud the world. If all of this is happening all around me, what might not happen next?

And so I stand here now in this subterranean place of prayer and it seems self-evident that there is more light in the night than darkness in the day. There is goodness breaking through, everywhere I look. And I'm praying for miracles tonight with greater faith than frustration for once. I can see creation rising like the moon above the Fall. Ultimately, almost inevitably, benevolence wins the day quietly.

I'm climbing the stairs to my car now, stepping out of the prayer room into the darkness. I'm driving home past houses and perhaps it's the music on the stereo, or the coffee, or the Spirit, but the city seems to me to have become the place of prayer.

Pete Greig, founding member of the 24–7 movement and director of prayer for Holy Trinity Brompton in a 24–7 prayer room in Guildford

Spend some time thanking God for the small miracles in the world around us.

EPIPHANY – DAY 46
A PRAYER OF FAITH-MISSION

1 Kings 8.22–30

A prayer of faith-mission
Lord God, be my defining *zeitgeist*. I'm desperate to discover and re-discover the abilities in me that come from you. Let the life-dreams you have given me become a tangible, actionable reality as I do the greater things that you said I would do when I live-you-out.

Lord, where my faith has lacked soul: revive my trust, and where my faith has no pulse: adrenalize my confidence. You are the energy of my hope, energy that is converted into kinetic motion enabling me to share your love.

Lord Jesus, help me to be reckless in my faith for you, because faith dignified is faith restricted. I'm resolved to lose control over my personal affairs and allow you to manage my estate. I'm ready to risk my life on an unseen reality, the realm of your kingdom. As I walk forward, led by your Holy Spirit I want to live for the eternal, that which the human eye can't see or value.

As I listen to your words and put them into practice shield me from the enemies of belief. Keep me from being consumed by temporary, unimportant goals. My house, my internet connection, and my holiday are not my god. As self-reliance tries to systematically dismantle faith, help me to remain dependent on you, for that is where my vulnerability finds its home. Thank you that I receive what I ask for in prayer, because I believe my faith finds its origin and completion in your all-sufficiency.

Though certain facts appear to dictate my present circumstances – in faith and in truth I will not embrace or live out my life according to that information. On the contrary, Jesus, when I remain focused on you I perceive the real facts not negative voices or material evidence hinged on human senses. Your words, your healing, your provision and your deliverance aren't reliant on what I taste, touch, see, hear or smell.

Help my every day to be founded on your truth and eternal reality; my God, show me how greater you are than my circumstances. I will neither be deterred by events in my past or trapped by a future predicted – my faith will not be bullied.

Lord, thank you that my mission is your mission; even if faith is like a safe with a time-delay lock, my faith will increase as I give myself in service to you. My life-faith isn't in a neat compartment but all of who I am, and finds substance when I live for others. And this is my response to you, my God, since you have faith in me to complete your work.

David Roche, France

Write a prayer of faith-mission to reflect your own calling and circumstances.

EPIPHANY – DAY 47
RESPONDING TO NEED

Luke 18.18–22; John 3.12,4.8

These passages show that Jesus related very differently to people according to their needs. Nicodemus was a teacher of the law, and so Jesus talked to him about quite complex theology. The paralysed man was healed spiritually and physically, but didn't get a sermon. Jesus asked the woman at the well for a drink and went on from there. If Jesus related to people in different ways when he was sharing the good news of the kingdom, then so do we!

Pray that we may have wisdom, sensitivity and respect in our dealings with those around us.

EPIPHANY – DAY 48
THE 'HONEYCOMB' GOSPEL

John 5.1–6

Traditionally, we've been encouraged to see the gospel as a set of simple truths that follow on from each other. We start at the top and end at the bottom and whoever we are talking to has then had the whole gospel. However, there are lots of different ways of explaining the gospel, and lots of different places that we can start. We could start with 'sin' – all of us are sinful and separated from God; Jesus died for our sins on the cross; to get right with God we need to repent of our sin and receive his forgiveness. Or we could start with 'creation' – God created a beautiful world for us to inhabit in relationship with him; the whole creation, including our relationship with God, has been spoilt by us going our own way; Jesus died to reconcile us to God and to restore the whole creation.

Those two explanations don't contradict each other but they start at two very different places. Pete Ward, in his book *Youthwork and the Mission of God*, suggests that a more helpful understanding of the gospel 'might be to see theological truth as a 3D honeycomb or cluster of ideas. Any one of the key ideas within the honeycomb can act as an entry point or doorway' to understanding the gospel. This model enables understanding of the gospel to develop in a more organic way, from one cell of the honeycomb to another in any order. When someone has understood all the key cells of the honeycomb and incorporated them into their lives, then they will be a disciple of Christ; the point at which they started is not important. This approach enables us to relate to people where they are and with the issues that concern them.

CSM 21M Resource

Lord – help us today to meet people where they are,
at their point of need –
in need of companionship,
of healing,

of encouragement,
of challenge.
Help us to meet with them,
and through us, may they encounter you. Amen.

EPIPHANY – DAY 49
A DOUBLE-EDGED SWORD

Hebrews 4.12

The Lumko method of action – reflection using the Bible
The method presented here was developed for neighbourhood gospel groups by the Lumko Institute, South Africa. From there, it has spread into many African countries and has been well-received in other countries as well. It deals with a method of communal, prayerful approach to the sacred scripture which may help us to encounter God and one another and to help us open our eyes to the presence and to the working of God in our everyday life. The Bible contains, is and imparts the word of God. It is a book that concerns us personally and likewise can make us concerned. This method provides the opportunity for allowing the Bible to speak to oneself first and, out of this perplexity, to share with one another (rather than just 'talk about' the Bible).

On the other hand, the Bible is a book that renders the faith experiences and faith testimonies of peoples from different times and cultures. We are standing in the living tradition of the people of God who have heard the word of God since Abraham and lived because of it. The Bible is therefore at times a strange and disturbing book. Hence, the meditative prayerful approach directed towards life is not the only one; rather it should be supplemented by biblical study.

Bible discussion and Bible meditation groups should not be too large. The ideal size is four to eight participants so that everyone may have the opportunity to talk. An atmosphere of quiet and calm is necessary. Just as important is an attitude of openness, of reciprocal listening in addition to the readiness to talk about oneself, that is, one's life and one's faith. The function of the facilitator consists only of this – that he or she announces the individual steps of the method.

The seven steps look very simple and indeed they are. Our experience in the dioceses of South Africa and elsewhere has shown us, however, that these 'simple' steps may also lead up to an encounter with God and our fellow humans.

Steps 1–4 help us to 'persevere' with God, to 'listen' to participate in the biblical action, 'to surrender ourselves to God'. **Step 5** brings us together as brothers and sisters because we risk sharing our experience with God with one another. This is not the most important step, but it gives great joy to all those who want to build and experience a deeply human community in God. In **step 6** we confront our life with the word of God. It is often the case that in this atmosphere of prayer, individuals discuss problems that they wish to resolve as a neighbourhood group. In **step 7** all are invited to share in spontaneous prayer.

Rose Uchem

Reflect on how you have allowed the word of God to challenge you in the last week.

EPIPHANY – DAY 50
INVITING THE LORD

Jeremiah 33.3

First step: we invite the Lord
Once the group settles down, the facilitator asks someone to volunteer 'to invite the Lord'. The belief in the living presence of the risen Christ in our midst is the presupposition and basis of our meditation.

We want to meet the Word who became flesh and dwells among us. We remember Jesus' promise: 'Where two or three are gathered in my name, I am there among them' (Matt. 18.20).

Do we believe that when we gather to study God's word with fellow Christians we are truly in the presence of the living Lord? How might our lives today be different if we invited Jesus into every aspect?

Come among us, Lord Jesus,
be in our meetings and our partings,
in our words and our silence.
Come among us,
and dwell in us today. Amen.

EPIPHANY – DAY 51
DWELLING ON THE WORD

Psalm 121

Second step: we read the text
The facilitator announces the chosen text. First the book, then the chapter. He or she waits until everyone has found the chapter and only then announces the verse. When everyone has found the passage, the facilitator invites someone to volunteer to read the text. A moment of silence follows.

Third step: we dwell on the text
The facilitator continues: 'We dwell on the text. Which words strike you in a special way?'

In doing so, almost the entire text is listened to again. The participants spontaneously read aloud the word or words that have impressed them. Whole verses are not read, only short phrases or individual words.

The participants are encouraged to repeat those words silently to themselves three or four times. It is extremely important that a moment of silence be kept after each person has spoken, allowing the message to 'soak in'. As a result of this step, 'simple' words often take on new meaning.

What words strike you in a special way from the verses read in Psalm 121? Take time to reflect on those words, allowing them and their meaning to 'soak in'.

EPIPHANY – DAY 52
GOD IS NOT FAR FROM US

Psalm 145.17–18

Fourth step: we are quiet
After spending time on the individual word, the entire passage is read again slowly. Then the facilitator announces a time of silence, giving the exact length of time, for example, three minutes.

We advise the people to spend this time in silence before God. 'We are open to God.' 'We allow ourselves to be loved by him.' 'We let God look at us.' A helpful practice during this silence is to repeat a specific word.

Read Psalm 121 again.

Meditation: Simply to be open to God, to wait for him, to be with him. Become aware that 'indeed he is not far from each one of us' (Acts 17.27).

EPIPHANY – DAY 53
SHARING FROM THE HEART

James 5.16

Fifth step: we share what we have heard in our hearts
After the time of quiet, the facilitator announces the next step: 'We share with each other what we have heard in our hearts.'

We do this to share with one another our faith experience and to help each other to grow in the faith. The entire sacred scripture is nothing less than a God experience which the people of Israel and Jesus 'share' with us.

It is somewhat strange that we can talk to friends about almost every aspect of our lives, yet when it comes to sharing with others our experience with God, we become shy. In this Bible meditation method, however, anyone can learn to 'risk' this sharing in a very natural and unpressured way.

Lord, give us grace, we pray,
to take risks in sharing with one another,
to confess to one another,
to acknowledge our needs to one another,
and to pray for one another
in the name of Christ. Amen.

EPIPHANY – DAY 54
SEARCHING TOGETHER

1 Peter 5.6–7

Sixth step: we search together
The facilitator announces: 'We search together.'

Now the time has come for the participants to examine their lives in the light of the gospel. At this stage, a basic community might discuss everyday problems, such as:

- Someone needs help in the neighbourhood . . .
- Children need instruction in the faith . . .
- Who will lead the Service of the Word next Sunday, since the priest will not be there? . . .
- How can we settle a discord that has arisen? . . .
- What can we do about getting the street lamp repaired? . . .

None of these problems needs to have a direct connection to the Bible passage that has been read and shared. However, they emerge and can be resolved because of the mutual confidence that now exists in an atmosphere of the presence of God. Things look different when God is allowed to be present.

Do we bring the most practical issues and problems we face to God, or do we consider them unworthy of his attention? Reflect on the practical issues that are troubling you or concerning you today. Bring them – however small – to God, allowing him to be present in the midst of our lives.

EPIPHANY – DAY 55
THE POWER OF PRAYER

1 John 5.14–15

Seventh step: we pray together.
The facilitator now invites everyone to pray.

The words of scripture, the various experiences of God's word, the daily problems – these all become fuel for prayer. Some find this form of sharing in prayer the easiest way to communicate with others.

The participants are encouraged to incorporate in their personal prayer whatever has been of special importance to them during the meditation.

Only at the end is a formal prayer known to everyone recited.

Lumko Institute, shared by Rose Uchem

O Lord, we beseech thee to deliver us from the fear of the unknown future; from fear of failure; from fear of poverty; from fear of bereavement; from fear of loneliness; from fear of sickness and pain; from fear of age; and from fear of death. Help us, O Father, by thy grace to love and fear thee only, fill our hearts with cheerful courage and loving trust in thee; through our Lord and Master Jesus Christ.

Akanu Ibiam, Nigeria

EPIPHANY – DAY 56
TOWARDS LENT AND EASTER

Luke 9.51

Take time to reflect on the image of Jesus below (from Beijing). Is it an image that appeals to you? Does it reflect the Jesus you read about in the Bible? How does it challenge you to think differently about Jesus?

Help us to follow you on the road to Jerusalem,

To set our faces firmly against friendly suggestions for a safe, expedient life, to embrace boldly the way of self-offering, of life given for others' gain.

Help us to follow you, Christ the Servant.

From a Litany of the Disciples of the Servant used in
Andhra Theological College, Hyderabad, India

EPIPHANY – DAY 57
THE ROAD TO CALVARY

Matthew 16.24–25

Take time to reflect on the image of Jesus below (painted by Miriam-Rose Ungunmerr, from the Northern Territory of Australia). The patterns on Jesus' body show the physical stress he is under. The circles on his head indicate the pain and sorrow locked up inside him. When Simon of Cyrene takes hold of the cross, his body merges with that of Jesus and the pattern on Jesus' head is open. This indicates a transfer of grace to Simon to strengthen him.

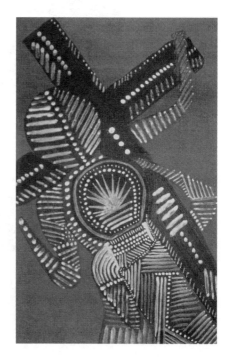

'The sun rose inside his head, his mind burst with a new belief, he became a new man. The resurrection had already begun.'

Lord, as we walk in the way of cross, may we find it to be none other than the way of resurrection, life and peace. Amen.

EPIPHANY – DAY 58
THE SUFFERING CHRIST

Isaiah 52.13–15

Take time to reflect on the image of Jesus below – created by the Peruvian artist Edilberto Merida. It shows Jesus as outcast, the one whom it is very difficult to love. 'Gargolyle-like', it reminds us that the suffering of the cross was dehumanizing and ugly. But it also serves to elevate the experience of all suffering people, who feel with Jesus. 'My God, my God, why have you abandoned me?'

What they were not told, they will see.
And what they have not heard they will understand.
Lord – grant us both seeing and understanding, as we look on your suffering and see in it the suffering of the world. Amen.

LENT – DAY 1

ASH WEDNESDAY
COMING HOME (AGAIN)

Luke 15.11–24

Contrary to what many may think or feel, a period of spiritual endeavour (during Lent, perhaps, or while taking part in a retreat) is a time of joy because it is a time for coming home, a period when we can come back to life. It should be a time when we shake off all that is worn and dead in us in order to become able to live, and to live with all the vastness, all the depth and all the intensity to which we are called.

Metropolitan Anthony Bloom

Do we dare to shake off all that is dead in us and live in the fullness of life God offers?

From the cowardice that dare not face new truth;
From the laziness that is content with half-truth;
From the arrogance that thinks it knows all truth;
Good Lord, deliver me. Amen.

From Kenya

LENT – DAY 2
JESUS, SON OF GOD – HAVE MERCY

Mark 10.46–52

I had no eyes
So I sat by the roadside
I had no name,
Only a surname.
I had no feet
With no light to guide them.
But I had ears
And a voice to shout
'Jesus Davidson, help me!'
He said, 'What do you want?'
I said 'To see again.'
He said, 'I'm bound for Jerusalem
To be scorned and tried
And scourged and crucified
Do you want to see all that?'
I said, 'Lord,
If I stay sitting here
How can I show I love you?'

K Hall

Jesus, Son of God, have mercy on me. Help me to see. Amen.

LENT – DAY 3
GRACE TO BE SEEN

Exodus 3.1–6

Grace comes to us through the senses.
We touch it, or it touches us, in an embrace
We smell it in freshly baked bread and morning coffee
We hear it in the ocean or Massive Attack
We taste it in a strawberry or a cold Belgian beer
We see it in the eyes of a child or the lines of an old person's face.

All our senses together like a huge neon sign saying
LIFE IS A GIFT!

This is how grace comes to us . . .
In the ordinary stuff of life, the everyday
Yet in our numbness, it's easy to miss this most simple of gifts
And go round with our eyes closed.

Mystics speak of awareness and its connection with prayer
Become aware of your own breath
Breathe in and feel the cold air on the hairs of your nostrils
Feel your pulse
Look at the skin on your hand
Slow down
Look around you
Notice details that you normally miss
Amazing things in your everyday world that you often walk by.

Maybe God is in the detail we normally miss.

You don't need eyes to see you need vision.

Jonny Baker

Throughout the day, make a conscious effort to recognize God in the detail we normally miss – food, creation, people, sounds. Thank God for the gifts of grace in the world around us.

LENT – DAY 4
WATCH AND PRAY

Mark 14.32, 38–40

As salaam alaykum (Peace be upon you).These words, *watch and pray*, have taken on new meaning for me. Prayer is influenced by culture; in Jordan most people pray standing up with their arms out and palms up, however, not so the deaf. The deaf really must watch and pray! It has been a shock to me, to keep my eyes open throughout. Also it is cultural for all the others to sign the prayer with those praying, a challenge but lovely. However, it has influenced my life. Now as I pray on the way to Amman, I look at the beauty of God's creation and the state of mankind, and pray! Now Jordan is so beautiful, radiant in green splendour and lush, many bright flowers dotting the hills. These are the hills of Gilead; I can see how it would inspire to song, though I'm not sure about the goats (Song of Songs 4.1, 6.5).

Michael Green, Jordan

Lord, open our eyes
to the beauty of creation,
to the pain of suffering
to the signs of hope before us.
Help us to watch and pray. Amen.

LENT – DAY 5
SEEING GOD'S HAND

2 Corinthians 4.8–12

Tension between Church and state worsened in 1976. Religious leaders, including Archbishop Luwum, jointly approached Idi Amin to share their concern. They were rebuffed. But Archbishop Luwum continued to attend government functions. One of his critics accused him of being on the government side and he replied: 'I face daily being picked up by the soldiers. While the opportunity is there I preach the gospel with all my might, and my conscience is clear before God that I have not sided with the present government which is utterly self-seeking. I have been threatened many times. Whenever I have the opportunity, I have told the president the things the churches disapprove of.'

On 16 February, the archbishop and six bishops were tried on a charge of smuggling arms. Archbishop Luwum was not allowed to reply, but shook his head in denial. The president concluded by asking the crowd: 'What shall we do with these traitors?' The soldiers replied 'Kill him now.' The archbishop was separated from his bishops. As he was taken away Archbishop Luwum turned to his brother bishops and said: 'Do not be afraid. I see God's hand in this.'

James E. Kiefer, www.jvstus.anglican.org

Give thanks for the faith and courage of many Christians around the world who face persecution and the threat of death because of their faith. Pray for courage and for peace for them – that they may see God's hand, even in the midst of danger.

LENT – DAY 6
STANDING FIRM

Mark 10.29–31

For months we have been praying for a young man who was researching Christianity. He asked many questions every weekend. Recently he decided to proclaim his Christian faith and was baptized in another town. He gave his chilling testimony just before his baptism, saying: 'When I was facing problems in my family, I reached the point of committing suicide – that was the moment when Jesus entered my life. He has saved me not only from physical death but has also showed me the way to eternal life.' He added: 'Jesus is my faithful friend – I'll never betray him.'

It was a huge change in his life but his family has not accepted it. His parents think that he has brought shame upon their family so they have publicly disowned him. They have removed his photographs from their home and also from the family albums. His mother has removed his name from the family inheritance so he will not get any share of it. He also receives regular (threatening) text messages from his brothers and relatives. A few days ago he received one text message from his brother saying: 'I hope you will die in an accident – don't dare to come back [to their country] and if you do, think you are dead. We will kill you.'

CMS Mission Partners

Pray for Christians facing tension in their families because of their conversion to faith. Pray for those who are supporting and discipling them. Pray for ourselves, that when we are called upon to take a stand for our faith we may not be found wanting.

LENT – DAY 7
BE CONTROLLED BY THE SPIRIT

Romans 8.5–8

Control. We all long to be in control. In control of our lives. In control of our bad habits. As parents, in control of our children! Living in Kampala is a real test to one's desire for control. The power goes off when you're expecting it to be on. There appear to be no rules on the road, with drivers battling each other for space, deep potholes that you need four-wheel drives to get out of and downpours that turn dirt roads into ice rinks with the risk of skating off into the ditch.

All these things are not only out of our control but lead to the temptation of allowing our emotions, thinking, and words to get out of control as we can get frustrated and irritated. But 'the mind controlled by the Spirit is life and peace'. How much we need to trust God and let him be in control of our uncontrollable situations, being filled with the Spirit and so experiencing the life and peace that only he can give, for 'those controlled by the sinful nature cannot please God' (Romans 8.6–7).

Angus and Helen Crichton, Uganda

Spend some time looking at your life and reflecting on where our emotions are out of control – where we react rather than respond, where we fail to allow God's Spirit to shape and lead us. Open your hands as a symbol of asking for and receiving God's forgiveness.

LENT – DAY 8
A FUTURE WE CANNOT SEE

Romans 8.23–25

The following morning we received news that Selua's nephew, who was three years old, had died overnight. This little boy had been very sick for at least a year. As a team of about ten 'Across' colleagues, we went to give our condolences and pay our respects. As we arrived, his tiny body was laid out on a bed outside, and the grief of those around was clear to see. His mother had only lost her nine-month-old in July, and here she was again, preparing to bury her second son. I cannot begin to understand the level of feelings or grief. As we arrived, Elunai, a colleague who is also a pastor, prayed, and we joined together in song. Some of us were also moved to tears – as we moved away to sit down, the boy's grandmother prayed the most heartfelt prayer I think I have ever heard. It was a prayer of real honesty, one that I have rarely heard prayed out loud in the UK. She shouted through her tears and wailing, 'Why O Lord do you give us children one day only to take them away the next? Why, why? Answer me Lord.'

We do not know the answers, and this side of heaven we never will; we can only hold on to him and trust that in his infinite mercy and goodness, he has a plan, he will comfort those who are grieving, and that he has us all in the palm of his hand. That is the beauty of faith, being sure of what we hope for and certain of what we do not see, as Paul puts it in Romans. It is a mystery, but one we can be confident in.

Ruth Radley, Sudan

We are so frequently confronted by situations we can neither control or understand. Are we able to express our questions and grief – and to live with the questions? Are we prepared to trust the mystery of God's plan and put our faith in things we cannot see?

Lord God, we pray for all those who grieve at this time,
for all those who cannot comprehend the path behind
and fear to face the path ahead.

Help us to name our grief with honesty.
Give them – give us, we pray – the faith to trust in what we cannot
see,
to believe in the hope that saves us.
In Jesus' name we pray. Amen.

LENT – DAY 9
LEARNING FROM LIFE

Psalm 32.6–8

This has been a remarkable year in many ways, beginning with fires when sparks from the main electricity cables set fire to the tinder dry grass beneath. Then an early morning attack by armed robbers/hired assassins; and later a couple of gales of hurricane strength that did much damage – the first passed us by, the second took the roof of the generator house into the next compound. But we are still here; the work of God is growing and we are all well. It has been a learning time, however.

We instinctively pray that all troubles will be kept far from us – but of course they come, and it is then that we know ever more clearly the power and the presence of God. As Oswald Chambers put it: 'An average view of the Christian life is that it is deliverance from trouble. It is deliverance *in* trouble, which is very different.' Life has changed. Perhaps we have changed; in some ways, I hope so, because we are in a poor way if we do not learn from the circumstances of life.

Susan Essam, Nigeria

Reflect on where God has been at work in the darkest places of life. How have you learned from the circumstances of life?

Father God, we thank you for all the circumstances of life,
for opportunities to learn in the midst of trouble,
for the challenge to live joyfully

and with trust to grow deeper in you.
Open our eyes to recognize your presence
not just in times of blessing
but in times of trouble. Amen.

LENT – DAY 10
VICTORY IS OURS

Acts 16.25–34

Preacher today: Paul in prison after being beaten. Midnight – the darkest part of the night, where we see no hope, no light, no future. And we are tempted maybe to start 'complaining'; have a 'pity-party'. Have you ever had a 'midnight' like this: all dark, 'looking lost', you trying your best, ending up 'beaten' in a dark place . . . ?

'Midnight' – the darkest part of the night – but suddenly God is at work. And he is working, preparing some of his most powerful witnesses in and through Paul's 'midnight'. And we have the same promise for our 'midnight': we are not beaten . . . 'The victory' is ours – in our Lord Jesus Christ.

Ruth Hulser, Tanzania

Goodness is stronger than evil;
love is stronger than hate;
light is stronger than darkness;
life is stronger than death;
victory is ours through God who loves us.

Desmond Tutu

LENT – DAY 11
MIRACLES

Mark 9.14–24

Lord God, you spoke into darkness and chaos and then
    there was light.
You imagined the earth in its complexity and beauty and
    called it into being.
You created humanity in your own image and gave us a home
    to live in.
We believe you can do miracles. *But even if you don't,*
    you are still God.

Lord God, you walked with Shadrach, Meshach, and Abednego
    through the fiery furnace.
You shut the mouths of hungry lions and kept Daniel safe
    until morning.
You gave Hannah a family when she despaired of ever having a child.
We believe you can do miracles. *But even if you don't,*
    you are still God.

Lord God, you changed water into wine so the wedding party
    could continue.
You calmed a storm and your disciples with words of quiet authority.
You transformed a boy's picnic into a meal for a multitude with
    plenty left over.
We believe you can do miracles. *But even if you don't,*
    you are still God.

Lord God, you healed a women from twelve years of bleeding
    and rejection.
You asked Bartimaeus what he wanted and then restored his sight.

You watched a paralysed man being lowered through the roof
and helped him to his feet.
We believe you can do miracles. *But even if you don't,
you are still God.*

Lord God, you called Lazarus from the tomb and restored him to life.
You walked past the mourners at Jairus' house and gave his
daughter back to him.
You suffered a horrendous crucifixion in order to defeat sin and death
and give us life.
We believe you can do miracles. *But even if you don't,
you are still God.*

Lord God, you told your disciples that they would do greater things
than you had done.
We hear and read stories of miracles in our world – of you healing the
sick, setting prisoners free, releasing drug addicts from their addiction, providing the right amount of money at just the right time.
We believe you can do miracles. *But even if you don't,
you are still God.*

And yet, Lord, we don't see many miracles happening around us.
We have friends with cancer, and we pray, and they are not healed.
We have friends who long for children, and we pray, and they
do not conceive.
Our doubt is mixed with faith, our trust is accompanied by questions.
We acknowledge the mystery of faith and prayer, and the
ways in which they are connected.
We acknowledge that you often do things differently to the way
we would do them.
We long to know you better, to understand more of your ways.
And we believe you can do miracles. *But even if you don't,
you are still God.*

Lord we believe. *Help our unbelief.*

Jenny Baker

LENT – DAY 12
LONG-SUFFERING LOVE

1 Corinthians 13.4–7

'Love suffers long and is kind; love does not envy; love does not parade itself, is not puffed up; does not behave rudely, does not seek its own way, is not provoked, keeps no account of evil; does not rejoice in iniquity, but rejoices in the truth; bears all things, believes all things, hopes all things endures all things' (NKJV).

Who are the long-suffering? They are people who wait and wait and wait. They show resilience in imperfect situations and with imperfect people.

Pakistan has had a difficult time of late. Often we question how it can survive the effects of corruption, terrorism and natural disasters. The monsoon flooding has meant prices have soared; many people are still dispossessed and awaiting aid. For aid agencies it has been very difficult to supply good quality corrupt-free aid and has been a frustrating process. Yet Pakistani people have shown great resilience in the past and probably will again in the future. For the minority poor, including the Christian poor, hardships are compounded by social oppression. They will suffer a lifetime of injustice, corruption, oppression and poverty. They know their treasure is in heaven. *Long-suffering is a lost art to many of us.* When things get hard, I want to run away.

David and Dawn Curran, Pakistan

We see ourselves, O God,
People of faith and faithlessness –
Dancing in the sun one day
And overwhelmed by our realities the next,
Joyfully announcing the gospel sometimes
And then trembling in its uncertainty.
We see the hope that lies among us –
And hope that we might care
And live in community with each other
And the world. Amen.

From Australia

LENT – DAY 13
LOVING KINDNESS

1 Kings 17.7–16

Love is kind. In my journal I have started writing about things I would never have experienced if I had not come to Pakistan. If I'd not come to Pakistan, I would never have known such kindness. In Pakistan I have discovered kindness coming from unexpected places. Our neighbours are so poor, and yet they are so kind. When we first arrived they fed us. They visit us. When we go near their homes they invite us to join them for chai. Pakistani's have hospitality down to a tee. To a guest they give their very best. It is from a heart of love.

David and Dawn Curran, Pakistan

Hospitality is a precious gift in many cultures. Reflect on how you have received hospitality from those who have few material resources, and yet give with kindness of what they have. Pray that, like the widow who fed Elijah, they may be blessed abundantly for their generosity.

The following prayer was suggested by a message delivered to the cabin of Bishop Lesslie Newbigin and his wife on their first embarkation for India. The sender asked for them the gift of 'verandah grace'; the verandah in India being the meeting place between home and the needy world outside.

We come to Jesus, whose unfailing gift was to welcome all who came to his door and table, and whose grace was such that no one had cause to fear overstaying a welcome. Aided by his presence and inspired by his example may we likewise have the good grace to welcome all who present themselves to us, even at the most inconvenient times, or in the most unattractive of guises. In all such circumstances, good Jesus, give us your verandah grace. Amen.

LENT – DAY 14
LOVE DOES NOT ENVY

Proverbs 14.30

Love does not envy. It does not put value in material things and so it doesn't want the possessions others have. This is hard for us arising from materialistic cultures, yet when I go to church I see people who are content. It seems sometimes that the rich are spoiled by envy. Last week I helped out at a jumble sale organized by someone at church. It is a yearly event for those of us who have a lot to redistribute to those who have less. There was so much stuff on sale and there were four or five stalls where items were priced from Rs 1 (1p) to Rs 25 (20p) with a few items of furniture priced at Rs 50–Rs 100. If after 15 minutes or so things hadn't been sold, they were reduced in price until they were free. I was amazed as while most things were sold quite quickly, some things like furniture and Western clothes, even when they were free, were not wanted. People don't want things for the sake of having them, only when things will be useful to them.

David and Dawn Curran, Pakistan

How can we learn to be content with what we need – and so be free to serve?

Lord – teach us to live simply, so that others may simply live. Amen.

LENT – DAY 15
EVERYDAY STONES

Luke 4.1–4

Jesus was hungry, really hungry.
Wanting bread, needing bread, not unreasonable in the situation.

But Jesus wasn't tempted by bread to break his fast.
Jesus was tempted by stones and the power he had to turn them into bread.
We all have legitimate needs and feelings of 'want' to express. Every day we are faced with the same temptation as Jesus. To fulfil our needs and wants by small, easy actions that are within our power but we know are wrong.
What are your 'everyday stones'?

Adam Baxter, adapted

Find a stone . . . hold it in your hand . . . offer your everyday stone to God. Then carry it in your pocket throughout the day, remembering each time you touch it that Jesus withstood temptation. Pray that God will enable us to do the same.

LENT – DAY 16
THE LANGUAGE OF LAMENT

Lamentations 3.1–18

In the ancient world, a rhythm of fasting and feasting was connected to the rhythm of the earth for important events and disasters. With people who are suffering, their incentive to cry for change is great. As part of that cry for change, in Hebrew and Christian traditions, a lament is accompanied by fasting and weeping, but it is maybe that in modern life, our collective lament takes a different form; this is a lament that accompanies the feast not the fast.

In a never-ending feast without the fast, living in the day without the night, in light without darkness and noise without silence, our lament takes a different form. It is hidden, unacknowledged, involuntary, but audible to those who listen to the sounds of the time. It is the sound of bewilderment to what is 'enough'. How do we know when we have done enough, spent enough, bought enough? How do we cope with the seemingly relentless and unstoppable demands on our time and energy? The ancient language of lament is in danger of becoming a lost language in a society that has made itself too busy to stop and face the forces of death that threatens to destroy us.

Lucy Winkett

Where do we hear the language of lament in our own context? Write your own prayer of lament – for yourself, or for your local context.

LENT – DAY 17
SALT AND LIGHT

Matthew 5.13–16

Salt and light: we had a discussion about this when our Thursday home group read the Sermon on the Mount. Does it refer to us as a community or to us as individuals? Or both? How can I be more salty – or indeed let *my* light so shine before men 'that they see your good works and glorify your Father in heaven'?

Then I thought, how have I been affected by the 'salt and light' of others? Or indeed how has our lifetime's ministry affected others by being different? There are at least a few answers to this sort of question. I really pray that our lives do demonstrate the difference that Jesus makes – it has shown at work before: if it is really true, why don't more and more people ask questions about what's different?

I was also reflecting yesterday, in the bright sunlight and lovely spring clear weather, that light both illumines and creates shadows (old street lighting was designed to make shadows visible rather than light things up). We may be light at times by creating shadows of contrast to the norm around us. Light also is both absorbed and reflected: maybe there are times when people take notice, and absorb what they see of us, and other times when our light is reflected and brightened by something or someone else.

Peter Hemming

How am I salt and light to those around me? How can I be more effective in mission today, so that people encounter me and recognize something different?

Lord, you placed me in the world to be its light.
I was afraid of the shadows;
afraid of the poverty.
I did not want to know other people.
And my light slowly faded away.
Forgive me, Jesus. Amen.

From Uruguay

LENT – DAY 18
A CULTURE-FULL GOSPEL

Genesis 2.4–9

I often heard as a young Christian 'Just give them the gospel!' I had the mistaken notion that the gospel was somehow culture-less. This puzzled me as the gospel seemed very wrapped up in the people who were presenting it. Through examining the first few chapters of Genesis, I came to understand God as the creator and sustainer of the universe, our world and our lives. As stewards of that gift, we create cultures that express God's intentions for his world and all its creatures. I began to see the gospel as being culture-full.

D. T. Niles, a Sri Lankan missiologist, once remarked that cross-cultural sharing of the gospel is like putting a plant enclosed in a clay pot into the ground. For a while the plant can survive off the nutrients contained in the pot. For it to mature and grow, however, its roots must expand, burst through the container and grow into the soil around it. This allows the plant to draw nourishment and propagate.

Christianity is a culturally specific faith. The incarnation of God in Christ is the supreme model for mission. God in Christ took human form. We sing, 'Veiled in flesh the godhead see', but we must be prepared to go further. Christ did not merely become human. He became a Jew. He was brought up within a Jewish–Galilean culture, shared a Jewish home and education and was entirely at home with its languages and customs. His ministry was confined almost entirely to a Jewish audience. All his original disciples were Jews. The salvation he brought is symbolized most powerfully in baptism and the eucharistic meal, rites with unmistakably Jewish roots. Here, then, is our warrant for affirming that ours is a culturally specific faith.

The gospel is always enclosed in a cultural wrapper and the Christian is called to celebrate that specific culture and see it as part of the gift of life that God imparts. However, a problem is created when the wrapper is marketed as more important than its content.

Paul Thaxter

We praise you, Lord God, that we are fearfully and wonderfully made,
unique beings, shaped and sustained by your hand and your grace.
We praise you for our different cultures,
for the richness that we enjoy.
Give us wisdom, we pray,
to understand and appreciate our own cultures
and the cultures that shape our sisters and brothers. Amen.

LENT – DAY 19
ENCOUNTERING A BIGGER JESUS

Acts 6.1–7

Christian expansion into other cultures demands translation – different wrappers. We can trace this principle in the book of Acts as the gospel, first believed and lived out by Jews, takes root among different peoples. This progress was not without much controversy. There was static between Hebrew and Hellenistic Jews who came to believe in Jesus (Acts 6). This continued throughout the Acts account culminating in the Gentiles being baptized in the Holy Spirit and water and triggering the Council of Jerusalem (Acts 15). The Church discovers it can retain its allegiance to Jesus without being bound to one specific cultural wrapper.

When we speak of gospel translation, it involves far more than searching for word equivalents in other languages. As the gospel is translated into the thought-forms, beliefs, customs and practices of a culture, there is an organic process taking place. The gospel acts as a catalyst – celebrating, challenging and changing a culture in the image of Christ. Cultures are dynamic systems that are always adapting to internal and external factors. If the gospel takes root within a culture, there is less chance that the gospel will be perceived as foreign.

Effective mission happens when the gospel is unwrapped, translation of words and ideas takes place and the Holy Spirit is received and works in the hearts, minds and imagination of people, enabling new possibilities in that culture. As the Holy Spirit works, cultures are transformed. Paradoxically, this process can lead to a greater appreciation of specific cultures and a broader appreciation of other peoples' cultures. People's image of Jesus is also transformed. We see this in the New Testament, as disciples perceive the Lord Jesus Christ in bigger and deeper terms.

Paul Thaxter

Pray that our image of Jesus may be enriched and transformed as we encounter Christ in other people and other cultures.

LENT – DAY 20
MISSION WITH CONTACT LENSES

Acts 17.22–31

Israel knew all about idols and foreign gods. Warned off them way back in exodus times, the people had nevertheless fallen prey to them and God had sent missionary prophets to redirect their hearts.

A Hebrew of Hebrews, Paul was distressed to see the 'very religious' Athenians worshipping non-gods, and used the altar to an unknown god as a starter or point of contact to teach the true God and his risen son. In other words, he set the gospel into a local context so it could be better understood – while maintaining the essential truth. A perfect example for doing mission across cultures.

Argentina's northern scrub plain, known as the Chaco, has been home to the Wichi people for centuries. The Wichi church, on the other hand, has existed for only thee generations and is made up of folk whose natural inclination is to animism. Demons, spirits in forest and river, things that inhabit the night – all are part of conversation and world view.

A fine Wichi pastor affirmed the reality of these one Sunday. But he then added that, 'your problems begin if you put your faith in them. If you trust them, they'll have you in their power. Believe they exist, for they do. But believe in Jesus for deliverance, well-being and durable greenness [= eternal life].'

The Wichi see people as composed of body, inner being and speech. Translating the famous Ezekiel 36.26, which talks about hearts, spirits and flesh, Juan wrote: 'I will give you new inner beings and new thinking. I will take from you your inner beings which are hard like stones, and I will give you inner beings which love me so that you do all my words that I tell you.'

A good translator thus maintains the sense while using words and concepts familiar and appropriate to his readers. Another example of doing mission across cultures.

Bob Lunt

What points of contact could you use with your neighbours in the community – of whatever faith or none? Are there words and concepts we use in church and when speaking about our faith that are somehow not 'familiar and appropriate'?

Lord God, open our hearts and minds,
that we may find the words to speak of your grace,
that are familiar and appropriate. Amen.

LENT – DAY 21
CONTEXTUALIZING THE GOSPEL

Romans 3.21–26

Currently, we have about 20 to 25 guests, mainly non-Christians, and they're divided into three groups to have the discussion in English, Thai or a mixture of both. I do most of the live talks and it's been a good opportunity to use some of what I've learned in my MA course in order to contextualize the gospel for Thai ears. Instead of going on about how sin separates us from God, which is something totally foreign to atheistic Buddhists, I spoke in terms of karma. We can never pay for all our bad karma, that's why Jesus had to die on the cross so that all our bad karma could be on him. When we believe in him, we enter into a relationship with him that gives us access to this karma-removing act (or in Christian language, the cleansing of sins).

Jane Lee, Thailand

What language would you use to express the gospel in different ways to friends, neighbours, those of other cultures? Think of someone with whom you would like to share the message of God's grace. How might you do that – by actions or by words? Spend time praying for someone with whom you want to share God's gospel of love.

LENT – DAY 22
TELLING IT SLANT

Isaiah 55.8–11

Tina Beattie, in her very readable book, *The New Atheists*, writes: 'It may be of the very essence of our humanity that we hunger for beauty as much as we hunger for food, and those who seek to do good in the world must be providers of beauty as well as of food to those in need.' Perhaps that's enough; humanity needs beauty and is fulfilled by it. Perhaps we don't need another layer of interpretation.

But let's follow the other path, the one that sees this response of wonder and 'reaching out' as a clue to a deeper longing still. The sort of longing Saint Augustine was referring to in his famous prayer, 'O God, you have made us for yourself, and our souls are restless until they find their rest in you.' If that's true, then the wonder and longing evoked by music or painting or poetry are taking us to the heart of contemporary mission. They're making a connection with huge numbers of apparently secular people.

So what do we do with this evocative possibility in the arts? Emily Dickinson, the American poet said, 'Tell the truth, but tell it slant.' I love that image. Telling it slant is what art does, and it's what the Church has done too for hundreds of years. It's used the arts to tell the story in religious drama, music, painting, architecture, stained glass, wood, stone, the sacred theatre of the liturgy and so on. Every way conceivable to tell it slant. Men and women have instinctively known that these were the richest ways they could find to convey spiritual truths, and that people would be drawn to these profound ways of telling the story.

'Telling it slant' is one way of describing it. 'Ec-centric mission' is another. Mission from a non-central, ec-centric place. To be eccentric means, literally, to have your centre somewhere else. Christian mission needs to start from that 'somewhere else' and the arts are ideal.

Anyway, let's return to the next stage of the argument I'm making for the role of the arts in mission. We've got as far as someone perhaps recognizing the source of the deep longing that's opened up in their heart and mind. When this happens, the crucial move for Christians is to avoid crashing in like a Monty Python foot with a triumphant 'here's the answer – my faith!' We've done far too much of that in the past and lost the trust of honest seekers and searchers. Instead, we have to listen to the questions, respect the journey the other is on, and simply let God be God and speak in God's own time and own way. You don't need to push a river; it flows by itself. God is the evangelist, not us.

John Pritchard

God – may we let you be God. Amen.

LENT – DAY 23
SEEING THROUGH DIFFERENT EYES

John 7.24

As Maurice and I were going out for a short walk a couple of weeks ago passing a new large building outside our compound, we began discussing how shocked we were that they are building a very high brick wall around it instead of using the traditional thorn bushes to guard it. The views from the windows were really beautiful looking out at a patchwork of fields with a variety of crops and trees. We spoke about how crazy it was to block the view and instead look out all day at a brick wall, not to mention the heat that would radiate from the wall in the summer. What a crazy thing to do!

Then, as we were talking it struck us, maybe it's all about world view, how we have been brought up and what different things mean to us. To us the countryside means relaxation, beauty, walks, leisure time, holidays. To us brick walls in Pakistan mean intense heat and, in this instance, the blocking of that beautiful scene. We realized to those brought up working the land this is very likely to appear as a scene of toil and hardship. To them bricks mean wealth, the sign of prosperous city life. It is so easy to quickly judge others and the things they do and so much more difficult to try to see these things through their eyes. God has challenged us through this.

Laura Connor, Pakistan

Reflect on the things you find yourself judging in others – choices, lifestyle, behaviour. How might seeing things through their eyes enable you to respond with grace and compassion?

Lord – you tell us not to judge, that we may not be judged.
Forgive our narrow-mindedness.
Help us to look at the bigger picture,
to see through the eyes of others,
and to have humility and openness to learn from them. Amen.

LENT – DAY 24
ROLLERCOASTER OF LOVE

Luke 17.20–21

We moved onto the Bournville Estate, an urban priority area in Weston-super-Mare, last September and being part of God's mission here has been a rollercoaster ride.

Thanks to a small amount of funding, we've undertaken intensive research into the culture and life of those growing up here. It's been a real joy to hear the voice of the faithful professionals who work so hard to serve people on the estate, and to get to know the young people nearby.

In the local play area we have a roundabout/see-saw. One day, I met a young boy who had never been on it. No one had ever put him on it, nor offered to push. It was a poignant moment, as he shrieked with laughter and shouted 'more', when we swung him round.

We're learning to take pleasure in the small joys, and to create moments that connect us. Armed with a stove, frying pan and sauces, we recently created a place of hospitality in the local park. Instead of inviting young people into our comfort zone, we asked to come into their space and share. And so that day we cooked pancakes for a group of six young people.

Life here is an experiment in being authentically Christian. It's an experiment in finding God again in a new way. It takes faith to believe that every place on the Bournville can be an encounter with the divine – but that's our dream; to know that every place is God's place. And so, with all our heart, we wish you well as you seek to discover God afresh in your own context.

John Wheatley and Dave Wilkie, www.streetpilgrims.org.uk

How can we create ways to connect with those around us? What would be good news for people living down your street?

Pray for young people like Tommy who long for the simplest pleasures in life, but who often miss out on some of the joys of childhood.

Pray for Dave and John and others like them who are living and working as part of the local community – that they may discover that the place is, indeed, God's place and that the kingdom of God is among them.

LENT – DAY 25
PRACTICAL PARTNERSHIP

Mark 16.15

In order to encourage the local people into something practical and building up community spirit, I often organize 'Southall community clean-up days', in conjunction with the Metropolitan police. It is usually simple, practical community work but effective enough to draw people from various ethnic and religious backgrounds. It opens doors for us to talk about our faith and the reason for organizing the event.

Kim and Khailean Khongsai, Southall

In what ways can we develop practical partnerships with others in our community, to build a sense of trust and belonging and to share something of our faith?

Lord God, help us to be creative and courageous in developing new friendships and partnerships. Open our eyes to see new possibilities in simple, practical ways. Amen.

LENT – DAY 26
SERVING AND LOVING

1 Peter 4.10–11

Being a mum is never easy. Added to that, many mothers we've got to know here are doing the job with added pressures of debt, addiction, ill-health or heartache. So the Saturday evening before Mothering Sunday, we wanted to let area mums know how special they are to us and to God. Around 40 mums were invited to an elegant evening in a local church. After being greeted at the door and assisted with their coats, they were ushered into a pampering room where they could have a massage and hairstyle, and get their portrait taken by a professional photographer or sketched by an artist. They were then treated to a three-course candlelit supper accompanied by music. Volunteers served them with the utmost care, treating them as honoured guests.

It was a huge amount of work, a bit like organizing a wedding reception, but it was also great fun and incredibly rewarding. At the end, one mother said, 'The night was a real encouragement. It makes me want to be a better mum.' Another told us she wanted to be more involved in our work here: 'Tonight's really made me want to give something back.' For us, the evening was a powerful image of God's kingdom, with the hurt and the bruised and the unconfident and the abused sitting down to eat.

Anna and Chris Hembury, Hull

So let us learn how to serve
And in our lives enthrone him;
Each others needs to prefer
For it is Christ we're serving.

This is our God, the servant King
He calls us now to follow him
To bring our lives as a daily offering
Of worship, to the servant king.

Graham Kendrick

LENT – DAY 27
THE FAITH OF YOUNG BELIEVERS

2 Kings 5.1–14

Recently, someone discreetly heard a 'Naaman' story (2 Kings 5) about a high-ranking Thai officer, who heard his Lisu house-girl singing, and paused to ask her what and why she was singing. She replied that it was songs of praise to the God in whom she believed. He wanted to know more, and mindful of Thai customs of seniority (and high language for his rank), she politely requested him to speak with her pastor. He came that very afternoon, and within two hours of conversation the Thai officer had invited the Lord Jesus into his heart, and promised to read God's word. Four days later he urgently requested to see the pastor again. He showed him two spacious rooms in his mansion and informed his guest that they used to be full of his hobby – a valuable Thai Buddhist image collection. 'As I read this book, I understood God does not like these. So, I burned all of the wooden idols, and disposed of all the metal ones. I feel so free!' For many folk who have ministered here for decades, this is a 'first'! Praise him for this young believer's faithfulness!

Shelagh Wynne, Thailand

Give thanks for the ministry of young people – so often undervalued in the Church. Pray that we may be open to receive their wisdom and their gifts – and to be challenged by them.

LENT – DAY 28
WATER OF LIFE

Psalm 36.5–9

Currently, to get safe drinking water people (ourselves included) would have to boil the water for at least ten minutes. This is very labour intensive as fuel wood must be gathered and then the water boiling supervised, and after all this a wife will often find her husband complaining that the water tastes too smoky! While safe drinking water is obviously beneficial for health, the smoke generated by boiling it is not. I was surprised to find out recently that more women and young children in Africa died last year from disease related to exposure to smoke from cooking fires than died from malaria! But there is another way of getting safe water, which requires less work and no smoke and gives water with a very good taste.

The process is called SODIS, and we have been doing it at home since we arrived here. Empty clear plastic or glass bottles are simply filled with water and left in the sun for six hours on a piece of metal painted black. This actually kills more bugs in the water than boiling for ten minutes! Plastic bottles are thrown away in huge numbers as rubbish here, so we are also recycling!

To introduce this simple technology to the villages I have been training Mothers' Union groups in each church, who then go house to house and train the women in how to use the technology. They also go to schools and teach the children. Alongside this they are also using this as an opportunity for evangelism. We have shown each group how they can introduce Jesus into their conversation as the 'water of life' and 'quencher of thirst', and thus these groups, which here are the heart of the church, are able to visit every household in the village with a solution for safe water, a way of reducing each woman's workload and the message of the gospel. For me, this has been the best development project we have been able to undertake so far, combining physical and spiritual outreach.

Andy Hart, Tanzania

Lord God, the fountain of living water,
we pray for those who thirst –
those who thirst for physical water,
and those who thirst for the living water of truth.
Give us grace to offer actions and words
to quench their thirst
and to lead them to the fountain of life. Amen.

LENT – DAY 29
A STORY TO TELL

Romans 8.26–28

Having very few TEFL resources, I decided to start using these sessions to study the Bible in English. We study a passage and use this to discuss grammar and vocabulary. The passage then serves as a basis for discussions about faith and life. We share our hopes and fears as mothers and wives. Each of the ladies in the group has a story to tell about life as a refugee or survivor of genocide, and it is with a sense of great privilege that I listen to them share some of this. It also helps me reflect upon my own experiences, particularly those more difficult or traumatic times. Through these English lessons each one of us has learned more about the love and faithfulness of God in difficult times. 'All things work together for good for those who love God, who are called according to his purpose.'

Sue Kellow, Rwanda

In all things God works for the good of those who love him . . . Spend some time thanking God for his hand upon your life – that in all things he is working for good, despite appearances at times.

LENT – DAY 30
KINDNESS AND PEACE

Romans 12.11–18

The number of Muslims in Rwanda has steadily been growing since the 1994 genocide. Why? In part the growth is due to the betrayal of those seeking refuge in churches. It is well documented that both Catholics and Protestants alike were betrayed by their own pastors, and it is not uncommon to hear that Muslims are peace-loving and kind-hearted and that Christians are not.

As we have travelled around Rwanda, on most main roads we see mosques. Frequently, when I ask Rwandan Christians if there are many Muslims in the country, the answer is that there are not. However, I wonder if the number is higher than is generally thought and if not, whether the number could grow more rapidly than expected. Either way, I think that complacency is not an option, but neither is fear.

Sue Kellow, Rwanda

Do we live up to the picture Paul paints in Romans – of people who are filled with integrity, honour, kindness, and peace? What do people see when they look at our lives?

Lord – let peace, kindness, integrity begin with me. Amen.

LENT – DAY 31
WITH COURTESY AND RESPECT

1 Peter 3.14–17

I recently had the opportunity to teach a diploma-level course which looked at this idea – that Christians need to be engaging with Muslims in Rwanda in a non-confrontational, diplomatic and loving way, which may then serve as a springboard for conversation about Christ at an appropriate time. It is true that there is much in Islamic practice, tradition and thinking that is very different from Christianity, but the course advocates that those befriending Muslims know both the differences between the two religions and also the similarities in thinking. These similarities could then be the focal point, at least in the initial stages of friendship with Muslims.

It also advocated that Christians do not primarily look at Muslims as 'targets' of conversion but rather as cousins who we are considerately seeking to influence for Christ. It is a focus of this course to inform simply the students, in order that (a) Christians may not be afraid of Muslims and think of them all as terrorists and (b) that Christians may become surer of their own faith. There is still disinformation, mistrust and a lack of clarity in the Church about other religions, and that is why this course is so important in the training of a new generation of Rwandan priests.

As is so often when we serve God, what we learn is sometimes equal or greater than what we teach! During the preparation and delivery of this course, Richard was interested to learn that the biggest growth in Islam in Rwanda is through conversion, rather than immigration; the reverse of the situation in much of the Western world. This has implications for the way in which Rwandan Christians interact with and approach their Rwandan brothers and sisters.

Sue Kellow, Rwanda

Lord, may we always be ready to give an account of our faith – with courtesy, respect and love. Amen.

LENT – DAY 32
MONEY IN SECOND PLACE
(VENN PRINCIPLES)

Hebrews 13.5–6

Venn principles – put money in second place, because money follows ministry; let prayer and study precede its collection.

One excellent non-profit manager . . . says that all the serious dilemmas in operating non-profit organizations relate to what she calls 'the three

Ms: mission, management and money'. The problem, she says, is that people tend to concern themselves with the wrong 'M' first. They tend to see most things in terms of money . . . But in fact, that is usually the last thing they should worry about. I believe that if an organization can define and articulate its mission in terms that are clear enough and compelling enough, and put in place structures and processes for achieving its goals that are obviously appropriate, then raising the money it needs will not be a problem.

Approaches to planning – strategic or otherwise – based solely on logic will prove incompatible with organizations that aim to be 'spiritually guided' in defining and fulfilling their mission. The religious organization that fails to employ prayer as well as analysis, that does not look at its spiritual resources as well as its technical capacities and environment in trying to determine its opportunities, goals and strategies will not long be effective in offering the witness of service. One of the most impressive aspects of the most effective organizations in the study was the way they recalled the need to seek divine guidance in all their activities; planning and prayer were often integrated, frequently part of the same meetings or conversations (as people recounted them). In the realm of planning, these organizations seemed always mindful that it was God's plans to which they ultimately needed to give the most attention.

Thomas H. Jeavons

Let nothing disturb you.
Nothing dismay you.
All things pass.
But God never changes.
Whoever has God lacks nothing.
If you have only God,
You have more than enough.

Teresa of Avila (1515–82)

LENT – DAY 33
MISSION FIRST!

Acts 2.44–47

Mission cannot wait for finance! If you press ahead with what you believe to be God's will, the money will follow – somehow. That is the theory – and we have found it to be true in practice many times.

Susan Essam, Nigeria

'Day by day, the Lord added new converts to their number.' Are we, like the early Christians, willing to step out in mission and trust that God will supply what is needful? Have we experienced that truth – that God will provide? How might God be calling us to put mission before money?

'God's work done in God's way will never lack God's supply.'

James Hudson Taylor (1832–1905),
founder of the China Inland Mission – later OMF

Lord – no one can serve two masters.
Help us to set the growth of your kingdom ahead of
   our growth in wealth,
the uncertainty of living by faith ahead of financial security.
Give us wisdom, we pray to discern your will
and the strength to follow your leading. Amen.

LENT – DAY 34
LAVISHLY OPEN-HANDED

2 Corinthians 8.1–4

We know we are going to work with people on the edge of society, and God has particularly spoken to us through the words of the missionary C. T. Studd: 'Some wish to live within the sound of a chapel bell; I wish to run a rescue mission within a yard of hell.'

The way people have responded when we have shared how God has called us has greatly encouraged us too. John shared what we were doing in a church for the homeless he had visited before, and they took a collection to support us. The folks who mainly live on the streets completely emptied their pockets of all they had in the world and it came to £140!

John and Gillian Robinson, Thailand

Are we prepared to be 'lavishly open-handed' and to give even beyond the limit of our resources?

Take my silver and my gold;
not a mite would I withhold.
Take my intellect, and use
every power as thou shalt choose.

Frances R. Havergal (1836–79)

LENT – DAY 35
MISSION AT THE HEART

John 12.1–5

Shannon Hopkins is an entrepreneur in mission with incredible energy. Her latest venture is a recycled fashion accessories business called Sweet Notions. She and a friend are collecting thousands of chic treats and selling them at unique boutique events. Shannon explains: 'I don't want to just generate income to enable mission work. Instead, I want the way we carry out Sweet Notions to be fully integrated with the kingdom as a missional act, living out the gospel through the social enterprise itself.'

How might our income generation and prayer, both so vital in supporting mission partners around the world, become part of mission so that others are drawn in and captivated by the gospel?

Servant Christ,
help us to follow you into the city,
to claim its whole life for God whose image we bear,
to confront the ambitions of those hungry for power,
the inhuman orthodoxy of the legalist,
with the startling message of your present action,
your living power.
Servant Christ, help us to follow you. Amen.

India: Litany of the Disciples of Christ the Servant

LENT – DAY 36
THE WIDOW'S MITE

Luke 21.1–4

Gaenor Hall writes about an experience when touring the UK with one of the miners from the Chilean mine disaster:

One venue, Kirkby in Ashfield, was economically destroyed by the miners' strikes and pit closures of the 1980s. Church work in that community became difficult. People were bitter and up to seven years ago, murders were still taking place within the mining network.

The first meeting with Jose and Alf that day was at Kirkby Miners' Welfare. The mining community would not come to the church – so the church went to them. It was standing room only. I found myself sitting in a corridor talking to a local minister. He was in tears, unable to believe that CMS would send the tour to 'an out of the way insignificant nothing of a place' and as a result of the meeting this minister rededicated his life to mission in his community.

As the meeting came to an end, I was stopped by a lady who wanted to make a donation to CMS – she took out her purse and emptied its content into the bag I was holding. Her friend asked what she was going to do as that was all the money she had until her pension was paid again.

The lady replied, 'God will supply. I know it is right to give.'

We praise you, Lord God,
for those who give sacrificially for the growth of your kingdom.
We ask you to deliver us from the love of money,
To make us content with what we need –
And to trust that you will provide. Amen.

LENT – DAY 37
A BETTER WAY?

Ecclesiastes 5.10

It is 9.30 pm on Friday night, and I am just back from the weekly 'prayer and fasting' at our church. The phone rings. It's Shiao Chi, and she wants to talk. We arrange to meet the following afternoon for coffee in Tamsui. Tamsui is several miles down the road, usually 25 minutes all round the mulberry bush on a bus. On Saturday afternoon it will be packed with tourists. The whole of Taipei will be there. They come for the night market, the river views, to ride bikes and look at the sunset.

Shiao Chi and I have been meeting this way for years – months of silence and then a phone call, 'can we talk?' She tells me the latest bad news of her family. It always seems like it can never get worse, but it usually does. She has spent the evening before at the police station, accompanying her mother to pay a NT$30,000 fine when her brother was caught over the alcohol limit driving a motorcycle in Taipei City. Last time he was caught he had actually stolen the motorcycle too. She is angry because her brother has no intention of changing his lifestyle, and her mother keeps on bailing him out. Thirty minutes after bringing him home from the police station he is back out on the streets with his mates.

Over the years, her tales of family life have saddened and disturbed me, but I listen again for signs of hope. Her childhood was filled with verbal abuse as her parents fought over money, threatened each other with knives, and chain-smoked, drank and gambled away what money they did have. Now divorced, they continue the verbal abuse by phone, while her father persuades her mother to open up ten or more credit card accounts so that he can borrow money from her. She tells me he's paid back only about half the money so far. Business is not good these days.

She tells me that she is the only one in her family who doesn't smoke, drink, gamble, and now the only one with a regular job. 'I don't want to be like them,' she says with conviction. She has come to Bible studies, church, met Christians and heard the gospel. When she asked her parents if she could become a Christian and be baptized, they told her to be loyal to the family and stick to the traditional religion of her parents. She tells me that Taoism and folk religion clearly hasn't worked for her family. They are totally obsessed with money, and no amount of temple worship, offerings and sacrifices seems to have helped them. She is challenged by my way of life and attitude to money. 'Maybe it's a better way,' she says hopefully.

Catherine Lee, Taiwan

Father God, may my attitude to money challenge and encourage others to discover what matters most in life – your son Jesus Christ. Amen.

LENT – DAY 38
WAITING . . . AND GROWING

1 Peter 2.2

The Orthodox Church here is well into the 'big fast' – 55 days of abstention from all meat and dairy products, and for the more committed, no food or drink until 3 pm each day and then still just beans and bread to look forward to! They are of course preparing themselves for Easter, the most loved of festivals. This year there were only five weeks between Advent and Lent, so it does feel as if the fasting just never stops (not forgetting a three-day fast to remember Jonah three weeks ago).

In many ways we too feel that since our last letter in November, God has been speaking to us about preparation . . . in terms of how our life and work here are all part of his plan of 'preparation' of us. Of course, we're not clear what his purposes are for our future, but what we do know from his word, is that he's in the business of seeing us grow, learn and mature . . . 'crave pure spiritual milk so that by it you may grow up in your salvation' (1 Peter 2.2).

We have recently been encouraged by *Detox Your Spiritual Life in 40 Days* by Peter Graystone. At one point in the book he talks about some of the great giants of faith and how a common theme was waiting and preparing. In the life of Paul, for example, there was ten years between his conversion and emerging as someone ready to lead the church.

For Moses there was 40 years as a farmer between his departure from Pharaoh's palace in disgrace and returning again to lead the people out. For Jacob there was 20 years between fleeing Esau and meeting again – by which time he was generous and ready to reconcile. How had Jacob learned so much?

Not from religious sermons, books or worship experiences, he learned, because he was acutely aware of God involved in his daily life . . . mostly he learned through hard, patient graft, work, success, being cheated. . . . We also grow through blunders, successes, heartaches, laughter and slog . . . and hopefully some dramatic revelations on the way!

Chris and Angela Chorlton, Egypt

Can you identify waiting or preparation periods in your life? Are you in one now? What might God be preparing in you?

Help us, Lord God, to be like new-born infants, craving pure spiritual milk. Amen.

LENT – DAY 39
THE CHOICE IS YOURS

Ephesians 6.10–18

As we meet with God and receive, think about taking the light out into the world and about what it might illuminate. Even if you're only a bright spark, kindle; kindle the life in the light you've received from the heart of the son. You might even get fired up. You might blaze a trail; stand up for others; seek out injustice; protest on behalf of the innocent; carry a torch for the unloved; demonstrate for love; demonstrate love itself.

Mary was also given a challenge; she was asked to carry the Word; the pulse of the cosmos within her. She literally carried God into the world. Mary said yes and changed the course of history; took a gamble on the divine; flouted the odds; evened the score with darkness; carried the light of the world and allowed it to shine so that we might see it and respond.

She had a choice, as we have a choice. Choice cuts, sometimes like a sword to the heart. It did for her. Choose carefully. Jesus was no robot; he made agonizing choices; stood up, stood out, and was crucified for it. 'Look where that got him,' they said. It got him all the way to us.

You can choose a lifestyle, or you can choose life. The choice, as they say, is yours.

Ana and Kevin Draper

Spend time reflecting on God's challenge to take the light into the world. What does that mean for you? How will you respond?

PALM SUNDAY
ENTERING INTO DEATH AND RESURRECTION

Mark 11.8–10, 15.9–14

We're writing this at Easter-time as we remember the defining events of Jesus' death and resurrection. Here in Southall it's been the Sikh festival of Vaisakhi, and on Sunday the streets were filled with more than 30,000 people celebrating, handing out masses of free food, playing loud Bhangra music, all with a wonderful party atmosphere. At our multiracial church we were celebrating Palm Sunday with our own more modest procession, but people really felt they were there in Jerusalem with King Jesus as we shouted out words projected onto a big screen – 'Hosanna!', 'Praise the Lord'. Then, shockingly, the words on the screen changed, and suddenly everybody was shouting 'Crucify him!' before they'd realized what they were doing.

We stopped and reflected on how easy it is to go along with the crowd – to worship Jesus when others are, but to keep silent or deny him when the crowd changes. In Southall, we're often a tiny Christian minority going against the flow in terms of what we believe, but actually the same is true across the UK today. The news in recent months has been full of signs that society is becoming increasingly intolerant of biblical values, and Christians will have to choose whether to simply go along with the crowd, or to go against the flow.

In many ways, what we're doing with A Rocha feels similar. Western society – including many Christians – still seems to believe we can keep aspiring to yet higher standards of living, consuming more, wasting more, destroying more and more of this fragile planet, while the poor starve, and wildlife becomes extinct. We're aware we've got an enormous way to go, but really believe it's time for us to 'go against the flow' in terms of our lifestyles. That's why we've set up www.arocha.org.uk/livinglightly as a lifestyle challenge. That's also why, this week, we remembered the darkness between Good Friday and Easter Sunday by having a complete fast from electricity and gas consumption (except for the freezer!), to identify with Jesus and the darkness of Good Friday, and also as a symbolic rejection of carbon-hungry lifestyles. The kids really entered into this, with candles and cooking outdoors, and somehow Easter Sunday was even more special this year.

Dave and Anne Bookless, Southall

Am I willing to 'go against the flow', not only with my words but with my lifestyle?

On Palm Sunday, Jesus enters Jerusalem to cheers and waving of palms. All too soon that changes and he is facing the reality of the cross. Pray that Christians throughout the world may enter afresh into Christ's death and resurrection this Holy Week and discover in a new way the life – for ALL creation – that springs from death.

MONDAY IN HOLY WEEK
OUR SOUL IS RESTED

Habakkuk 3.19

25 March 1965, Montgomery, Alabama

Last Sunday, more than 8,000 of us started on a mighty walk from Selma, Alabama. We have walked through desolate valleys and across the trying hills. We have walked on meandering highways and rested our bodies on rocky byways. Some of our faces are burned from the outpourings of the sweltering sun. Some have literally slept in the mud. We have been drenched by the rains. Our bodies are tired and our feet are somewhat sore.

But today as I stand before you and think back over that great march, I can say, as Sister Pollard – a seventy-year-old Negro woman who lived in this community during the bus boycott – said when one day, she was asked while walking if she didn't want to ride. And when she answered, 'No,' the person said, 'Well, aren't you tired?' And with her ungrammatical profundity, she said, 'My feets is tired, but my soul is rested.' And in a real sense this afternoon, we can say that our feet are tired, but our souls are rested.

They told us we wouldn't get here. And there were those who said that we would get here only over their dead bodies, but all the world today knows that we are here and we are standing before the forces of power in the state of Alabama saying, 'We ain't goin' to let nobody turn us around.'

Martin Luther King (1929–68)

Give thanks for those who, like Martin Luther King, have fought tirelessly to see transformation of society – who have stood up against injustice despite the cost. Pray for those today who are engaged in the struggle for a world reflecting God's justice and equality – that their strength may be renewed today, that they will soar as on eagle's wings. Pray as we walk with Christ through Holy Week, that God will give us all the strength and the passion to be a part of transforming the world.

TUESDAY IN HOLY WEEK
UNLESS A GRAIN OF WHEAT . . .

John 12.24–25

March has seen a continuation of such activities but has also been marked by some very sad events over the last few weeks, for which I would love your prayer. First of all, the oldest son of a German couple who are working on a development project for the Catholic Church started having problems with his eyes; by the time he returned to Germany they found that he was virtually blind.

Then last week, the 18-month-old child of the local catechist from the Anglican church next to the clinic drowned in a small pond. At 10 am he was alive, at 11 am he was found drowned and at 5 pm his shocked parents had to bury him. There were over 100 people present and funerals for children get done quickly as it is so expensive to feed all mourners for the days and nights that they stay.

And then last Saturday, very suddenly, the wife of the second officer in the development office fell ill and within six hours died of a ruptured ectopic pregnancy. The funeral will be today.

Living here, and sharing in these sudden and not so sudden tragedies, keep us close to our God, searching for him daily. And it has brought home in an unforgettable way the truth of my sermon text for last Sunday:

'Truly I tell you, unless a grain of wheat falls to the earth and dies, it remains just a single grain; but if it dies, it bears much fruit. Those who love their life will lose it, and those who hate their life in this world will keep it for eternal life' (John 12.24–5).

Ruth Hulser, Tanzania

Unless a grain of wheat falls into the ground and dies it remains only a single seed – but if it dies, it produces many seeds . . .

Spend some time reflecting on what these words mean for you in your life of mission.

WEDNESDAY IN HOLY WEEK
GOD'S LOVE POURED INTO
OUR HEARTS

2 Kings 4.1–7

The Living Waters Church in Recife, Brazil is pouring out God's love in a deprived and dangerous area – and whole families are being changed.

Gabriel was an alcoholic and abusive towards his wife, Maisa, and their children. His addiction caused him to lose his job and the family had to move closer to Olinda, a shanty town on the edge of a huge rubbish dump. With no income, they began to starve. The three children began scavenging on the dump for things to sell for food.

One day the children were befriended by a team from Living Waters Church nearby. The church's pastor, CMS Latin partner Siméa Meldrum, recalled, 'As the children became regulars at our Sunday services, the parents saw their new courage and joy. One day they agreed to come to church and that was when the change in Gabriel began.'

Maisa said she can remember Siméa's sermon that day. 'She was preaching on the widow and bottle of olive oil from 2 Kings 4.2. Then she gave everyone in great need a bottle of oil to take home, symbolizing that God could do in each house as he did in the widow's. I took it home and put it in a special place and every day I was filled with faith and joy.'

Gabriel began attending church, turned to Christ and became a founding member of the Association of Recyclers of Olinda. The family no longer lacks food.

During a Maundy Thursday service the children forgave their father for his past abuse and washed his feet. 'We felt the love of God being poured into our hearts,' Maisa said.

CMS Publication

Give thanks for God's promise of new life – that even in the midst of seeming crisis his hand is at work to bring about change and renewal. Pray for those you know who are currently going through a time of crisis, that they may experience new life and hope this Easter-time.

MAUNDY THURSDAY
A RECONCILING HEART

John 13.1–15

I, a Palestinian, recently helped lead a group of 27 young Christians origi-
nally from opposing backgrounds – Israelis, Palestinians and Americans –
on a week-long Jordanian desert trek. The trip was part of a programme
sponsored by CMS's strategic partner Musalaha (reconciliation), which
promotes peace between Israelis and Palestinians through a shared love
of Jesus.

On arrival everyone greeted each other and shared stories, followed by
a meal, worship and prayers. The next day we set off at sunrise, mounted
on camels and started to explore the desert. We stopped for Bible study
and talked about our identity, our responsibilities and forgiveness. On
the Thursday night before Easter, an Israeli participant, Itav, asked me,
'What are we reconciling about? I did not know you before this encounter and I have nothing against you.' Within a few minutes, most of the
group had gathered around Itav and me as we talked about his question.
We concluded that we need reconciliation because we have ignored our
responsibilities as children of God – in the way we behave towards each
other, talk about each other and stereotype each other.

Later that evening, one of the guys talked about washing feet and
the example Jesus showed us in humility and service. Some commented
on how in Middle Eastern culture it is a hard thing to do, as only servants wash their masters' feet. Suddenly an American, an Israeli and a
Palestinian brought a bucket of water over and started washing each
other's feet. Immediately, everyone else did the same. It was a night full
of worship, tears, love and humility.

I was sitting next to a policeman – a young Jordanian Muslim who was
assigned by the government to protect the group (a normal procedure in
Jordan). Jamal's English was not good enough to understand everything
that was going on, so I offered to translate. He was shocked by what he
saw and heard. He had misconstrued ideas about Christians. But I could
see the passion in his eyes and his questions started going deeper – asking

about faith and salvation. Then suddenly his mobile rang and he said that he had to go and pray.

I said to him, 'Why don't you pray with us?' He hesitated, but left. A bit later, a woman in the group came and asked me if I could bring Jamal into the tent and wash his feet. I said to her that I was happy to do so, but I could not ask him in front of his friends he was praying with, and that we needed to wait for God's timing. Five minutes later, Jamal moved away from his friends and came to watch us washing each other's feet. One of the male participants took Jamal by the hand, prayed for him and washed his feet. God's work is beyond our thinking and power; we just need to trust him and take our identity in him more seriously.

Tanas Al Qassis

Father – we are all your children. Help us to trust you and take our identity in you more seriously. Amen.

GOOD FRIDAY
RIPPING THE FABRIC

Mark 15.33–38

As Jesus dies we are told that the Temple curtain ripped. This curtain was what separated the Holy of Holies from the people – and even the High Priests had to undertake thorough cleansing rituals before they could enter it. So the death of Jesus rips the fabric of religion, it ruptures the structures and blows wide the gates! The glory of God is now immanent – it is here, there and everywhere, within everybody's reach (as Paul says to the Athenians in the Areopagus) . . . but if we go back to the birth narrative, we find the glory of God present on earth outside the Temple/ religious system already! So it seems that Jesus' incarnation as well as his death is part of this action – by his birth, not just by his death the system becomes defunct, by his birth we are able to exist within the glory of God, by his birth we are forgiven, and by his death it is completed and open to everyone.

Mark Berry, SafeSpace Telford

Give thanks to God that in the death of Jesus the gates are blown wide open and that salvation is for all people.

HOLY SATURDAY

WAITING . . .

Mark 15.42–47

A couple of years ago one of our friends suggested we read W. H. Vanstone's book *The Stature of Waiting*. In his book Vanstone observes that in Mark's Gospel, up to the time of his betrayal, Jesus is the one who makes things happen; he never simply observes events, he initiates them. But from the time of his betrayal Jesus appears to *do* nothing; even his words no longer seem to have the effect they once did. Jesus is still the focus of the action, but now he 'passes from doing to receiving what others do, from working to waiting, from the role of subject to that of object and . . . from action to passion'. Vanstone notes that the Greek word from which the word 'passion' is derived means, not suffering as people often think, but 'to be done to'.

For most of Lent Allan, having recently broken his ankle, had tended to be the object rather than the subject, although as Lent moved towards Holy Week things improved a little. We were both able to do some productive work and even found a physiotherapist for Allan. Miraculously, two crutches and one foot finally became no crutches at all and two feet. That was the week before Holy Week.

The following days of Holy Week were like a rollercoaster but we will tell the tale in Allan's words: On Monday we went to the office at Diocesan HQ but I continued to feel negative and desperate. Nothing was right, everywhere seemed like a disaster area, there was nothing positive, and repeated expressions of concern about how my ankle was getting on infuriated me.

We had been invited to a special Holy Week service and lunch at the college at Ringili on Tuesday lunchtime. Anne suggested we should go, but I had no wish to go anywhere particularly. Reluctantly, I agreed and used my newly acquired driving ability to pick up Anne from the School of Nursing. When we arrived at the turning to the college, however, we discovered some minor road works, several workmen and two cones blocking our route. One of the workmen rather rudely refused to allow us access, and we had to return home since I couldn't walk that far. I was ridiculously angry. The next few hours were bad. It seemed as though my own effort to be positive had been met by a 'Road Closed' sign. What future was there in continuing? I was at the end of my resources. 'I don't want to carry on. I give up. I want to go home.'

During Lent it seemed that a broken ankle was the cause of *being done to* rather than *doing*. And this Holy Week we have been brought to the point where we have had to say *'I give up, I have no more resources to offer, I am broken.'* It is the point of powerlessness, but the place where we can begin to learn to stop *doing* and start *being done to* by God.

Allan and Anne Lacey, Uganda

Have you experienced 'waiting times' in your life? Are you experiencing one now? What might God be preparing you for?

Lord, as we wait for resurrection,
give us grace to come to you empty handed,
to stop doing and start 'being done to' by you. Amen.

EASTER DAY
RECONCILING THE WORLD WITH GOD

Mark 16.1–8

Over Chinese New Year, I had the opportunity to visit New Zealand. On the last Sunday I joined my friends for worship in their home church in Paraparaumu (that'll test your Maori pronunciation!). The church itself is built right next to a small airport, used mainly by light aircraft. The large window behind the altar was of clear glass, and through the window there was a view of trees, hills and sky.

That Sunday morning, as we were praying the final post-communion prayer (the one where we are sent into the world in the power of the Spirit, to live and work to God's praise and glory), suddenly through that altar window I saw in the distance a helicopter plummeting head first towards the ground, followed by pieces of wreckage. The few of us in the congregation who saw it knew that a crash was inevitable, with almost certain death for the pilot. Later we discovered that a light plane had collided in mid-air with the helicopter, both then crashed onto neighbouring houses and shops, and all three people onboard died.

Six days later, I was back in Taiwan, and attending the thanksgiving service for the new stained glass. The artwork is magnificent, full of blues, yellows and reds; with a Jacob's ladder sculpture hanging down towards the altar from the centre. The altar itself is of marble, and usually left bare, reminding us of the stone that Jacob slept on when he had had his dream of the angels ascending and descending the ladder. The top of the sculpture, the flat part of the ceiling, is covered in mirrors, giving an impression of never-ending ladders, going on and on, up and up into eternity. The whole artwork vividly depicts the glory of God and the light of Christ, with the ladders calling us to come closer to God in prayer, joining heaven and earth in one glorious whole.

What a huge contrast between those two images. One glass window invites us to look out at the world; the other invites us to look up at the glory of God. Through one window I saw images of death and destruction; in another I saw images of the glory of God and the light of Christ.

Holy Week and Easter! Yet in both church services I heard words of how God sends us to take his light out into the dark world, and I also heard words of invitation to bring the concerns of the world to him in prayer. We are indeed called to do both, to do our part in reconciling the world with God, and God with the world.

Catherine Lee, Taiwan

Lord, on this resurrection day, send us out again, inspired, refreshed and renewed to do our part in reconciling the world to you. Amen.

EASTER – DAY 2
OPEN GRATITUDE

2 Corinthians 5.18–21

The highlight of our Easter celebrations was again attending the Easter Sunday sunrise service outside the parliament building in Dhaka along with hundreds of believers.

We've been reflecting over the last few months about thankfulness as we have seen again and again friends and colleagues showing gratitude publicly, in a way that we often don't see in our culture. This Easter we were struck anew by how much we have to be thankful for and what an amazing gift we have been given.

David and Sarah Hall, Bangladesh

Certainly something to celebrate!

Thank God for the public displays of celebration shared by Christians around the world. Pray for courage to share the Easter gospel more openly with our friends and neighbours, that we may be true ambassadors for Christ.

EASTER – DAY 3
BY THE WAY – JESUS IS ALIVE!

Philippians 3.10–11

By the way, Jesus is alive.

Isn't that the best 'by the way' ever? How amazing and life changing and hope restoring and death defying is that news!

If I didn't believe in the resurrection I would have given up on the Diocese of Muhabura (and life?) years ago. By the time you get this letter Easter Day will be behind us according to the calendar. Never mind, every day should be Easter Day.

My prayer for you and for us is that every day that remains of the year will be a fresh experience of resurrection life in Jesus Christ.

Jenny Green

How often do we fail to live in the power of the resurrection? Spend time thanking God that he never gives up on us – and never will. Pray that we may know Christ and the power of his resurrection every day of the year, not just on Easter Day.

EASTER – DAY 4
A NEW CREATION

2 Corinthians 5.16–17

The coming of Christ has opened for us the possibility of being part of an *emerging new culture*. The effect is similar to a stone being dropped into a pond, creating ever-increasing ripples in the water.

A mission partner

What might this 'emerging new culture' look like? What part am I called to play?

Find a stone, and if possible a pond – if not, a large bowl of water will do. As you drop the stone into the water and watch the ripples spreading, pray for God's Church throughout the world and in your own context, that our faith in Christ might create ripples of hope in new ways throughout our world.

EASTER – DAY 5
THE COST OF RENEWAL

Mark 8.34–38

How do we spell out this renewal? It is likely to be increasingly costly if it is to mean anything in the present, unjustly divided, conflict and famine-ridden, oppressed and tormented world, over which looms the growing threat of nuclear war. Those struggling for a new humanity in Christ in such a setting realize increasingly that it means nothing less than entering deeper into Christ's death and resurrection.

There were traditionally in the ancient Church two types of martyrdom. A 'red martyrdom' was the laying down of one's life, and a 'white martyrdom' a deep repentance and brokenness, a surrender of one's being through which God's love can flow to others.

Martyrdom then becomes a part of *matryria*, the word from which it springs, 'witness'. To encourage each other across the world in this witness, this life out of death, both corporately and individually, is an urgent necessity for Christians now if they are responsibly to seize hold of a moment for crucial, unprecedented opportunity for witness in every part of the globe. This may mean a breaking and remaking of our institutions, a loss of our 'physical plant', our buildings, our prestige.

Jocelyn Murray

What does God call me to surrender? What might the Church be called to 'break and remake'?

Lord – there is so much that we hold dear (too dear):
our traditions,
our prestige,
our sense of self-worth and importance.
Lord – take us, break us, remake us,
so that we may truly be your witnesses throughout the globe. Amen.

EASTER – DAY 6
WIDE AWAKE PEOPLE

Ephesians 1.7–10

In his book *Surprised by Hope*, Tom Wright talks of Christians and Christian communities living as Easter people, but more expressively as 'wide awake people'. At its core the Church is called to be a community of people caught and held by the fact that, in Christ, God is renewing the whole of creation, and calls human beings to share in this task of renewal. Certainly, if, as followers of Jesus, we are to live in this way we will need to be alert and attentive not only to the pain and the needs of the world around us, wherever that 'around us' may be, but also 'wide awake' and alert to the possibilities and opportunities that the risen Christ brings with each new day. A longing for justice and the right ordering of society, a deep concern for creation and care for the environment, a seeking after truth and beauty, a concern for each person, especially those who are rejected, stigmatized or marginalized, a longing for each individual to discover something of God's grace and love, are all significant in their own right, but take on an even deeper significance when they are seen as part of God's longing and purpose – 'to bring all things in heaven and on earth together under one head, even Christ'.

Chris Neal

Lord, may we be alert and attentive to the possibilities
of each new day.
May we have a longing for justice,
a deep concern for creation,

a seeking after truth and beauty,
a concern for every individual,
and a desire to participate in the vision you have set before us. Amen.

EASTER – DAY 7
CREATION: FOLLOW THE WORD OF GOD

Leviticus 26.3–5

CMS mission partner James Pender, as part of his work on helping the Church respond to the challenge of climate change, has had the opportunity to lead some workshops for youth on responding to climate change and on care for creation. One of these was a church youth seminar at the small rural village of Khamamaria in drought-prone western Bangladesh that attracted 40–50 young people from local Lutheran churches, Catholic churches and a few from other faiths as well as from the Church of Bangladesh. Another couple of workshops were led at the South Asian Christian Youth Network (SACYN) conference in Pokhara, Nepal with 50 young people from various churches in Pakistan, India, Nepal, Bhutan, Sri Lanka and Bangladesh. It was great to be able not only just to talk and explain about climate change and what we can do about it, but also to lead Bible-based discussions in which the youth saw the link between the 'environmental crisis' to sin, how God cares for his people in times of 'natural' disaster, our call to value all God has created, as well as to turn our encounters with the beauty of the natural world into prayer and worship. At the end of the workshops statements, songs or poems were written to express their feelings; my favourites include this one below and the reading tomorrow.

James Pender

We are in lack of food,
All around us
We are killing our mother earth,
By cutting trees
We are destroying our land,

By our own hands
It is the time to think in a different way:
If you want a peaceful world,
If you want a green earth,
Follow the words of God.

Bangladeshi youth in Khamamaria and translated from Bengali

Do we see caring for creation as an essential part of God's mission?

Father, may we treat the world you have wonderfully created for us with
the wonder and respect it deserves. Amen.

EASTER – DAY 8
FOR THE BEAUTY OF THE EARTH . . .

Psalm 65.6–13

Beautiful mountains with snow caps,
rivers, valleys, forests and deserts,
trees, rocks, animals and birds,
show us how much God loved the world.
For unto us he has given this earth,
to live in it and to take care of it,
so why do we pollute and destroy it?
We must take care of it, love it
and thank God for this lovely world.
O Lord, how beautiful is your world?
My words are not enough to express it.
Let us get together as one family and take care of it
throughout our lives!

Sudarshi Nonis, Sri Lanka, written at the SACYN conference in Nepal

*Today take time to stop and look more closely at God's creation – the
intricate pattern of a leaf or flower, or the expanse of hills or mountains.*

Pray that we may grow in appreciation of creation and all its wonders – that God will give us eyes to see and appreciate the beauty surrounding us.

EASTER – DAY 9
SUFFERING CONSEQUENCES

Ezekiel 34.17–20

In Tanzania we mainly depend on electricity that is generated by water power in one or two dams and also over two or three rivers. The main reliable river in Morogoro had totally dried up, so we have had fourteen-hour electricity cuts on alternate days since February. That played havoc with everyone's businesses and is very bad for the economy. In my case it meant that our laboratory was struggling getting through our diagnoses as we use electricity as the main light source for the microscopes. To keep our vaccines cool became an added challenge, and I was getting incredibly frustrated as all my administrative work is on computer. Internet had more or less become impossible as our internet provider had electricity on alternate days to the diocese.

Water became severely rationed, but as that coincided with some rain falling in Tabora, the effect was not so noticeable to me. More worrying is that the dams that give water to Tabora town for the dry months have only filled 11 per cent, which may mean very severe water shortages later this year, if there are no further significant rainfalls.

So you see the weather has a great influence on practically everything.

Ruth Huelser

The reason

Why has the weather changed? For many generations the rains on the whole have been quite reliable while in recent years we have noticed a definite change in the pattern. The experts say that this is the reality of the climatic changes in worldwide weather.

*It is ironic that the people affected severely here are those who have nei-
ther cars, electricity or are users of any fossil energy and therefore have
not themselves contributed significantly to global warming.*

*Pray for those throughout the world who are suffering as a result of cli-
mate change. Pray that we may be challenged to recognize the seriousness
of the situation – and to change.*

EASTER – DAY 10
RIVERS INTO DESERTS

Psalm 107.33–34

In March I visited the village of Kanainagor, in southwest Bangladesh.
It is in the coastal region, close to the port of Mongla (south of the city
of Khulna) and just north of the majestic Sunderban forest – the thick
mangrove jungle where the tigers live! I went at the request of the bishop
in response to the local church's plea for help to solve problems with
drinking water. I quickly realized from discussion with villagers that the
problem with drinking water and for agriculture is caused by the same
thing – salt! The ponds where people have traditionally obtained fresh
water have gradually been becoming more saline over the past 20 years.
The villagers I spoke to blame the Faraka Dam on the Ganges in India,
constructed in 1975. Because of this dam less water flows down the river
in the winter season, and the reduction of fresh water from inland allows
the sea water to come further up the rivers. This salty water has gradually
seeped through the ground, contaminating ponds and reducing agricul-
tural output.

But while things might have been getting tough, at least they were
bearable. That was until the two devastating cyclones in the past three
years (Sidr in November 2007 and Aila in May 2009). These cyclones,
especially Aila, drove a huge amount of swirling sea water across the
land, filling up ponds and leaving salt on the fields. As a result, the few
remaining fresh water ponds were turned saline, and fields are now so
saline that trees have died and no crops can grow.

Mr Sader, a 50-year-old farmer who has lived in Kanainagor all his life, told me that 30 years ago he used to be quite wealthy, growing rice, vegetables and keeping cattle. Now he grows only a few vegetables and has two cattle, although due to lack of crops he struggles even to feed them. As he succinctly put it: 'We used to be wealthy, now we survive hand to mouth.' I asked about the future, and he said that his children do not want to come back as there is no income or job. As for himself, he said: 'This is my native land. Though there are many problems, we do not want to leave from here. This is my house, my land, my property, I can't leave here.'

As I reflect on this situation, I am struck by an interlinkage of global and local factors causing such environmental degradation. In this case, the problems seem to be caused by regional (river dams) and local (fish farming) factors in the first instance. But these are only exacerbated by global factors (climate change causing increased cyclones). Climate change can't be blamed entirely for the problems at Kanainagor, but at the very least, it is making an already difficult situation much worse. And as I reflect further, I see that climate change simply highlights the injustice inherent in this world. The rich Western countries are rich largely because of industrial activity which has produced, and still produces, vast quantities of greenhouse gases. And it is these gases that are now causing climate change, which is likely to inhibit Bangladesh's development. And even within Bangladesh it is the poor people who are worst affected and who suffer most.

David Hall, Bangladesh

Pray for the poorest people in Bangladesh who are affected by these issues.

EASTER – DAY 11
IF ONE PART SUFFERS . . .

1 Corinthians 12.26–27

Results are showing that there have been significant changes in seasonal patterns over the past 20–30 years, and now all kinds of crops (from rice to vegetables to jute) are now planted one or two months different than before. But it is not even that simple – when filling out the table, there is always plenty of discussion on the variability of the seasons, where there can be drought one year and flooding the next. It seems there is much more seasonal variability now than there was before.

These results shocked me, as I realized that climate is not just something to fear in the future – it is happening NOW. I think of the individuals it is affecting – of Mr Sader, a farmer in Kanainagor, who said: 'We used to be wealthy, now we survive hand to mouth.' I think of Mr Hossain, a poor farmer in Faridpur, who commented on the lack of rainfall that reduced his rice yield, saying: 'It wasn't always like this. Ten years ago the seasons were regular and predictable and farming was better.' And I realize that these two people are not isolated examples – they represent the majority of people here, people who live off the land and are struggling to come to terms with a changing climate and varying seasons.

All this makes it frustrating to see the global debate on climate change go nowhere, with discussion only around the small areas of doubt. I heard a scientist on the radio recently who said we had to return to the facts that we do know: that carbon dioxide in the atmosphere causes a warming effect; that the level of carbon dioxide in the atmosphere is much higher than it was 50 years ago; that burning of fossil fuels releases carbon dioxide to the atmosphere. Therefore we know that human activity over the past 50 years has caused a warming of the atmosphere to some degree. It struck me that this alone should be enough to lead Christians to action. We are called to be stewards of God's creation, to look after it, and so we should try to avoid any detrimental impact where possible.

In 1 Corinthians 12.26–27 Paul writes to the church in Corinth: 'If one member suffers, all suffer together with it . . . You are the body of Christ, and individually members of it.' We are all part of the same human family with people such as Mr Sader and Mr Hossain. As the required global action seems further away than ever, please let us pray, lobby elected representatives and act to reduce the impact on the earth from our daily actions, helping to prevent an increase in suffering.

David Hall, Bangladesh

Lord – lead us beyond words to action, so that we may understand, experience and respond to the suffering of fellow human beings. Amen.

EASTER – DAY 12
ALL THINGS WERE CREATED . . .

Colossians 1.15, 19

After long and thoughtful prayer, Kim and I decided to initiate a community food growing project. In fact, we have come across many official reports, and have witnessed that Southall and Hayes areas have little knowledge about a healthy diet, growing local food and suffer from a lack of community spirit. Our main objectives are to stimulate social interaction, promote healthy eating, organic growing, reduce food miles (reduce ecological footprint), as well as promote regular exercise and recreation. So I contacted the allotment manager to ask if he had a space for us, but there were a few false starts. However, with God's help we managed to find a space after two months – an overgrown site at Bixley Field, Southall. We thank God for giving us just what we needed.

We started the project with £20. As the site was extremely overgrown with wild grasses and bramble thorns, it demanded lots of hard work! We were concerned that this could put off some people, so Kim and I cleared some of the worst parts to make the site look better. A few days later we thought of launching the first community food growing project open day (8 May 2010), but it was pretty daunting as nobody had done a practical community garden project in the area before and I was very much concerned how people would respond to this project. However, to my surprise, the day attracted over 70 people and the event went really well . . . I was silently thanking God all day long. So far we have held three open days, and have drawn over 120 local people to be on board (people from various faith and ethnic backgrounds – Sikh, Muslim, Hindu, Christian, Buddhist, Chinese, Caribbean and African). Since the very first open day people have been involved in various capacities from clearing and digging to planting and general maintenance. It is incredible to see people braving extreme weather and working throughout the day in the community garden. We have planted potatoes, coriander, lettuce, basil, rocket and sweetcorn. Some local residents who are unsure about being involved in physical activity still turn up and contribute food and drinks, and offer funds for buying seeds. Kim usually looks after the children, and involves them in planting and sowing seeds, after the soil is well prepared.

Khailean Khomgsai, A Rocha, Southall

Pray for creative ways to feed and nourish people both physically and spiritually.

EASTER – DAY 13
'GROW' ZONES

Ephesians 3.14–19

I am helping the team behind Grow Zones, a community growing project that helps people work together to grow their own fruit and veg; and connect with each other and the environment. It is a great way for churches to nurture community and deepen their mission engagement.

There are great reasons to grow your own fruit and veg; it is fresh, local and can be cheaper than the alternative – and gardening keeps you fitter.

How does it work? Someone from a local church or neighbourhood obtains a Grow Zones kit and forms a team. People are introduced to a natural growing method known as permaculture and redesign their gardens so they can grow more of their own food. Each team is offered insurance as part of the package, and sets out on a series of visits, where they work on one another's gardens. The commitment is deliberately light; just four mornings make up the whole course.

Grow Zones teams are springing up all over the country. No experience is necessary – the Grow Zones Kit guides you through the process from start to finish. Grow Zones have proved to be an amazing community-forming project; it seems easier for people to make friends over shared work.

One participant said: 'I have longed to do something really positive about caring for creation ... It seems to me that reconnecting with the land, and with growing our own food, is an extraordinarily powerful means to help us reconsider how we are living and to build fresh expressions of community life. There was a sort of implicit and deep spirituality that pervaded our experience of Grow Zones . . . as if God was there among us as we worked together.'

For more information on how to start a team: www.growzones.com.

Matt Freer

Lord, as plants are rooted and grounded in soil,
we are called to be rooted and grounded in your love.
Bless us as we enjoy your creation,
as we wonder again at the miracle of growth
at your provision for us through the goodness of the land;
and may we see you among us as we work together. Amen.

EASTER – DAY 14
PROCLAIMING THE RESURRECTION

John 20.11–18

After meeting with the Bishop of Perpignan, we had been given permission to start meeting in a Catholic chapel that wasn't used on Sunday mornings, and we were waiting for the keys. Due to a shortage of priests, many local chapels are empty on Sundays as everyone congregates in one of the larger churches.

Well, we're pleased to announce that this all passed smoothly, and we have been meeting at église Saint Vincent for a few months now. We have felt that this is a significant move for us as a Christian community for several reasons. We feel that being connected with the Catholic Church here in France is a key to building unity and authentic friendships. Our sense is that this is making local history as we are unaware of anyone else in similar circumstances to ourselves. Our Catholic brothers and sisters in Christ have made every effort to welcome and encourage us. We have found their practical love humbling, and it's such a privilege to use their building and share a commonality of faith.

On Easter morning, they decided to hold their service at église Saint Vincent rather than their main church; this gave us just a 30-minute turnaround. As they exited the church, we were waiting patiently in the car park on a mission to make a rapid entry, go in and set up. However, we were astonished by their celebratory and affectionate Pâques greeting. There in the car park they greeted us with handshakes, hugs and *'bisous'* and cries of *'Alléluia Il est ressuscité!'* and *'Jésus est vivant!'* We weren't expecting such an unashamed, unreserved and exuberant greeting; our hearts were warmed by their raised voices declaring *'He is Risen!'* and *'Jesus is alive!'* Their worship, faith and passion was impressive and an encouragement to us.

David and Amy Roche, France

'Jesus est ressuscité! Christ is risen!'

Thank you, Lord God, for the new life you have won for us. May those words – Christ is risen! be our shout of celebration. Amen.

EASTER – DAY 15
FINDING YOUR GALILEE

Matthew 28.8–10

On Easter Sunday I was preaching in Maridi Cathedral. I was very challenged by Matthew 28, about how Jesus wanted people to move on with their lives. The women were lost in their grief and pain as they went to the tomb, expecting to find the dead body of Jesus. Jesus wanted them to move on. They were the first to witness the resurrection of Jesus, but would others believe them, as in those days the witness of women was not usually accepted or believed?

But at the tomb, Jesus was putting women in a position of honour in the eyes of the world, as they were entrusted with the news and told to go and tell others. Part of their message was that they and the disciples were to go to Galilee – Jesus was going there ahead of them, and they were to meet him there.

What was the significance of Galilee? It was a place of new beginnings and fruitful ministry. They needed to move ahead, and Jesus was already there. What is your Galilee? What new beginning is God giving to you?

What new fruit are you going to bear for him? How does God want you to move ahead, or do you wish to stay put where you are?

Patricia Wick, working in theological education in Sudan

Spend time reflecting – where is your Galilee? What new beginning is God presenting you with this Easter season?

EASTER – DAY 16
AN INTEGRATED LIFESTYLE

Galatians 3.15–17

A sense of community became so important to me during my ten years as a mission partner in Thailand. I think before I went to Thailand I led a compartmentalized life – work, family, church and perhaps mission were somehow divided. Thailand taught me to live in a more integrated way.

The challenge for me now, having returned to the UK, is to continue to live this integrated mission lifestyle. I love the recognition that mission is not just something mission partners or 'professionals' do – it's a call to everyone – not a task but a lifestyle. We're often good at coming up with programmes, activities, initiatives – my experience in Thailand showed me that these have much more impact when they are born out of a sense of community.

Thai culture is very communal – more relationship-orientated than task-orientated. It's not just a question of getting things done efficiently, but more about getting things done together. In the childcare centres where I worked, the thing that impacted people most was not the quality of education (although that was important) but the relationships between our staff, the children and their families. Many of our staff came to faith in Christ through being part of this community. And people were inspired to get involved when they felt part of a bigger picture.

Gail Philip, Thailand

Lord, as you have entered into our life and death,
and in all the world,
you call us into your death and risen life,

forgive us our sins;
and draw us, we pray,
by the power and encouragement of your Spirit
into an exchange of gifts and needs,
joys and sorrows, strength and weakness
with your people everywhere;
that with them we may have grace
to break through every barrier,
to make disciples of all peoples
and to share your love with everyone
for your glory's sake. Amen.

CMS community prayer

EASTER – DAY 17
FINDING THE HEART

Romans 12.1–2

Often the reality of the Christian community, and even our own expressions of discipleship, seem disconnected from the world in which we live. We long to live out of a deep integrity, to be part of a community that encourages authenticity and that dares to challenge us into a fuller understanding of what it truly means to follow Jesus Christ in his world. The questions posed by such aspirations are – 'How do we discover such a way of life?' and 'How do we create such communities?'

In his book, *The Witness of God*, John Flett suggests that for so long the Christendom understanding of Church has been shaped by the primacy of worship and that mission has been reduced to a secondary activity which the Church does on behalf of God, rather than recognizing that mission is integral to the very nature and person of the God who calls us to participate in his work. The apostle Paul, in his letter to the Romans, encourages his readers to offer their whole lives as a living sacrifice, in order that their minds might be renewed, and they would know the good, pleasing and perfect will of God (see Rom. 12.1–2). It is as we recognize the all embracing nature of worship that we will begin to discover what it might mean to be led deeper into the heart of God, finding ourselves, individually and corporately, being shaped by him and prepared in new ways for participation in his mission.

If we want to know and experience this mission heart of God then we need look no further than Jesus himself. In him we encounter the integration of the acknowledgement of the Father's will for his life, the centrality of prayer, and a life consistently and continuously shaped by the Father's mission heart. It was this integrity at the heart of his life that enabled Jesus to demonstrate the kingdom, a demonstration that brought both life and hope to the many, but also challenge – a challenge that was so great that it eventually led to the cross.

Chris Neal

Lord, let it not be that I follow you merely for the sake of
    following a leader,
but let me respond to you as Lord and Master of every
    step I take. Amen.

Prayer used in Pakistan

EASTER – DAY 18
MISSION IN COMMUNITY

Luke 10.1

Once we get past the rebellious or reactive countercultural paradigm and muster up the courage to try living in new ways, most of us find that community is very natural and makes a lot of sense, and that it is not as foreign to most of the world's population as it is to us. Community is what we are created for. We are made in the image of a God who is community, a plurality of oneness. When the first human was made, things were not good until there were two, helping one another.

The biblical story is the story of community, from beginning to end. Jesus lived and modelled community with his little band of disciples. He always sent them out in pairs, and the early Church is the story of a people who were together and were of one heart and mind, sharing all in common . . . But that doesn't mean community is easy. For everything in this world tries to pull us away from community, pushes us to choose ourselves over others, to choose independence over interdependence, to choose great things over small things, to choose going fast alone over going far together.

Shane Claiborne

Spend some time reflecting on the communities in which God has placed you (work, home, church, neighbourhood, social networks) and give thanks for the people who support and sustain you in your walk of faith. Ask God to bless and guide you as you develop new relationships and as you begin to explore what being part of a global, mission-focused community might mean.

EASTER – DAY 19
WAITING FOR EASTER . . .

Philippians 2.1–4

Are we purely Orthodox? Yes, we are, and we try to follow the Orthodox tradition and spiritual discipline as instructed by the Orthodox faith. But if we are open to the other Christians, if we strive for common understanding and Christian values, then we could also be seen as all-Christian, too. Last week our Western Christian friends celebrated Easter and we, the Orthodox, are going to celebrate it one month and four days after the 'Western' Easter.

Christians in the world differ in many things, and the differences may be obvious or may be too small to be noticed or considered. But the calendar is the most obvious difference for the outside observer. And now we are again struggling when we experience this difference; our Western Christian friends have now fully celebrated the resurrected Lord, and they serve in their churches, joyous worshipping that follows Lent and Easter. At the same time we, the Orthodox, continue our spiritual discipline and fasting, without any joy, or feasts, or other merry celebrations or events. In fact, during Lent we do celebrate different events but they all are intended to strengthen our spiritual longing for heavenly blessings: we celebrate the Sunday of the tax-collector and the Pharisee, the Sunday of the prodigal son, the Sunday of the cross, and other Sundays of saints, such as the Sunday of St Mary of Egypt, the Sunday of St Gregory Palamas or the Sunday of St John of the Ladder. Our Lent is rich with so much spiritual guidance.

Anyway, in a month's time we will celebrate the Lord's resurrection and again fully enjoy our meetings and contacts with our friends and our mutual spiritual striving.

Valentin and Daniela Kozhuarov, Bulgaria

May we be of one mind in you, O Christ.
May we have the same love.
May we be one in spirit and purpose, despite our differences.
May we look to the interests of one another,
And may we learn together as part of your body here on earth. Amen.

EASTER – DAY 20
WALKING (TOGETHER) IN INTEGRITY

Psalm 101.1–2

Like missiologists-in-residence before me, I live in House 244 – the CMS community house in Oxford. Sharing a common life has been a most enjoyable part of my immersion into CMS. I am grateful for the welcome accorded me and for the inspiring sisters and brothers who have supported and challenged me.

The house is spacious and comfortable. We are eleven people, with eight belonging to two families who live in small apartments on the top floor. Most leave during the day – me to CMS or the Bodleian Library, parents with children to a park or nursery, others to workplaces. Improving weather, however, has made our backyard a lovely sanctuary for relaxation while children play.

We have an impressive vegetable garden along with some hens. I have appreciated our common efforts to embody stewardship of creation through our purchases and consumption patterns.

As a Catholic priest normally living in a student residence at my university in the US, I am not used to living with children. At times I find myself grateful for my small apartment (read: refuge – from clamouring play and shrill voices that sometimes echo about the house). Much more prevalent, however, has been an appreciation of the sweet liveliness of the small ones and the loving attention given them by their parents.

We gather most evenings for meals that we take turns preparing. We meet and pray together weekly. We laugh often and easily, sometimes over miscommunications caused by the astonishingly many mistakes in English English (why 'rocket' for arugula? Why 'courgette' for zucchini?).

Appreciative of friendships formed, I have drawn strength from the integrity with which we, singly and together, try to walk our paths faithfully in Christ.

Paul Kollman

We praise you, O God,
for humour and homes,
for meals and mercy,
for fellowship and faith. Amen.

EASTER – DAY 21
UNIQUE BUT TOGETHER

Psalm 139.1–12

Lord, we thank you that we are fearfully and wonderfully made.
You formed us each in your own image, and you made us all special.
Our voices, our faces, our bodies, our habits, our talents, and our failings.
All the same and all unique.

You search me and you know me.
You search us and you know us.

We each have our private stories, feelings, our places, our hopes,
   our joys.
Our secret fears, resentments, insecurities doubts
Which we bear alone or we bear together.
Help us to hold our individuality with our place in community.

Search me and know me.
Search us and know us.

Jesus, you walked alone in the desert,
You shared a life and ministry with your twelve disciples.
You were surrounded by massive crowds,
You spoke to individuals and to multitudes
You suffered alone on the cross.

Search me and know me.
Search us and know us.

We come to you as individuals,
We come to you as a community
In the silent of night, the brightness of morning,
The turbulence of the rush hour
In our church buildings, in our workplaces and homes.

Help us to be one with ourselves,
One with each other, and one with you. Amen.

Jackie Elton, *Grace Pocket Liturgies*

God of companionship and solitude
Of natural spaces and places built with human hands –
Help us to be one with ourselves,
One with each other, and one with you. Amen.

EASTER – DAY 22
ANOTHER WAY OF DOING LIFE

Romans 12.9–10

On the second evening I was present for their campfire, and it was a privilege to hear their stories and understand a little more about their lives. One talked about how she had felt so alone but now had friends who could share her experience; another talked about the loss of her grandmother who had brought her up for most of her life. While we were there to give the young people opportunity to talk, the learning and transformation that went on was not limited to them only, and it was so encouraging to hear some of the Ugandan staff team sharing around the fire too – by giving them a chance to think about their lives, they will be more able to listen and help and advise the young people. It felt like we were learning together with a deepening sense of friendship and family.

During our last session before we returned to the hospital everyone present was invited to sign a declaration – a commitment to the Afaayo 'family', to their friends and, for us as staff, to them. For me it was a very emotional moment just thinking of how far they have come and the hurdles they have overcome. To have HIV positive teenagers who are still alive is in itself a success, and I've seen so many of them in different stages of health and sickness, so to see how they have progressed is humbling, exciting and tragic all at the same moment.

I am well aware that this is a small group and there are countless others whose lives are equally grim – both HIV positive and those who are not. It would be easy to be totally overwhelmed by need and think why do so much with one small group when there are so many others – but I firmly believe these are the ones God has put across my path, so my desire is to draw alongside them and show them there's another way of doing life . . . as Jesus says in John 10.10: he has come to bring them a rich and satisfying life . . . so let's help them find it!

Alison Fletcher, working in Uganda with teenagers living with HIV/Aids

Pray for young people around the world facing the challenge of living with HIV/Aids, that through the love and commitment they share with others, their lives may be transformed in hope.

EASTER – DAY 23
LIVING IN HARMONY

1 Peter 3.8

One of the things you see when you look around creation is that God loves diversity. God could have made us all alike, but he didn't, so this can make getting along a problem! Peter suggests four attitudes that, if built into our life, will bring dramatic improvement in our relationships.

Be sympathetic: To sympathize means to understand, validate or affirm someone's feelings. When you're sensitive to their feelings, you don't belittle them or put them down and say, 'You shouldn't feel that way.' Instead, when you validate somebody else's feelings you're being sympathetic. The first step in diffusing conflict is understanding where people are coming from, their background, their temperament, the circumstances that have shaped them. When you do that you'll be more sympathetic.

Love as brothers and sisters: Family love is about being committed to the relationship, having the mindset that we're on the same team and in this together. We don't compete with but complement and co-operate with each other. This is an important ingredient in reducing relational conflict. When I get irritated with someone, I can focus on the problem and forget the value of the relationship. Loyalty says, 'Let's stop attacking each other and let's attack the problem together.' Rather than seeing the person as the enemy, say 'We're on the same team, how can we work on this problem, together?'

Be compassionate: Compassion is love in action – it takes sympathy one step further and demonstrates it practically. What can I do to help you? We show compassion by what we say to other people, with words that build up and that make the other person feel good. Don't let your talk be toxic, filled with bombs and verbal arrows that destroy. We also show compassion by the things we actually do. Compassion says with actions,

'How can I make life easier for you? What can I do that will make your life a little bit easier?'

Be humble: Humility is being honest with my weaknesses, my needs, my failures. It's not assuming I know it all or understand everything you're saying. If I'm humble, I can say phrases like, 'I need your help', 'I was wrong' and 'Please forgive me.' These are hard words to say, especially in our culture. This takes humility.

How do you rate yourself on these four attitudes? Why not identify one to work on especially today! God made us all differently and did it on purpose. None of us has the total picture and perspective on life; that's because we need each other. So God puts different parts of his truth in different personalities and wants to use our differences to enrich us, rather than to divide us. It will enrich you if you practise these four attitudes.

Paul Morris, Vicar of St Peter's in the City, Derby

Spend time asking God to show you how/where you need to live in greater harmony.

EASTER – DAY 24
BEING KNOWN

Ephesians 4.1–2

When I imagined living in community, I envisaged myself turning over-night into a paragon of virtue, simply by sheer force of will. I would leave behind my bad habits, my judgemental attitudes and any tendency towards gossip. I would never make myself vulnerable by exposing my weaknesses, because I wouldn't have any. I believed that in order to find my place in the community I would need to be perfect. A year in, I have found that it is precisely in times when our weaknesses are exposed by close communion with others that we are transformed in more than a cosmetic way. God uses others to knock rough edges off us and refine our characters. As humans we have a deep desire to be known, even in all our imperfection. The relief in living closely with others and finding that they are not perfect is magical. The acknowledgement that you don't have to be perfect to be loved and accepted is an important step in healthy Christian growth and transformation.

Emma Woo

Do we dare to take off our masks, risk vulnerability, and allow ourselves to be known (and loved)? How might being a member of a Christian community enable that to happen?

Lord – may we have the courage to love and be loved,
to give out of who we really are,
to recognize and share our weaknesses,
to live as communities filled with your grace, so we can grow together
and be transformed as we travel together. Amen.

EASTER – DAY 25
BROKEN BLESSING

John 20.24–29

May you be blessed as you engage with others, as you find the time to participate and give others the chance to do the same.
May you have the courage to create and take risks, and may you find your rest in God.
May you be blessed, as you show your weaknesses and accept God's grace.
May others see that you are fragile that they might join in your fragility.
May our broken edges fit together to become one body.
As Christ kept the holes in his hands and feet having risen from the dead,
may we keep our wounds even after we have healed.
May you be blessed, as you are healed by Christ's own wounds.
May you become broken in order to become whole.
May you become whole by knowing you are broken.

May you remember your wounds and embrace your hurt.
May you go into the places that scare you.
May you deal with anger and with sadness.
And may God be with you all the way.
May you be blessed, that you are perfect in your imperfections –
as you are forgiven, but never forgotten.
May you be blessed, as you are accepted as you are.
As you are broken.
As you are wounded.
As you are hurt.
As you are loved.

Harry Baker, adapted

Lord – we often fear our doubts and places of weakness,
and yet – like Thomas – we discover that those moments are often our
    greatest teacher,
moments when we encounter you and the power of your resurrection
    like never before.
Lord – may we find you in our places of brokenness and fear.
Meet with us, we pray.
Reach out and touch us,
enable us to reach out and touch you,
and bless us with courage and peace. Amen.

EASTER – DAY 26
CALLED BY NAME

Isaiah 43.1–2

The spring has been an incredibly busy time with lots of opportunities to
minister God's love and hope. At the beginning of April I put on an art
installation at Kingston University. My creative team artistically explored
experiences of growth and change using the idea of metamorphosis. It
was fantastic that I could work with others and help them develop their

ideas into something that the students could be blessed and challenged by. This is a model that I would like to continue with and I plan to put on an 'Arts as Mission' conference in the autumn to identify and envision other creative people in Kingston who might become team members on future Sacred Space projects.

A lot of time and effort went into activities for this year's May Merrie in Kingston town centre on Bank Holiday Monday, 2 May. On the green outside the parish church, I set up a tent where children could make name bracelets and name plates for their bedroom doors, and in the church there was an art installation exploring the importance of our names and the names of God.

In the marketplace there was an opportunity to have a free spiritual reading using Ruach cards that use biblical and Celtic Christian symbolism to bless and reveal God's love and purpose in Christ to spiritual seekers. It was a great day with lots of sunshine and good conversations with the 150 or so people who engaged with one or more of these different expressions of mission.

Andrea Campanale

Lord God, we praise you for your constancy and faithfulness,
that you create us and call us by name.
Give us grace to share that love with others in open and imaginative ways,
that they too may discover themselves to be known and treasured by you. Amen.

EASTER – DAY 27
PERSEVERING IN FAITH

Hebrews 10.23–25

Every year we seem to go through a phase of growth, and this year is no different. However, it is harder for people to be committed to God and his Church, and we have had a number of folk coming and going. Some leave the city, some may go to another church, and some may just stop attending. But over the past few months, we have also seen quite a number of folk starting to attend our church, so we are looking in good standing for next year.

Hebrews 10.25 says: 'Let us not neglect to meet together, as is the habit of some, but let us encourage one another – and all the more as you see the Day approaching.' Therefore going to church can be a good habit, if we are not doing it from a sense of obligation.

David and Gina Hucker, Chile

Take time to reflect on your commitment to meeting with other Christians. Does your commitment stem from a desire to encourage one another and spur one another on to deeper faith, or from a sense of obligation?

Lord, give us grace to keep on keeping on,
to spur one another on to good deeds and deepening faith,
to encourage one another,
to appreciate one another,
to love one another,
as you have loved us. Amen.

EASTER – DAY 28
CELEBRATING LIFE

Acts 4.32

Looking to the future I think the very good news is that we can create a new way of life that is less stressed, that is more festive, more celebrative. We have got to reduce our footprint in terms of our use of energy and money. The only way we can do that is re-examining the single-family-detached or semi-detached model – people treat it like it came with the Ark of the Covenant.

It's the most land-intensive, energy-intensive way to live, and for people under 40 it's becoming such an expensive model. If people can significantly reduce their living costs and increase their community, then there's a much better chance they're going to be missional.

Most of all we need to hear God speaking to us through the needs of others. As Mother Teresa said, 'Jesus Christ is thinly disguised in the poor and the suffering of the world.'

Tom Sine

How might we model a way of living differently as Christians to begin to address some of the huge issues facing our world in the future?

Lord, may we see you in the poor and suffering of the world,
and may it inspire us to live differently,
to create a way of life that is less stressed, more festive, more celebrative for all. Amen.

EASTER – DAY 29
TRELLIS AND VINE

John 15.1–8

I'm writing this while at a conference with Chilean pastors and church leaders led by the Australian author of *The Trellis and the Vine*. His thesis is that we need trellises that help order, administer and give structure to the vine. However, the danger is that the vine – the ministry of the gospel of Jesus empowered by the Holy Spirit – is dwarfed by the trellis; so we need to focus on enabling the vine to grow so that the trellis disappears into the background and much fruit is borne.

Daniel and Ellelein Kirk, Chile

Reflect on your experience of church. Does the trellis dwarf the vine? How can we focus on enabling the vine to grow – both locally and at a global level?

Lord God, we thank you for the trellis which supports and trains the vine.
Where it overshadows the vine and prevents growth,
give us grace and wisdom to respond and to refocus on the vine,
so that we may bear much fruit. Amen.

EASTER – DAY 30
ALL THINGS ARE COMPLETED IN CHRIST

Ephesians 1.22–23

'World church' – the gift of Christ to which we belong – stirs up anxieties for some. Rather than experiencing a sense of enrichment from it and embracing it to strengthen local mission, they acknowledge that it triggers guilt feelings because we are aware of our Western materialism and affluence, over against the poverty of so many countries. Simultaneously, in Britain the mantra keeps echoing in our ears – 'the Church is in decline', and there are only a few churches where the statistical evidence contradicts this. But it is only part of the truth, and we must not use guilt trips or the expansion of the Church in other countries as a rod for our backs in Britain. They are in a different 'place'. And when you look outside the stable embrace of our traditional structures and patterns, it is amazing where you find the Holy Spirit at work in this country, resonating in people who are leading others to transformed lives through faith in Christ. How vibrant we might all become when we resonate with the whole body of Christ and with God's mission heart for the whole world.

Gill Poole

For the Church where it is strong,
that it may prefer nothing to Christ;
for the Church where it is weak,
that it may know God's power to save;
let us pray to the Lord.

From a Benedictine vespers

EASTER – DAY 31
MANY DIFFERENCES . . . BUT ONE TRUE GOD

Galatians 3.26–29

It is difficult to compare church life in England and in Bangladesh, as the whole setting is different, one being historically and majority Christian and the other having a very small minority Christian community (the Church of Bangladesh has fewer than 20,000 members in a country of 150 million people).

Church services, of course, reflect the culture of the country. In Bangladesh generally, people remove shoes at the door, sit on the ground (men on one side and women on the other) and indigenous music is used. But although the whole 'feel' of services may be different, it is wonderful to realize that we all believe and worship the same God. It is one of the real privileges of being mission partners to be able to share worship and communion with people in different churches in different countries and to see differing cultural expressions of the one true God.

David and Sarah Hall, Bangladesh

We thank you, Father
that we are all your children –
whatever our culture, background or tradition.
We thank you that in Christ the barriers which divide
    are broken down,
and that we are truly one in Christ Jesus. Amen.

EASTER – DAY 32
BROTHERS AND SISTERS IN CHRIST

Romans 12.3–5

Just as all the readjustments of returning were beginning to become over-
whelming, I was able, at last, to get out to the villages and make contact
with the pastors and the people I had been working with. The welcome
I received was wonderful and really lifted me. I was constantly told how
everyone in those small mud churches had been constantly praying for
Rosie and for our safe return while many of them were suffering a failure
of the rains and their crops for the third year in a row. It is humbling that
these congregations were thinking and praying for us in their own time of
adversity and also a fantastic picture of how we are all brothers and sisters in Christ throughout the world, whether worshipping in a small mud
church with rain coming through the thatched roof, or a central-heated
church with the latest sound system in the UK. We can often all too easily
think that we in the West are the ones praying and supporting the Church
in the rest of the world but it really is a two-way, or multi-way, process.

Andy Hart, Tanzania

Father, we thank you that we are brothers and sisters in Christ throughout the world.
Forgive our arrogance and pride that leads us to want to give, to
   support
without recognizing our own needs and having the grace to receive.
May we live as global disciples, faithfully walking together
and enabling one another to grow deeper with you.
In the name of Jesus Christ we pray. Amen.

EASTER – DAY 33
SHARING THE LOAD

Galatians 6.2

'Are you sure we should bring Coke?' We were saddened to hear that our friend Christine, who works for the Kigali Diocese guest house, had lost one of her two remaining children. Christine's family has lived most of their lives as refugees; they returned to Rwanda only a month after the genocide ended. Sue visited Christine's family at their home. When she asked what she should bring, local people advised her to take a box of food for the family and bottles of Coke and Fanta. It seemed strange to take soft drinks, which are usually associated with celebrations. However, the family has had a great number of callers, and they find it financially difficult to provide for them. They feel obliged to offer soft drinks, especially to Westerners, so by bringing Coke as a gift we were all able to enjoy the treat together. It was humbling to sit in the house that they've established themselves in their own homeland. Stories from the Bible about the exiled Israelites returning to the Promised Land come alive when one has friends who have lived for years in refugee camps. We were also challenged by the community support at this time of grief. Surely this is something we in the often relationship-poor West can learn from our African brothers and sisters.

Richard and Sue Kellow, Rwanda

Richard and Sue's story sums up the heart of our shared faith – we are enriched by one another in so many ways. Spend some time thanking God for Christians from different cultures who have shaped and enriched your Christian journey. Pray that God will make us ever more open to receive from one another.

EASTER – DAY 34
REDISCOVERING JESUS

Revelation 7.9–12

The model of Jesus in the Gospel record is not just for his day; it is there to shape us in our mission thinking and engagement, as we seek to live out our lives as part of his body around his world today. For many in this Western context our understanding of the significance of Jesus has been minimized through the pressure of the relativity of truth, and the fear of the big story embracing the whole of life. Many of us would recognize something of his eternal significance, and look for our own resurrection and promise of heaven, but the global significance of Jesus is a deeper challenge. If we are to understand and then engage in and with God in his mission in the challenges of the twenty-first century, then we need to explore not just the eternal but also the global significance of Jesus.

Being part of a global community (like CMS) constantly reminds one of the need to recognize that Jesus is acknowledged as Lord by many different tongues and in many different cultures. This reminder is not just the acknowledgement of Jesus as Lord by these many different tongues, but recognition that each culture will bring its own perspective and understanding of who he is, and so stretch and, hopefully, deepen the understanding of us all. Reflecting on this, the missiologist Andrew Walls has said:

> The very height of Christ's full stature is revealed only by the coming together of different cultural entities into the body of Christ. Only 'together' not on our own can we reach his full stature. The Church . . . is a celebration of the union of irreconcilable entities, the breaking down of the wall of partition brought about by Christ.

It is as we celebrate and enter into this deeper understanding of the person of Jesus Christ that Christian communities, and individual disciples, will begin to participate more fully in the mission of God.

Chris Neal

Lord – enlarge our vision,
that together we may see you
and work together in your mission. Amen.

EASTER – DAY 35
IDENTITY IN CHRIST

Isaiah 1.18

One day the king of the birds sent out an invitation to collect taxes from all the birds and the bat said: 'I am not a bird. Have you seen a bird giving birth and suckle its young one, a bird having ears and teeth like mine?' With this question, the bat was able to dodge paying taxes.

Later on, the king of the animals again sent out emissaries to collect taxes from the animals, and the bat said: 'I am not an animal. Have you ever seen an animal flying?' Again, the bat dodged paying taxes for the animal kingdom.

One day, there was a heavy rain with hailstones and it killed the bat. His dead body was found lying on the ground by some of the birds. The birds quickly took the message to the animal king saying: 'Come and collect the dead body of bat. We found him dead and his body is lying down on the ground.' But the animal king said: 'The bat does not belong to the animal family; instead, he belongs to the bird family.' The birds' king in turn rejected the dead body, since he did not belong to the bird family. Thus the fruit bat was rejected by both the animal and the bird kingdoms because he was neither an animal nor a bird. The bat had had an identity crisis.

There are Christians, who have identity crises. They are neither Christians nor pagans. They are just there in the middle of the world. These people live the life the bat lived. If you die one day, where do you belong? Are you going to be with God in heaven or with Satan?

Amule Emmanuel Timothy, Diocese of Kajo Keji, Sudan, shared by Gary Ion

Lord, we may we truly know our identity as your children, purchased by your blood. Amen.

EASTER – DAY 36
OUR TRUE HEART IN CHRIST

Ephesians 2.4–7

A certain man went through a forest seeking any bird of interest he might find. He caught a young eagle, brought it home and put it among his fowls and ducks and turkeys, and gave it chicken food to eat even though it was an eagle, the king of birds.

Five years later a naturalist came to see him, and after passing through his garden said, 'That bird is an eagle, not a chicken.'

'Yes,' said its owner, but I have trained it to be a chicken. It is no longer an eagle, it is a chicken, even though it measures 15 feet from tip to tip of its wings.'

'No,' said the naturalist, 'it is an eagle still: it has the heart of an eagle, and I will make it soar high up to the heavens.'

'No,' said the owner, 'it is a chicken and it will never fly.'

They agreed to test it. The naturalist picked up the eagle, held it up, and said with great intensity: 'Eagle, thou art an eagle; thou dost belong to the sky and not to this earth; stretch forth thy wings and fly.'

The eagle turned this way and that, and then, looking down, saw the chickens eating their food, and down he jumped.

Then the owner said: 'I told you it was a chicken.'

'No,' asserted the naturalist, 'it is an eagle and it still has the heart of an eagle; only give it one more chance, and I will make it fly tomorrow.'

Father, we are your children,
Called and set apart by you.
Yet we are so easily led astray and 'domesticated' by the world around
    us.
Help us to know ourselves more fully,
So that we may live in your fullness of life. Amen.

Traditional folk tale

EASTER – DAY 37
RISING LIKE EAGLES

Isaiah 40.28–31

The next morning the naturalist rose early and took the eagle outside the city, away from the houses, to the foot of a high mountain. The sun was just rising, gilding the top of the mountain with gold, and every crag was glistening in the joy of that beautiful morning.

He picked up the eagle and said to it, 'Eagle, thou art an eagle; thou dost belong to the sky and not to this earth; stretch forth thy wings and fly!'

The eagle looked round and trembled as if new life were coming to it; but it did not fly. The naturalist then made it look straight at the sun. Suddenly, it stretched out its wings and, with the screech of an eagle, it mounted higher and higher and never returned. It was an eagle, though it had been kept and tamed as a chicken!

Traditional folk tale

Lord, renew my strength,
that as I look to you I may soar on wings like an eagle;
that I may run and not grow weary,
that I may walk and never faint. Amen.

EASTER – DAY 38
IDENTITY: PEOPLE OF GOD

1 Kings 2.1–4

One weekend last summer we brought eight teenagers together for some mountain biking, canoeing, fencing and an assault course. But the trip was also about recognizing differences – and similarities – in beliefs because four of the lads were Muslim, and four Christian. All were from around Birmingham. The theme was 'What does it mean to be a man of God?'

On Saturday night, the group made five commitments to work towards being peaceful men of faith: to tell people positive things about the other faith; to offer to do chores daily; to avoid X-rated material on TV and internet; not to use foul language; and to pray at least once a day. It was great to see the forging of friendships across boundaries of difference. Sometimes it's the less obvious barriers that keep people apart. One of the Muslim guys said he'd never listened to rock music before. Pointing to his nu-metal Christian roommate, he said, 'If I'd seen someone looking like him I'd have just thought he was weird and avoided him. I realize he's actually really cool.' It was also good to hear some of the Christian lads challenged to be more serious about their faith. Just one very small example of relationships being forged, misunderstanding being overcome, and faith playing a vital part in a way that recognizes similarity and difference.

Richard Sudworth, Birmingham

What five fresh commitments to faith can you make to set you apart as a person of God? Spend time reflecting with God on where he is leading you to be 'more serious' about faith.

EASTER – DAY 39
IN THE FOOTSTEPS OF SAINT BRENDAN

Isaiah 41.10

St Brendan and the chosen brethren then decided to make a fast of 40 days, at three days' intervals, and afterwards to take their departure. Those 40 days having elapsed, St Brendan, affectionately taking leave of his monks, and commending them to the special care of the Prior of his monastery, who was afterwards his successor there, sailed forth towards the west, with 14 brethren, to the island wherein dwelt St Enda, and remained there three days and three nights. Having received the blessing of this holy father and all his monks, he proceeded to the remotest part of his own country, where his parents abode. However, he willed not to visit them, but went up to the summit of the mountain there, which extends far into the ocean, on which is 'St Brendan's Seat', and there he fitted up a tent, near a narrow creek, where a boat could enter. Then St Brendan and his companions, using iron implements, prepared a light vessel, with wicker sides and ribs, such as is usually made in that country, and covered it with cow hide, tanned in oak bark, tarring the joints thereof, and put on board provisions for 40 days.

St Brendan then embarked, and they set sail towards the summer solstice. They had a fair wind, and therefore no labour, only to keep the sails properly set; but after twelve days the wind fell to a dead calm, and they had to labour at the oars until their strength was nearly exhausted. Then St Brendan would encourage and exhort them: 'Fear not, brothers, for our God will be unto us a helper, a mariner, and a pilot; take in the oars and helm, keep the sails set, and may God do unto us, his servants and his little vessel, as he willeth.' They took refreshment always in the evening, and sometimes a wind sprung up; but they knew not from what point it blew, nor in what direction they were sailing.

Navigatio Sancti Brendani Abbatis, translated from Latin by
Denis O'Donoghue, 1893

What comfort zones or places of security might God be calling us to leave behind?

Shall I abandon, O King of mysteries, the soft comforts of home? Shall I turn my back on my native land, and turn my face towards the sea?

Shall I put myself wholly at your mercy, without silver, without a horse, without fame, without honour? Shall I throw myself wholly upon you, without sword and shield, without food and drink, without a bed to lie on? Shall I say farewell to my beautiful land, placing myself under your yoke?

Shall I pour out my heart to you, confessing my manifold sins and begging forgiveness, tears streaming down my cheeks? Shall I leave the prints of my knees on the sandy beach, a record of my final prayer in my native land?

Shall I then suffer every kind of wound that the sea can inflict? Shall I take my tiny boat across the wide sparkling ocean? O King of the Glorious Heaven, shall I go of my own choice upon the sea?

O Christ, will you help me on the wild waves?

Prayer of St. Brendan

EASTER – DAY 40
ASCENSION DAY

Luke 24.50–53

Lord, a thin drizzle of humanity is penetrating us. We are not the axis of life as our self-centredness falsely claims. We travel through life like blind persons; we did not choose life before embarking on it nor do we know the day when we shall depart from it. Life is larger than we are, and your ways extend beyond the horizon of our vision.

Bolivia

Lord our God,
You have raised your Son to be with you,
And we sing to you in joy.
Send your Spirit, as he has promised us
To free all people from hatred and from fear
And so give us the peace of Christ, our Lord.

France: Cistercian vespers

EASTER – DAY 41
INTERCHANGE: FELLOW CITIZENS OF CHRIST

Ephesians 2.19–22

Interchange can produce mutual benefit, enrichment, learning and sharing, which links back to Ephesians 2.19–22. Paul uses the metaphor of us all being built into 'one holy temple in the Lord', so none of us can reach Christ's completeness on our own – each culture is a building stone that needs the others to grow in the fullness of Christ.

The changes in people's lifestyles and their commitment, after short-term mission visits, express themselves in highly individual ways. One girl, a team member this summer felt challenged to initiate fair trade practices at work. Her canteen and staff room adopted them, so she spearheaded something that affected her entire workplace community. Another, Hannah, returned from Russia very keen to do her dissertation on Exodus, a drug rehabilitation project she'd encountered – her mission experience has affected her ongoing study and she'd love to return there. Yet another, Emily, returned and started working at a homeless shelter in her local community.

Debbie James

Interchange challenges us to consider, 'What am I giving to God and to other people, locally and elsewhere, in my life?'

Lord, we are called to be built into a holy temple
with you as our cornerstone.
May we inspire one another to grow in faith
and challenge one another to see a bigger picture
by your grace. Amen.

EASTER – DAY 42
SEND HIGH CALIBRE PEOPLE
(VENN PRINCIPLES)

Lamentations 2.18–19

Only people who are constantly being changed can bring change to others. Through them the message of the wounded Servant God in Christ might become 'a story whose hour has come'. We are moving towards a melting pot of all cultures and ethnic groups in the next millennium, a kind of breaking and remaking of humanity, in the midst of which the cross can gently but surely be planted to spring up as a tree of life for all faiths.

But those who present that message must be people who are humbled, gentle, profoundly spiritually motivated, radiant, more of a Celtic than a Western imperial spirit. My greatest experiences at CMS were encounters with such people, pilgrims often on the edge of many different worlds of faith, spiritual pioneers, unconventional figures, leading small, growing companies of fellow seekers into the way of the cross. They were 'watchers on the walls' not ceasing to cry out, as it were, 'Jesus have mercy'.

Simon Barrington-Ward

Almighty God, the Giver of Wisdom,
without whose help resolutions are vain,
without whose blessing study is ineffectual,
enable me, if it be your will,
to attain such knowledge as may qualify me
to direct the doubtful and instruct the ignorant,
to prevent wrongs, and terminate contentions;
and grant that I may use that knowledge which I shall attain,
to your glory and my own salvation.

Samuel Johnson (1709–84)

EASTER – DAY 43
'MIDWIVES' OF THE GOSPEL

1 Corinthians 1.26–30

In one Arabian Peninsula city, an Ethiopian pastor trains every one of his church members as a missionary. There are 35,000 Ethiopians working in that country; 96 per cent of them are young, female, domestic workers living on a few dollars a week. The Christians among them, like every other young Ethiopian woman, are hoping to send home a little money to support their families. They also discover that God has placed them in a key mission context.

In just 11 months these young women have taken the Jesus film and Arabic New Testaments into 800 homes where they are able to share the film with children and read the Bible with their mothers. Sadly, these women, who are actively engaged in evangelism in one of the most closed mission contexts in the world, will never appear in any statistics of 'foreign missionaries'. They will attract little prayer or financial support from minority world (Western) churches so concerned to 'reach the unreached'. This is why we need to radically revise our understanding of who a missionary is in the contemporary, globalized world. In fact, we also need to revise much of our mission history in order to take a much more realistic account of who really have been the 'midwives of the gospel' over the past 2,000 years.

Mark Oxbrow

Spend time thanking God for the many people who spread the gospel almost unnoticed. Praise God for the way he can use us in our ordinariness and weakness. Pray that all Christians will recognize their place in God's mission – starting with us.

EASTER – DAY 44
A DIFFERENT DANCE

Matthew 9.37–38

It is not only Western Christians who forget that refugees, merchants, monks, and civil servants can be missionaries. Addressing the mission community of the World Evangelical Alliance in 2006, Duncan Olumbe, director of Kenyan-based Mission Together Africa, warned his majority world colleagues of the dangers of seeking to join the European choreographed 'power dance', 'imitation dance' and 'position dance'. In other words, the professional missionary paradigm has become so pervasive that even those who have a much stronger missional rhythm in their spiritual bones feel constrained to do mission in the European style.

Many majority world churches would struggle to support one traditional, 'professional' missionary family, but how many of their members could be resourced as refugees, migrants, businesswomen, overseas students, or traders in cross-cultural mission? Olumbe continues, 'I long for a different dance! However, how can we allow space for the different dancers – African, Asian, European, American – with all their different rhythms, beats, and paraphernalia?'

Olumbe's question is addressed to mission leaders in North America and Europe, as well as those in Asia, Africa and Latin America. While rejoicing in all that 'professional' missionaries continue to achieve for Christ's kingdom, we need to create space for the other dancers. This will involve reallocating resources; for example, to fund the training of the 400,000 Filipino Christians currently working as migrants around the world.

This requires partnership on a global scale, where power relationships are renegotiated and resources are pooled. My greatest hope is that as the majority world begins to control the dance tune and discover new steps and rhythms, we in the minority world will at last escape our blinkered professionalization of mission.

Mark Oxbrow

Lord – help us to long for a different dance,
so that we can bring good news to all. Amen.

EASTER – DAY 45
LOOKING TOWARDS PENTECOST –
THE HOLY SPIRIT IN HISTORY

Ezekiel 37.1–14

Throughout its history the Old Testament witnesses to the character and
work of God's Spirit, reflecting every facet of God's revelation of himself,
and always pointing forwards to the great fulfilment in the person of
Jesus Christ. In Jesus the age of the Spirit has dawned in all its fullness.
We must be ready to explore that fullness, to allow the Spirit to touch
our lives as he wants, and to allow him to fill us afresh with his hope as
we look for the completion of his work.

Chris Neal

*The power of the Holy Spirit helps us to see God at work in the present
moment. Are you willing to allow the Holy Spirit to fill and renew you
day by day?*

Lord, so fill me with your Holy Spirit that I might know your living hope
both for the present and for all eternity. Amen.

EASTER – DAY 46
LOOKING TOWARDS PENTECOST –
THE HOLY SPIRIT IN JESUS

John 14.15–21, 25–27

Jesus knew that his earthly ministry was just the beginning and the wider ministry could not come in all its fullness and potential until he had made it possible through his death and resurrection. Only then could the power of sin and death be defeated and the possibility of knowing the power of the Holy Spirit in a personal and continuing way be given to men and women. As his ministry drew to its close Jesus began to speak of the future and to talk about the promise of the Holy Spirit.

Chris Neal

Jesus Christ longs to fulfil his promise of the Holy Spirit in your own life. How do you respond to this truth?

Come down, O love divine,
Seek thou this soul of mine.

Bianco da Siena (d. 1434)

EASTER – DAY 47
LOOKING TOWARDS PENTECOST –
THE HOLY SPIRIT IN THE
NEW TESTAMENT

Galatians 5.22–25

Three days after his startling meeting with the risen Lord Jesus, Paul was met by Ananias who prayed with and for him, and laid hands on him. Paul received his sight back and also received the gift of the Holy Spirit. From that moment he realized that his life was not his own, nor was his life self-motivated. He recognized that the rest of his life would be lived out in the power of the Holy Spirit who gave him the life of Jesus.

In Galatians he wrote: 'I have been crucified with Christ, and it is no longer I who live, but it is Christ who lives in me' (2.19). And again: 'The Spirit produces love, joy, peace, patience, kindness, goodness, faithfulness, humility and self-control' (5.22). The fruit of the Spirit gives the very life of Jesus to the believer. Paul, from the road to Damascus to his final trial in Rome, was a man who knew the Spirit empowering his ministry and filling his life.

Chris Neal

In what ways do you know the peace, purpose, passion and power that the Holy Spirit wants to give you?

O thou who camest from above
The pure celestial fire to impart,
Kindle a flame of sacred love
On the mean altar of my heart.

Charles Wesley (1707–88)

EASTER – DAY 48
LOOKING TOWARDS PENTECOST –
THE HOLY SPIRIT IN AN INDIVIDUAL

Ephesians 5.15–20

In his letter to the Ephesians Paul exhorts his readers to 'go on being filled with the Spirit' (5.18). As with so many aspects of discipleship, receiving God's Spirit should be an ongoing daily experience. Each day as I rise to greet the new morning, I need to ask God to fill me afresh with his Holy Spirit so that I might walk closely with him, shine in his light, and seize every opportunity to share his good news. Perhaps it has been a long while since you knew the joy of the Lord Jesus filling your heart and life. Begin again today by humbly asking the Lord to fill you.

Chris Neal

The Holy Spirit longs for you to come to the point where you are ready to open yourself to his power, either afresh or for the first time. How do you respond to this truth?

Lord Jesus Christ,
thank you that you long to pour out
the gift of your Holy Spirit
upon all who will receive.
Please forgive me for the times I have grieved your Holy Spirit
or refused to allow him to rule in my life.
Please forgive me for the times
I have been afraid of your Spirit
and not trusted your love.
Today, I ask you to pour your Spirit into my life.
Help me to know your love in my life,
to experience your peace and joy,
and give me power boldly to proclaim your gospel. Amen.

EASTER – DAY 49
LOOKING TOWARDS PENTECOST – THE HOLY SPIRIT IN THE CHURCH

1 Corinthians 13.13

The greatest gift the Spirit brings to the heart of the disciple and the community of God's people is the gift of love. In Romans 5.5 Paul says: 'God's love has been poured into our hearts through the Holy Spirit that has been given to us.' That love is the love of Christ which moulds and welds the different members together. To describe this Christian love, the Church used the word *agape*, a love which reflected God's willingness to give of himself . . . It is vital that the exercise of the gifts of the Spirit is deeply rooted and grounded in the love of Christ. The gifts replicate his ministry. That can only be done with any integrity if they are used in the context of the love of Jesus, shining through each believer and dwelling at the heart of his Church (see 1 Cor. 13).

Chris Neal

How much do you see the gifts of the Holy Spirit in your local expression of church? Do you believe they should be sought and exercised? Why are we so often afraid of the gifts God wants to give? How can you play your part in ensuring they are used in love?

Lord Jesus Christ,
as you pour out your Holy Spirit upon the Church,
help us to recognize all the gifts you are giving,
and teach us to use the gifts with humility as well as love.
For the glory of your name. Amen.

EASTER – DAY 50
PENTECOST – THE HOLY SPIRIT
IN MISSION

Acts 2.1–12

It was the Holy Spirit who led the early Church to climb over human divisions and proclaim the kingdom on the other side of the frontier. If the Church today is to be empowered in the same way, it is crucial that it should be willing to wait upon the Lord and expect the Spirit to lead it forward.

One of the reasons that we may find it easier to stay behind the barriers is because to move across the frontiers brings change and challenge. Peter rejoiced that Cornelius and his household experienced God's grace in the gift of the Spirit (Acts 11). However, Peter had to face the leaders of the Jerusalem church who were at first hostile to what had happened. All of us find change difficult to handle and cope with. For many, living in a world of bewildering change, church life becomes a bastion of stability. This is not God's way or desire.

We need to learn a willing obedience and to realize that our true stability is in him alone and not in the structure of church life, which all too frequently becomes a barrier to God's mission in his world.

Chris Neal

Do you find change difficult – if so why? How can the Holy Spirit help you to be prepared to change and move on? Are there frontiers you are unwilling to cross?

Lord, thank you that in your love
you crossed the greatest barrier,
the barrier of my sin,
and brought me back to yourself.
Give me the courage,
by the power of your Holy Spirit,
to cross every barrier I know
to bring your love to others. Amen.

ORDINARY TIME – DAY 1
LET YOUR SPIRIT BREAK IN

Joel 2.28–32

On your last days on earth
You promised
To leave us the Holy Spirit
As our present comforter.
We also know
that your Holy Spirit blows over this earth.
But we do not understand him.
Many think
He is only wind or a feeling.
Let your Holy Spirit
Break into our lives.
Let him come like blood into our veins,
So that we will be driven
entirely by your will.
Let your Spirit
Blow over wealthy Europe and America,
So that men there will be humble.
Let him blow over the poor parts of the world
So that men there need suffer no more.
Let him blow over Africa
So that men here may understand
What true freedom is.
There are a thousand voices and spirits
In this world,
But we want to hear only your voice
And be open only to your Spirit. Amen.

From a young Ghanaian Christian

Lord, may we hear only your voice and be open only to your Spirit. Amen.

ORDINARY TIME – DAY 2
SEEK FIRST THE KINGDOM

Matthew 6.33

When Bishop Hilary of Yei (Sudan) returned from Ireland recently we heard him preach. He shared his experiences with the 500-strong youth congregation at the 8 am service in Yei. 'It would be impossible to find a congregation like this in UK . . . so young . . . so many.' He shared how he had preached in big churches designed for thousands of people but there was only a congregation of about 50. He said he had told the people in the UK 'you have good reason to love Jesus Christ, you have creativity, innovation, all the wealth of the world . . .' He went on to relate how people in the UK have houses full of things, even just for two people, and he had asked what they needed all these things for.

The message he had given in the UK was 'seek first the kingdom of God'. The message he gave in Sudan and Uganda is 'They have a problem over there.' Christians in the Sudan are praying for the people in the UK.

CMS mission partners

Lord Jesus Christ,
Alive and at large in the world,
Help me to follow and find you there today
In the places where I work,
Meet people, spend money
And make plans.
Take me as a disciple of your kingdom
To see through your eyes
And hear the questions you are asking,
To welcome all with your trust and truth,
And to change the things that contradict God's love
By the power of your cross
And the freedom of your Spirit.

ORDINARY TIME – DAY 3
MAKING MISSION A LIFESTYLE

Malachi 3.8–10

There is still a huge lifestyle challenge too many Christians seem oblivious to. On the evangelical and charismatic side many still have discipleship wrong. In the US, a lot of middle-class people, including a lot of committed Christians, have been bingeing on borrowed money which of course is not sustainable. One wonders where the teaching of the Church was to help these good people really question to what extent they have to have the mega mansion houses, vehicles and expensive holidays.

I think part of the problem here in Britain, Down Under and in the States is the teaching on tithe stewardship. It would be wonderful if everyone gave a tithe, which of course very few do these days. The problem I see is frankly that as soon as people give 10 per cent or some portion thereof, then they are kind of off the hook. They tend to think what they do with the rest of their time and their money is pretty much up to them, their taste, preferences, class, where they like to party, where they like to holiday. I think that's a serious mistake.

Tom Sine

Spend time reflecting with God on what we have and what we really need. Are there areas of our lives and giving where God is challenging us to make courageous changes?

ORDINARY TIME – DAY 4
DO NOT WORRY ABOUT TOMORROW . . .

Matthew 6.31–34

Some friends have commented to me about Nepali people that 'they seem happier and more content than many at home are. They've got less to worry about.' How to compare or judge the happiness of another, especially from such a different world? I know that many here suffer from grinding poverty, ill health and have had little or no opportunity to be educated, yet perhaps do not suffer from the pressures of time and money that many in the West do. Are they happier than someone in the UK hit hard by the current credit crunch? I don't know. I suppose that there is some kind of a middle ground that some have achieved – whether it's in Nepal or the UK – but is elusive to most. It does strike me, however, that the more simple your lifestyle is, the less affected you are by outside factors. Perhaps many people here are less anxious about tomorrow because they are too busy managing for today.

But I am reminded of those well-known verses: 'Therefore do not worry, saying, "What shall we eat?" or "What shall we drink?" or "What shall we wear?" For it is the Gentiles who strive for all these things; and indeed your heavenly Father knows that you need all these things. But strive first for the kingdom of God and his righteousness, and all these things will be given to you as well. So do not worry about tomorrow for tomorrow will bring worries of its own. Today's trouble is enough for today' (Matt. 6.31–34).

Paul and Jean Dobbing, Nepal

Lord God, in the birth of Jesus,
you show your preference for all that is humble and poor.
May this mercy save us
from illusions of grandeur and power,
and lead us to love simplicity of heart.
Through Christ, our Lord. Amen.

From France

ORDINARY TIME – DAY 5
GOD'S HEART FOR THE POOR

Luke 19.1–10

We are in a battle where the enemy wants us to quit and to stop pursuing God's love for the poor: economical immigrants are mostly poor. In his book, *The Call to Conversion*, Jim Wallis calls them 'victims' because of the structures of this world that are so unbalanced economically, mainly due to original sin. Wallis's prophetic voice tells us that the main victim is Christ, who took on himself all this suffering when he died on the cross for us to break the power of sin in our lives. He has experienced and truly understands how immigrants and asylum seekers feel to be in exile, to have fear and to be abandoned.

Even though Christ loves everyone, he favours the poor, and he tells us that if we help one of them, we are helping him. That's why being a Christian transforms our lives and we cannot omit the care for those who are in need. It's what happened with Jesus' encounter with the tax-collector who, when he met Jesus, gave back to the poor over and above what he had taken and received salvation. One of the major factors of today's 'crisis' has been idol worship: MONEY. This god tries to keep us away from God Almighty through greed and over-consumption, and guess who is more affected . . . the poor and the disenfranchised. We need to keep our eyes on the things that will last for ever; we need to awake, as one day all of us will have to give account to God.

Felipe and Sarah Yanez

Father of all,
may we recognize the challenge of consumerism,
the temptation of greed
and the call to repentance.
Like Zacchaeus,
may we be ready to give over and above the call of duty
and keep our eyes fixed on things that will last for ever. Amen.

ORDINARY TIME – DAY 6
RESPONDING TO NEED

Luke 18.18–23

For us, one issue that continues to raise its head time and time again is the issue of giving. To give you an example: When we first arrived here we were immediately approached by some Nepalis we had never met before. They were 'full-time' Christian workers who were, and still are, doing a great job out in the community. They received 80 per cent of their funding from several expatriates. However, the expatriates were leaving, and consequently the funding was coming to an end. We were asked to help fill this funding gap. As Westerners we are viewed very much as being rich, which, in Nepali terms, we certainly are. This issue of being approached for funding is one that has happened several times, and something that we still struggle with. It is not that the amount needed is big. It isn't. That is definitely not the issue. The issue is the fact of creating a dependency culture; creating people totally dependent on the West as a source of income or funding. In our time here one thing that has been quite disturbing are the negative examples of how Western money and assistance has *not* helped individuals to develop themselves. Rather it has created an atmosphere of 'expecting' Westerners to help and provide for them.

Nowadays, the word 'sustainability' is certainly a buzz-word in development work circles. Any given project must be 'sustainable' within the local community after the initial input and investment has been withdrawn. Compared against the world's definition, this scenario would definitely not be deemed 'sustainable'. Whenever these requests for funding arrive, all the above issues relating to sustainability come flooding in, together with the negative legacy of dependency I can see. I ask myself, 'If I agree to help finance this request am I just adding to the fires of dependency that are already burning?' 'Are we taking over something that should in fact be the responsibility of the Nepali Church?'

Yet, among all these very practical thoughts and global perspectives about sustainability, comes the Bible's perspective. Jesus tells us to give to the poor, and never mentions the word 'sustainability'. The thought comes to me, 'Is God using us in this situation to meet a need?' 'Is he using our access to financial resources to help fund his work in Nepal?' After all, grassroots Nepali–Nepali ministry is far more effective than expatriate–Nepali style ministry. If I take the 'sustainability' analogy and apply it to Tracy and me, are we not being supported ourselves by churches and individuals back home? Our work here in Nepal would in no way be seen as 'sustainable' according to the world's definition – we'd have been closed down a long time ago! This issue has no easy answers, but instead throws up lots of complicated and often contradicting issues to grapple with. Our experience here has suggested that each case has to be judged separately. There are times when we need to say 'No' and pull back from offering assistance, while at the same time not becoming so negative and focused on the issue of 'sustainability' that we miss the times when God says 'Yes' to us. There are definitely times when God wants us to use the resources he has given us, while still being wise about the decisions we make.

Jason and Tracy Day, Nepal

Lord – give us wisdom as we reflect on what we have and how we use it. Amen.

ORDINARY TIME – DAY 7
ASKING TOUGH QUESTIONS

1 John 3.16–17

Trying to make sense of the extreme poverty and wealth displayed in Pakistan is very difficult. Many times it seems unjust. Then thinking about how even the very poor in Britain would be wealthy here sends your thoughts into a tailspin. How can God let such injustice occur? How can we and the Church let such injustices occur?

Prior to coming to Pakistan, I read a very challenging book by Brian McLaren called *Everything Must Change*, which looked at these issues. Unsurprisingly, it gave no clear answers to these questions, but it caused me to think deeply about the subject. How can we in Britain who have three cars, a comfortable home, a flat-screen TV, a dishwasher, holidays abroad and who throw out unused food festering at the back of our fridge react in an appropriate way to this poverty? In the grand scheme of things, it seems that our lifestyles are unjust, unmerciful even. To quote a U2 song: 'Where you live should not decide whether you live or whether you die.'

As Christians what should we be doing? How can we respond? I certainly don't hold the answer to this question. Jesus has a special heart for the poor as we see throughout the Gospels. 1 John 3.16–17 (NIV) reads: 'This is how we know what love is: Jesus Christ laid down his life for us. And we ought to lay down our lives for our brothers. If anyone has material possessions and sees his brother in need but has no pity on him, how can the love of God be in him?' This is a clear challenge to Christians everywhere. We should all be doing something, through practical assistance and regular prayer; if we are not, then how can the love of God be in us as we claim? Jesus commands us to love our neighbours as ourselves. We may be tempted to ask who is our neighbour; the family living next door, anyone who lives in our street, anyone who lives in Europe? Indeed, a Pharisee asked Jesus this same question as detailed in Luke 10.25–37. Jesus answered him with the parable of the Good Samaritan, which effectively explains that our neighbour is just about anybody in need, even our enemies, like the Samaritans and Jews were to each other in New Testament times.

Often we can see the gospel as only being about telling people how they can be saved from their sins and be assured of going to heaven by believing in Jesus. This is of course true, but is only the beginning of the gospel message and what God wants to do through his Church. He wants the kingdom of God to be seen on earth, and Jesus instructed us to pray in the Lord's Prayer: 'Your kingdom come, your will be done on earth as it is in heaven.'

David and Dawn Curran, Pakistan

This is how we know what love is: Jesus Christ laid down his life for us. And we ought to lay down our lives for our brothers and sisters. If we have material possessions and see our brother or sister in need but have no pity on him, how can the love of God be in us?

ORDINARY TIME – DAY 8
'GOD WITH US'

Proverbs 14.31

We are often confronted by the realities of poverty and suffering here, which puts our own problems into perspective. One such example is Beauty, who works as an *ayah* (nanny) in one of the schools Sarah helps in, and who was recently widowed. Her husband worked as a carpenter, but was struggling financially – largely due to different customers not paying him on time for his work.

One day, despite feeling unwell, he felt he had no choice but to try and get some of the outstanding money owed to him, and so caught a bus across Dhaka to a previous customer. It seems the customer again refused to pay until later (unfortunately a common practice towards poorer workers such as this). As a result, he did not even have enough money for the full bus fare home, and so paid all he could, expecting to walk the rest of the way home. However, while he was still on the bus, he died of a heart attack. He leaves behind Beauty, their two daughters and significant debts.

The actions of the local church in Mirpur were a great example to us of how we need to come alongside those in need. The minister and the headteacher of the school (who is also involved with the women's work in the church) both went with Beauty to identify the body, visited her regularly in her home and have helped her financially. In Bangladesh when someone dies they are returned to their village to be buried, and this is an additional financial burden as a vehicle has to be hired. But the church were able to assist in this too.

Forty days after his death, friends and family met together again in church to thank God for his life and to continue to pray for the family. Again it was encouraging to see the love and support offered by the church as they came alongside – a practical example of 'God with us'. Beauty continues to struggle without her husband's income to supplement her own, but through the help of many she is slowly beginning to adjust to life on her own.

David and Sarah Hall, Bangladesh

Lord, by our kindness may we honour others and thereby honour you. Amen.

ORDINARY TIME – DAY 9
HONEST DOUBT

Psalm 44.23–26

I heard one preacher say that as far as he was concerned God sent the tsunami as a reminder to the world that he was God and that we must repent. Conrad and I felt this was so judgemental and lacking in love. The Archbishop of Canterbury, on the other hand, was reported as saying that it is right for people to ask where God is in the midst of such disasters. Good on you, Rowan! After all, we are only human, struggling with our faith.

I read something I liked: 'There lives more faith in honest doubt, believe me, than in half the creeds . . .' – Tennyson's lines from 'In Memoriam'. It is OK to doubt. It's not surprising we do, and grapple with issues, but perhaps our faith is strengthened if we honestly question and allow ourselves to doubt.

What I do know for sure is that the God I believe in does want us to act in love, and stand up and help one another, and an awful time like this gives us a chance to do that, rather than stand up in a pulpit wasting time speculating. We will never know here on earth why what happens happens. It has been wonderful to see how much people have genuinely wanted to help one another.

Conrad and Liz Foote, Cambodia

Bring to God your areas of doubt and questioning, asking that through grappling with the questions, we may find our faith strengthened and deepened.

ORDINARY TIME – DAY 10
MAKING ALL THINGS NEW

Isaiah 58.6–8

Neema Crafts Workshop, which I set up with the diocese to provide handicrafts training and employment for deaf and physically disabled people, is now four years old and continues to grow, grow, grow. Early in the year we were invited to send five people with disabilities to Dar es Salaam for a month to learn how to make recycled glass beads from bottles and jars, which are usually dumped or buried. During the course, which was given by four Ghanaians, the trainees learned how to hand-build a kiln from clay, make moulds, fill them with crushed bottle glass and fire them into new beads. We are now the first – and only – organization within the Iringa region to be recycling glass. As Christians, we should be at the forefront of developing environmentally sustainable practices in our communities, yet how often is this the case?

We see daily in Tanzania, first-hand, how people in developing countries are suffering as a direct result of climate change due to carbon emissions and over-consumption of resources by the West. See Isaiah 58 if you are in any doubt about our God-given responsibility to care for the poor and be challenged to think about how the environmental damage we do directly affects people who can least afford it in countries such as Tanzania. Neema Crafts is proud to be a witness in the community of the importance of recycling resources and caring for the environment.

Susie Hart, Tanzania

Father, give us creativity
to use resources wisely,
to find new ways of addressing issues,
to see others through your eyes. Amen.

ORDINARY TIME – DAY 11
EYES OPENED

Luke 5.12–16

We really thank God for this place, where we have found hope. We were the hidden people in our society, even our own people abandoned us and considered us nothing, but now we feel alive! We can now plan for our future; we are sure to care for our children through our own wages, which is a wonderful thing for us. There will be no more dragging ourselves around the town begging in the streets and markets with lots of insulting words from people. Hopefully our society will start opening their eyes to us now too.

A Neema Crafts participant, Tanzania

Pray for communities of hope like Neema Crafts, which reach out and touch people in the name and love of Jesus. Pray that God will open our eyes to the suffering of individuals.

ORDINARY TIME – DAY 12
KNOWING AND LOVING

Luke 14.12–14

I asked participants who claimed to be 'strong followers of Jesus' whether Jesus spent time with the poor. Nearly 80 per cent said 'Yes'. Later in the survey, I sneaked in another question, I asked this same group of strong followers whether they spent time with the poor, and less than 2 per cent said they did. I learned a powerful lesson; we can admire and worship Jesus without doing what he did. We can applaud what he preached and stood for without caring about the same things. We can adore his cross without taking up ours. I had come to see that the great tragedy of the Church is not that rich Christians do not care about the poor but that rich Christians do not know the poor.

Shane Claiborne

How do we model Jesus' compassion, not pity, for the poorest in our societies? Is this at the heart of our faith? How might being part of a community of mission help us to engage with different people and different needs?

God of compassion,
help us not simply to know *about* people but to know people;
help us not just to care *about* people but to care *for* people.
Break down the barriers that divide us
and help us to walk together as your children. Amen.

ORDINARY TIME – DAY 13
BELONGING TO CHRIST

Matthew 19.16–21

Lord,
Because you have made me,
I owe you the whole of my love;
Because you have redeemed me,
I owe you the whole of myself;
Because you have promised so much,
I owe you all my being.

I pray you, Lord,
Make me taste by love
What I taste by knowledge;
Let me know by love
What I know by understanding.

I owe you
More than my whole self,
But I have no more,
And by myself I cannot render
The whole of it to you.

Draw me to you, Lord,
In the fullness of love.
I am wholly yours by creation;
Make me all yours, too,
In love.

Anselm of Canterbury (1033–1109)

Lord – make me all yours. Amen.

ORDINARY TIME – DAY 14
RENEWING DISCIPLESHIP I

Philippians 1.1–2

Even in these opening verses of Philippians 1, Paul reminds us that discipleship is about participating in Christ, and finding ourselves committed to one another because we are committed to him. The church in Philippi was the first that Paul planted in Europe, and this letter is witness to the fact that the gospel of Jesus Christ is for all cultures and all times and cannot be contained by any one culture or time. It is God's longing that all will discover his grace and peace, and be counted among the saints.

Chris Neal

Do I recognize the great privilege of participating in the life of Christ, and am I willing to recognize that he is not only for every generation, but for every race. Does my daily life reflect these great truths? Can Christ be seen in me, and am I open to and welcoming of the stranger? Am I willing, if he calls, to cross frontiers in Christ's name?

I take God the Father to be my God.
I take Christ the Saviour to be my Saviour.
I take the Holy Spirit to be my sanctifier.
I take the word of God to be my rule.
I take the people of God to be my people.
I dedicate my whole self to the Lord.
And this I do deliberately, sincerely, freely
and for ever. Amen.

ORDINARY TIME – DAY 15
RENEWING DISCIPLESHIP 2

Philippians 1.3–6

For Paul, participation in Christ, finds its true expression as we discover a deep partnership with him and one another in sharing the life of the gospel. In his letter to the Colossians Paul recognizes that this gospel is bearing fruit all over the world (1.6). In his encouragement of the Philippians, Paul points to the eternal nature of the gospel and that Christ will complete the good work that he has begun, both in them and through them.

Chris Neal

Am I willing to recognize the corporate nature of the gospel and the mission to which it calls us? Where do I share with others in this mission of God? Am I willing to allow him to continue his work in me, knowing that this is for eternity?

I take God the Father to be my God.
I take Christ the Saviour to be my Saviour.
I take the Holy Spirit to be my sanctifier.
I take the word of God to be my rule.
I take the people of God to be my people.
I dedicate my whole self to the Lord.
And this I do deliberately, sincerely, freely
and for ever. Amen.

ORDINARY TIME – DAY 16
RENEWING DISCIPLESHIP 3

Philippians 1.9–11

This prayer of Paul is a pattern and model for our own prayer life – as we pray for others as well as for ourselves. Paul prays not only for the Philippians to abound in love, but, perhaps even more importantly, that this love may be shaped and informed by a depth of knowledge that can only come from God himself. Out of this deep understanding comes a true discernment that enables us to live a life that is not only pure and blameless but demonstrates the righteousness of Christ. This alone is the foundation for a community of mission service, for it is only in the love, knowledge and righteousness of Christ that true transformation can be discovered and shared.

Chris Neal

Do I allow my life, day by day, to be shaped by the love and knowledge of God? As I meet with people and interact with them, and as I deal with the situations that face me, do I seek to reflect the Lord's love and grace; does my life speak of and point to eternal realities?

I take God the Father to be my God.
I take Christ the Saviour to be my Saviour.
I take the Holy Spirit to be my sanctifier.
I take the word of God to be my rule.
I take the people of God to be my people.
I dedicate my whole self to the Lord.
And this I do deliberately, sincerely, freely
and for ever. Amen.

ORDINARY TIME – DAY 17
RENEWING DISCIPLESHIP 4

Philippians 1.12–14

For many the experience of being imprisoned would have brought questioning and doubt. For Paul, chained to a series of guards during the course of 24 hours, it was a key opportunity to share his love of Christ, and to explain the significance of the gospel for all people. Not only has the gospel been shared, but the Christian community, despite this seeming set back, has been encouraged by Paul's passion, and has done likewise. The experience of the one had a real impact on the lives of many, both on those within the Christian community and those beyond it.

Chris Neal

Am I prepared to allow my life to be shaped by this same passion for Christ and his gospel? Am I willing to try and turn every circumstance to his honour and the blessings of others? Do I realize that all my actions, however small and insignificant, have an impact and influence on the lives of others?

I take God the Father to be my God.
I take Christ the Saviour to be my Saviour.
I take the Holy Spirit to be my sanctifier.
I take the word of God to be my rule.
I take the people of God to be my people.
I dedicate my whole self to the Lord.
And this I do deliberately, sincerely, freely
and for ever. Amen.

ORDINARY TIME – DAY 18
RENEWING DISCIPLESHIP 5

Philippians 1.15–17

Seeking to participate in the life of a community is never easy, even if it is focused on sharing in the mission of God! Human nature soon intervenes, and jealousies and rivalries can soon become the order of the day. For Paul, chained in prison, this must have been a very painful experience, particularly as he realized that the gospel itself was being used for personal ambition. These three very poignant verses begin to take us to the heart of what it means to be a community committed, as servants, to the mission of Christ. Each member has to decide whether to allow the way of Christ to shape their thinking, attitudes and priorities, and to remain true to that commitment no matter what the cost imposed by others within the community.

Chris Neal

Who or what do I allow to shape my personal ambition and consequent attitudes and lifestyle? Do I allow Jesus to be at the centre of all that I am and do, or am I more concerned about my position within a community? Am I willing to begin to explore what it means to become more like Jesus, in the way of his service and cross?

I take God the Father to be my God.
I take Christ the Saviour to be my Saviour.
I take the Holy Spirit to be my sanctifier.
I take the word of God to be my rule.
I take the people of God to be my people.
I dedicate my whole self to the Lord.
And this I do deliberately, sincerely, freely
and for ever. Amen.

ORDINARY TIME – DAY 19
RENEWING DISCIPLESHIP 6

Philippians 1.18

This verse, of course, follows on from the struggle of community that was the focus of reflection yesterday. From the community, Paul again looks to Christ and rejoices that whatever the motive of the individual, Christ is preached, the gospel proclaimed and the purposes of God fulfilled. Paul is able to see beyond the immediate pain of a broken community, to the centrality of Christ, and that in him all things can and will work together for good. An individual disciple and the Christian community can only remain true to the mission call of God as it maintains this centrality of Jesus Christ.

Chris Neal

As I reflect on my life and discipleship, can I recognize that the central focus is Jesus Christ and the call to share in his way? Do I live my discipleship in such a way that the Christian community of which I am part is enriched and blessed, and encouraged to find the whole of its life flowing from Christ?

I take God the Father to be my God.
I take Christ the Saviour to be my Saviour.
I take the Holy Spirit to be my sanctifier.
I take the word of God to be my rule.
I take the people of God to be my people.
I dedicate my whole self to the Lord.
And this I do deliberately, sincerely, freely
and for ever. Amen.

ORDINARY TIME – DAY 20
RENEWING DISCIPLESHIP 7

Philippians 1.19

At the end of this part of his letter, Paul recognizes the coming together of the prayers of the Philippians and the work of Christ's Spirit. Here is the deep and humbling mystery of a God who gives himself to his people to partner with them in his mission. There can be no community of mission service unless it flows from this mystery, and allowing it to be lived out in the reality of everyday experience and life; only in and through this partnership can there be the transformation for which we long. There is, of course, a paradox in Paul's words. Will the deliverance be physical freedom from incarceration in prison, or is it the final deliverance in Christ? It is as we live in the tension of this paradox, not demanding the easy and comfortable way, that we are taken deeper into sharing God's mission in and to his world.

Chris Neal

Am I willing to explore the mystery of participating with God and his people? Do I demand the easy and the comfortable route, or am I willing, as Paul, to allow the purposes of God to be worked out in my life no matter what the cost?

I take God the Father to be my God.
I take Christ the Saviour to be my Saviour.
I take the Holy Spirit to be my sanctifier.
I take the word of God to be my rule.
I take the people of God to be my people.
I dedicate my whole self to the Lord.
And this I do deliberately, sincerely, freely
and for ever. Amen.

ORDINARY TIME – DAY 21
BEAUTIFUL ENCOUNTERS . . .

Luke 14.15–24

I am passionate about mission among those most marginalized. I volunteer at a drop-in centre where I and others make friends with people whose lives are affected by poverty, homelessness, addiction, abuse and exploitation. The drop-in place is Christian in ethos and my developing role is to support the foundational spirituality there, both in its environment and in relationships.

Places where those who gather are acutely aware of their own brokenness are potentially very special. They can open up some profoundly beautiful encounters wherein compassion and grace can bring sustaining life and hope – both for those seeking friendship and help and those who give it. It is a privilege to serve those relationships by imagining new (and rediscovering old) ways to explore prayer and how to communicate worth and love.

Karlie Allaway, a pioneer training on the CMS Pioneer Programme

Spend time reflecting on Jesus' many encounters (often over meals) with the poor and marginalized. How can we develop relationships – 'beautiful encounters' – where we not only give but receive from one another?

ORDINARY TIME – DAY 22
OUR SHIELD AND DEFENDER

Psalm 18.1–3

At a service I recently attended we sang the well-known hymn 'We trust in you, our shield and defender'. I was particularly struck by the third verse, which summed up how I was feeling, as I was about to return to work here after my break:

> We go in faith, our own great weakness feeling,
> And needing more each day your grace to know;
> Yet from our hearts a song of triumph pealing,
> 'We trust in you and in your name we go'.

Now and always. Amen.

Francesca Elloway, Democratic Republic of Congo

Thank God for his protection, even in the midst of our weakness and fear. Pray for courage to continue in trust.

Give me the supreme courage of love, this is my prayer – all courage to speak, to do, to suffer at thy will; to leave all or to be left alone.

Give me the supreme faith of love, this is my prayer – the faith of the life in death, of the victory in defeat, of the power hidden in the frailness of beauty, of the dignity of pain that accepts hurt but disdains to return it. Amen.

Rajkumari Kaur, India

ORDINARY TIME – DAY 23
TREASURE IN EARTHEN VESSELS

2 Corinthians 4.7

I know that although I will be spending time in the 'limelight', public speaking isn't something I am comfortable with. I understand, though, that this is the Lord's mission, so I pray that I may draw on his strength. In the same way someone once told me: 'Just remember you are *not* taking God to Africa; God is taking *you!*'

Garry Ion

Father, we thank you for our weaknesses
which lead us to depend on you;
We thank you that we are like clay vessels
that the glory goes to you. Amen.

ORDINARY TIME – DAY 24

MAY HE ADD . . .

Genesis 30.22–34

'May he add' (Gen. 30.24). This was the prayer of Rachel at the birth of
her first son, Joseph, and it is our prayer. Rachel's prayer was answered
in both quality and quantity as Joseph became a man who brought salvation to others, through allowing God to work in his own life. Rachel had
a second son, Benjamin. She came from a dysfunctional family. She had
faults and made mistakes, but because her prayer was aligned with God's
heart to save his people, she was in partnership with God and her prayers
were answered. In mission we also feel that we present ourselves as very
imperfect people but if God has honed our desires and motivations, then
we will see answers to our prayers.

A CMS mission partner

Lord God, thank you that you accept us as we are
with our mistakes, our faults, our pride, our mixed motives.
Like Rachel, we pray – 'May you add'
to the honour and glory of your name. Amen.

ORDINARY TIME – DAY 25
TRUE WORTH IN CHRIST

Ephesians 1.4–5

It is wonderful to know and be serving a God who uses every situation for our good. Even when we are unsure of what is happening around us at least we know that nothing we give to God will be wasted. Our God is a God of surprises. Just when I was rejoicing in the process of settling into my flat and thinking I would at last have some stability in my life, I suddenly found myself needing to leave Kiev and living in very different circumstances. In a review at the end of last year I was advised to work through the Genesis Process fully for myself, so that I can work through the exercises more fully in my own life and that my teaching of it would become more effective, with more personal examples and a greater demonstration seen in my life. Therefore at the beginning of January I joined the Gilead Foundation's rehabilitation centre in Devon for their five-month programme. (A reminder that the Genesis Process is a course to help people overcome destructive habits that can range from addiction and codependency to anger and anxiety.)

Teaching this course has become one of my main projects in both Ukraine and Russia. Though I am not here to address chemical addictions as most of the residents are, I am gaining from the attention to my character. Gilead was chosen with the hope that I will be able to receive from them ongoing counsel for implementing the Genesis Process in rehab centres in Russia and Ukraine. While going through this deeper self-evaluation I have come to realize how much I have found my value/sense of worth in what I do rather than in who I am in Christ. In my mind I know that who I am has greater influence on my effectiveness for the gospel than what I do; however, it's harder to amend character than programmes.

Alison Giblett, Russia

Praise God for his grace.

Praise be to you, the God and Father of our Lord Jesus Christ!
You have blessed us – you continue to bless us – with every spiritual
blessing in Christ.
May we know ourselves as your children, chosen and loved, precious
and honoured in your sight and may that knowledge be the bedrock
of our lives. Amen.

ORDINARY TIME – DAY 26
UNEXPECTED MIRACLES

Revelation 3.20

The first few months of the year were very difficult, what with struggling
to complete the thesis amid church commitments. Moreover, I had even
less time than my classmates, because I spent the whole of December
training the dancers for a Christmas extravaganza at church. It was a
very stressful period and I was beginning to wonder if doing a masters
degree was not such a good idea after all.

Then a miracle happened. One day in February, a Thai girl who special-
ized in another field of study at the university, but whom I got to know
from a shared lecture, came up to me and asked me if I was a Christian
(which was obvious from my thesis topic). Yes, I answered. Then she said
she wanted to go to church with me and become a Christian. I stared at
her, open-mouthed, and almost asked her if she was sure. Now I know
what it feels like to reap where I have not sown.

Apparently, Tan (which means sugar) had been having recurring night-
mares of being lost in a building. There were many doors in the building
and she just couldn't find the right one. But in her dream, she knew that
she had to go to church and ask the people there which was the right
door. And that was how she turned up at my 'doorstep'. She's now in my
cell group, and we're discipling her. She has since brought her younger

sister to church, who has also accepted Christ after being touched by God during the worship.

Jane Lee, Thailand

We thank you, Lord God,
that you so often surprise us,
that you break into our lives
and the lives of others.
Help us to respond. Amen.

ORDINARY TIME – DAY 27
ADOPTED IN LOVE

Galatians 4.4–7

I am not God. Apparently. As you can imagine this has come as a huge shock to me. Obviously I did not admit to anyone, much less myself, that I had been labouring under this misapprehension, but it has been recently revealed to me that I had in fact thought this to be the case.

I guess the little things gave it away. Taking too much responsibility for other people's choices, wondering why people or situations didn't change, and being affronted by my inability to affect situations. Coupled with this revelation of my humanness, has been an awareness of my mistakes and omissions. Before I left to come here, I was often told how brave and extraordinary I was. Claims I dismissed easily as I know myself to be ordinary and not unusually brave. I return to the UK on home leave at the end of this year after two and a half years of living among the people of Central Asia. I return as I came, an ordinary person with fears, limitations and a new-found humility and sense of my limitations and mistakes, as well as joys and good times and a greater awe at the mystery and greatness of the true God.

Not only have I come to realize more profoundly I am not God. I have also come to realize I have no claim on Jesus. He is not 'my' Jesus, I have no share of him or a monopoly on him. As a friend put it: 'He is not so much "mine" as he is "he" (or, "I AM"). So he is not "mine" to create in my image (ination); but "mine" to discover; to get to know, and fall in love with.' It has actually come as a relief that 'he' is not mine, but his own, I am not here to promote him, or to force him on other people, but be a witness to him – nothing more and nothing less, to seek and to see where and who he is.

A CMS mission partner

Lord, may we be witnesses to you –
Nothing more and nothing less. Amen.

ORDINARY TIME – DAY 28
RENEWING DISCIPLESHIP 8

Philippians 1.20

The way of Christian discipleship is not a call to an easy life, however we might long for it to be so. Paul was suffering imprisonment because of his commitment to Christ, but even in this captivity he longed for his Lord to be exalted in his life and even in his death. This longing and conviction was underwritten by the expectation and hope that he had in Christ, and knew that as he held to that hope he would be enabled to witness to the transforming love of Christ. It is fruitless for us to look for the transforming work of Christ in others until we are willing to allow that transformation to happen in us. Such transformation can only happen as we, with Paul, put all our hope and expectation in Christ.

Chris Neal

Do I seek an easy and comfortable discipleship, or am I willing to allow the way of Christ to shape my thinking and actions, even if that means walking the hard way of suffering? Am I willing to allow the transforming power of Christ to be mine even in the midst of suffering, and to allow that transformation to touch, and in turn, transform the lives of others?

Lord, in your love and mercy,
You are still calling sinners to repentance,
calling stray sheep to the fold,
calling prodigal sons to come home,
calling all who labour and are heavy laden,
calling new disciples to follow you.
Lord of Glory,
in your love and mercy say the word – and we will come. Amen.

ORDINARY TIME – DAY 29
RENEWING DISCIPLESHIP 9

Philippians 1.21–24

The total conviction of the resurrection and reality of Christ shines through every word in this short passage, and yet Paul is torn in the decision he has to make. For his own comfort, to depart and be with his Lord is the most attractive option. Yet, he recognizes that to remain in his earthly body and continue in his ministry will bring blessing and encouragement to the Philippians. He is motivated by this desire to continue to share Jesus in such a way that the lives of others can continuously be transformed and renewed. Such a servant heart can only be possessed by one who has experienced the service of the one true servant – Jesus Christ.

Chris Neal

Do I share with Paul an assurance of the presence of the risen Christ, and do I allow that to shape my deepest desires, my inner attitudes, and my outward actions? Am I willing to give up my self for the sake of others, in order that they might know the transforming love of Christ? Do I allow Christ to be my servant, in order that I might serve others?

Lord, in your love and mercy,
you are still calling sinners to repentance,
calling stray sheep to the fold,
calling prodigal sons to come home,

calling all who labour and are heavy laden,
calling new disciples to follow you.
Lord of Glory,
in your love and mercy say the word – and we will come. Amen.

ORDINARY TIME – DAY 30
RENEWING DISCIPLESHIP 10

Philippians 1.25–26

In his inner struggle, Paul comes to the point where he is willing to remain in this present age in order that the young disciples in the church in Philippi might grow in their faith, and do so with a real sense of joy, even though they might experience the suffering that following Jesus often brings. At first sight, there may seem an arrogance, as Paul suggests that their joy will overflow because of his presence. However, it is important to recognize that the true joy flows not from Paul, or even the relationship that they share, but from their common life and fellowship in Jesus Christ. The primary focus of all Christian community must be Christ, and the recognition of his supremacy; it is from this and this alone, that everything else will follow.

Chris Neal

While we may not find ourselves in the challenging situation of Paul, it is always important to ask whether we are prepared to use every circum-stance to God's glory and honour and the blessings of others. Does our presence and the contribution we bring enable others to grow in their knowledge of Christ, and therefore in their discipleship? Do we look to the centrality of Christ as we experience and seek to build his community, recognizing that he alone is the true source of joy?

Lord, in your love and mercy,
You are still calling sinners to repentance,
calling stray sheep to the fold,

calling prodigal sons to come home,
calling all who labour and are heavy laden,
calling new disciples to follow you.
Lord of Glory,
in your love and mercy say the word – and we will come. Amen.

ORDINARY TIME – DAY 31
RENEWING DISCIPLESHIP II

Philippians 1.27

The next four days present four challenges to the individual disciple and the whole Christian community, as Paul continues to remind the Philippians that their life together must be shaped by the life of Christ himself. In this verse, Paul is clear that the conduct of the believer must reflect the gospel of Christ. The word 'gospel' is used some 75 times in the New Testament, and becomes shorthand for the whole of God's purposes for the whole of creation, centred on and expressed through the person and work of Jesus Christ. In his own discipleship, Paul recognized both the depth and mystery of this gospel, and the continuing challenge to allow that gospel to inform and determine our conduct.

Chris Neal

When was I last excited or challenged by the mystery and depth of the gospel? In what ways do I allow that gospel to inform and shape the motivation of my life and subsequent attitudes and actions? In the daily conduct of my life do people see the grace and love of Jesus? Am I helping the Christian community of which I am part to grow in this way?

Lord, in your love and mercy,
you are still calling sinners to repentance,
calling stray sheep to the fold,
calling prodigal sons to come home,
calling all who labour and are heavy laden,
calling new disciples to follow you.

Lord of Glory,
in your love and mercy say the word – and we will come. Amen.

ORDINARY TIME – DAY 32
RENEWING DISCIPLESHIP 12

Philippians 1.27b

Yesterday, Paul encouraged the Philippians to allow their conduct to be shaped by Christ; today they are encouraged to stand firm! Now, as then, disciples of Christ will be tempted to allow the prevailing culture to shape them in their lifestyle, both their attitudes and actions. Often this is very subtle and hard to recognize. It is only as we allow the gospel to continue to renew our minds that we can begin to see the issues clearly, and so allow it to change the way we live. This is a hard and ongoing process, and it is only as we encourage each other in one spirit, and know the encouragement and accountability of the wider body of Christ, as the Philippians did in their relationship with Paul, that we can 'stand firm'.

Chris Neal

Do I find myself being blown about by the prevailing culture and attitudes, or am I allowing my mind to be shaped by Christ, shaping my attitudes and actions? Do I recognize my responsibility to and my need of the body of Christ, so that together we learn to stand firm? Where am I experiencing that kind of accountability with a local Christian community and with the wider Church?

Lord, in your love and mercy,
you are still calling sinners to repentance,
calling stray sheep to the fold,
calling prodigal sons to come home,
calling all who labour and are heavy laden,
calling new disciples to follow you.
Lord of Glory,
in your love and mercy say the word – and we will come. Amen.

ORDINARY TIME – DAY 33
RENEWING DISCIPLESHIP 13

Philippians 1.27c–28

As this first chapter draws to a close, Paul again highlights the cost of discipleship, the alternative nature of the Christian community and that in its very life it is called to be a sign of God's judgement and the eventual renewal of all things. As members of the Body of Christ, we are called to live the gospel life in a way that reflects the unity we have in him, and in this unity discover courage even in the face of opposition. As the Church lives the countercultural life that the gospel inevitably requires, there will be those who are challenged by it and then challenge the message of Jesus and those who seek to live by it. This is the heart of discipleship as we witness to what will be and share in the present struggle between the forces of good and evil.

Chris Neal

Do I recognize the significance of all we are called to be and do as disciples of Jesus? Do I live a radical Christian lifestyle which challenges the values of this present age? Do I encourage the Christian community to stand together in unity, and even in the face of opposition, to continue to contend for the gospel?

Lord, in your love and mercy,
you are still calling sinners to repentance,
calling stray sheep to the fold,
calling prodigal sons to come home,
calling all who labour and are heavy laden,
calling new disciples to follow you.
Lord of Glory,
in your love and mercy say the word – and we will come. Amen.

ORDINARY TIME – DAY 34
RENEWING DISCIPLESHIP 14

Philippians 1.29–30

As has been apparent in all of these reflections, Paul is clear that struggle and suffering are at the heart of the experience of Christian discipleship because they are at the heart of the experience and ministry of Jesus. This is going to be a recurring theme throughout the letter. Paul recognizes that the individual disciple, and therefore the Christian community has at the heart of its vocation a sharing in and a reflection of the life of Jesus – at the heart of that life was the example and the ministry of the cross. To share Jesus and to call others into the way of discipleship is no light or easy task. To share Jesus with others means that first I must be prepared to share in his life for myself, with all the consequent challenge and risk of misunderstanding, rejection and suffering that might well follow. This does not mean that we seek suffering for its own sake, but have a willingness to allow our lives to be lived in the way of service that Jesus modelled. Paul also calls the Philippians to see their oneness with him in the mutual experience of suffering for the sake of Christ.

Chris Neal

How willing am I to share Jesus in the way of his service and therefore in the way of his cross? Do I seek to share Jesus with others in the light of this call, or am I too concerned for my ease and comfort? Am I willing to recognize the suffering of disciples around the world, and stand with them in their witness?

Lord, in your love and mercy,
you are still calling sinners to repentance,
calling stray sheep to the fold,
calling prodigal sons to come home,
calling all who labour and are heavy laden,
calling new disciples to follow you.
Lord of Glory,
in your love and mercy say the word – and we will come. Amen.

ORDINARY TIME – DAY 35
PROPHETIC MISSION – THE VENN FAMILY

Amos 7.10–17

CMS was born in revolutionary times in eighteenth-century Britain. It emerged out of the Evangelical Revival that helped to prevent a revolution such as the French experienced in the 1790s: there was an England 'before and after Wesley'. During this period leaders emerged who enacted prophetic roles: as moral guides, social reformers and mission pioneers.

The Venn family represents such prophetic leadership and were involved in forming and developing CMS. Henry Venn (d. 1797) turned the Evangelical Revival into a way of life for making disciples and transforming society. His family life was well known for its love, piety and practical Christianity. John Venn, his son (d. 1813), was the founder of the world mission society we now know as CMS, and was also one of the Clapham Sect who challenged the slave trade and set up the free state of Sierra Leone. Henry Venn, his son (d. 1873), was the CMS general secretary who developed the world mission strategy of planting churches that were self-supporting, self-governing and self-extending. CMS has been involved in planting or supporting up to two-thirds of the Anglican Communion.

The Anglican Churches of Britain and Ireland remember these three leaders on 1 July. One of the set Bible readings is from the prophet Amos (7.10–17), who challenges the people, king and clergy to be true to God's covenant, calling them back to the Lord. The prophetic dimension was incorporated into the very foundation of the Church's self-understanding at Pentecost: this was a prophetic community that interpreted Jesus and the Jewish scriptures with new prophetic insight, lifestyle and foresight about God and his plan of salvation.

Jesus' pattern of prophetic mission is holistic: it includes deed and word. Jesus' deeds were as prophetic as his words, and included his moral holiness, his travels, miraculous signs (personal and creational) and his hospitality. Jesus' words were poetic, everyday stories and didactic; they showed insight and foresight about us and about God's world. Jesus' unique prophetic perspective and practice were brought together in the cross: the greatest deed and word – the prophetic revelation of God's loving way of life: *living through dying* by which Jesus has transformed the world.

It is said that when Henry Venn the elder was told by his doctor he was about to die, it cheered him up so much he stayed alive another fortnight! May the Holy Spirit so inspire us with the life of living through dying that we become followers of Jesus in his prophetic pathway of transformation.

Tim Dakin

Gracious God, whose divine Spirit moves over the world to teach, challenge and comfort, we give you thanks for the Venn family who encouraged so many to obey the call to mission at home and abroad. Inspire us by their vision so that we too may commit ourselves in the prophetic mission of Jesus, whose loving sacrifice transformed the world; we pray this through the power of the one Spirit that raised Jesus from the dead and glorifies the Father in all the world. Amen.

ORDINARY TIME – DAY 36
DEPEND ON THE HOLY SPIRIT
(VENN PRINCIPLES)

John 16.13–15

The difficulty is for us to believe in the indwelling Spirit . . . To trust the Spirit seems to us a desperate act . . . We are indeed afraid of liberty. We are afraid of it because we do not know what our converts would do if they were at liberty . . . we have no real confidence that they would continue to employ the forms which we have imposed upon them.

Roland Allen (1868–1947)

O Lord, I do not know what to ask of you. You alone know my true needs. You love me more than I myself know how to love. Help me to see my real needs, which are concealed from me. I dare not ask either a cross or a consolation. I can only wait on you. My heart is open to you. Visit and help me, for your great mercy's sake. Strike me and heal me, cast me down and raise me up. I worship in silence your holy will and your inscrutable ways. I offer myself as a sacrifice to you. I put all my trust in you. I have no other desire than to fulfil your will. Teach me how to pray. Pray yourself in me. Amen.

Metropolitan Philaret

ORDINARY TIME – DAY 37
WALKING WITH GOD

1 Kings 3.5–12

When asked what is the one thing he desired, Solomon asked God for wisdom. But wisdom was not enough. Even with all of his wisdom, he still failed to find satisfaction in life. The one thing Solomon's father, David, asked of God was to walk with God. Our daily walk with God must supersede wisdom in our relationship with wealth. Worship as a preoccupation with seeking his presence and glorifying him in all we do, must be our foundation.

Dennis O. Tongoi

Enable us, O Lord God,
to walk in your way
with integrity and cheerfulness,
faithfully believing your Word
and faithfully doing your commandments,
faithfully worshipping you
and faithfully serving our neighbour;
through Jesus Christ our Lord. Amen.

J. W. Poole

ORDINARY TIME – DAY 38
BECOME LIKE LITTLE CHILDREN

Matthew 18.2–4

I recently had a very poignant conversation with Ruby that really made me think. Ruby, Libby and I had had a very difficult afternoon culminating in me shouting at them and marching them up to bed. I felt that I had behaved badly towards them, so I apologized and then the three of us knelt down to pray. I explained to the girls that as we prayed I would say sorry to Jesus for shouting and ask for forgiveness.

They understood, we all prayed and then Ruby said: 'Now Mum, it's forgiven and forgotten. You don't need to think about it anymore.' I was amazed at her grasp of the essence of the gospel, but also caught myself thinking 'could it really be so easy?'

As adults, we complicate everything, but when you look at God through the eyes of a child, the beauty and love that you see is amazing. No wonder Jesus tells us to 'change and become like little children' (Matt. 18.3).

Tracy Day, Nepal

We praise you, Lord God, for the gift of children,
for their openness to your grace, beauty and love.
May we become more like them,
as we walk in trust with you. Amen.

ORDINARY TIME – DAY 39
LOOKING FOR BEAUTY

Isaiah 61.1–3

'Miss Alison, what has happened to your back window?'

'Oh that! Some naughty children threw a stone at it and broke it.'

'But, Miss Alison, look, it's beautiful – it's all sparkly.'

And sure enough the car window, which we had up until then seen as shattered and imperfect, was a beautiful glittering piece of art as the sun shone through it. However, it took a six-year-old to show us that there really is beauty in everything. Maybe we sometimes look at life as shattered and imperfect when we should be looking for the beauty of God.

Peter and Alison Roots

Pray that we may see the beauty of God in the midst of the pain and shattered hopes of life – the oil of gladness instead of mourning.

ORDINARY TIME – DAY 40
GRACE IN THE MAKING

Psalm 8

Grace in the making

Creativity and imagination are divine gifts that get to the heart of what
  it is to be human.
God's image bearers.

It is of course possible to deny the gift
Or grow out of the habit

Or recite the mantras 'I'm not creative', 'I haven't got the gift', or
    'I haven't got time'
But such denial won't wash –
It's the road to numbness

Cook a meal
Plan a pilgrimage
Make some music
Form a garden
Pull off a skateboard trick
Tell a story
Take a picture
Design a web page
Write a prayer

Grace is in the making

We have got used to passivity
To consuming what others have made
To sitting and watching
To processed and pre-packaged
To fast food
To reality TV

Consuming isn't bad
It's what you do with it and who can get in the shops that's the
    problem
Even shopping can be creative

Create
Make something
Surprise yourself
Play
Wake up
Encounter grace

Jonny Baker

Create something . . .

ORDINARY TIME – DAY 41
THE POWER OF FORGIVENESS

Matthew 18.21–35

I gather that old wounds have been reopening, yet I hear that seminars have been held bringing together perpetrators and victims and that God has done an amazing work of reconciliation. Wherever I have been, I have been conscious of this need for reconciliation. In Australia between indigenous and white races, in Israel between Jew and Palestinian and between the different strands of Christianity. Last Sunday I heard two different services taking place at the same time in the Church of the Holy Sepulchre! What example are we giving when we cannot even present a united front to the world? The lessons we have been learning in Rwanda are needed everywhere: to see people as human beings, people created by God for whom Jesus the Messiah died. It is so easy to dehumanize our enemy. I urge you to see the film *Hotel Rwanda*, which so clearly shows the demonizing process at work. The reconciliation process starts as we listen to each other's story and learn that we are not unique in our pain. As we transfer our pain and anger to Jesus who carried it all on the cross, we are set free to forgive and to be reconciled.

I have had several dealings with my student, John, whose daughter was raped. He was worried that she might have some physical trauma, so I drove them over to Shyira, where she was examined under anaesthetic by a paediatrician and a gynaecologist. Fortunately, all is well, and also she has tested negative for HIV. On the way, John told me that he had visited the rapist in prison. He said that his situation is appalling with no one bringing him meals, so he has decided to arrange this. I am constantly amazed at the depth of forgiveness these people can display.

Meg Guillebaud

Father, we praise you for stories of forgiveness,
of lives restored, relationships renewed.
We praise you for those who work for peace,
who bring together perpetrators and victims

in the hope of new beginnings.

May we be inspired to work for peace and reconciliation in our homes,

our communities, our places of work. Amen.

ORDINARY TIME – DAY 42

BLESSED ARE THE PEACEMAKERS

Matthew 5.9

We affirm the special role of the Church in Sudan in working for the genuine reconciliation necessary for sustainable peace. We challenge ourselves and our churches to present a true and clear gospel message of peace and reconciliation and to demonstrate this in our lives. As Christians, we declare to all our people that we are to forgive one another and seek forgiveness ourselves. We are to humble ourselves so that God can heal the wounds within us. Blessed are the peacemakers (Matt. 5.9).

Church Leaders in Sudan, pastoral letter

Give thanks for the Sudanese Church's commitment to reconciliation. Pray for the Church throughout the world, that we may be faithful to our calling as peacemakers, able to model a new and different way of being.

ORDINARY TIME – DAY 43

MINISTERS OF RECONCILIATION

Matthew 18.15–16

Most of the members in my cell group are in their early to mid-twenties. Since I'm one of the older ones, the girls tend to look up to me as an older sister. I thank God for the opportunity to share their joys and tears, while I also dispense advice on anything from fashion to boys. They are so gracious to allow me to speak into their lives and to disciple and mentor them.

Just a few days ago, I had to sit two of the cell members down to clear the air between them. Basically, the girl likes the guy, but it isn't reciprocal. Instead of telling her directly, he tried to pass the message through a third party. That went wrong somehow, and everything took a turn for the worse in the last two weeks – hurtful remarks were traded and other cell members were being affected. So I got both of them together for a chat, while I mediated.

I've never played peacemaker before, and the end result was beyond my wildest expectations. God was in the middle of the whole discussion. Both parties were frank and open with each other. Misunderstandings were cleared up, apologies offered and forgiveness extended. At the end of the four hours, there was so much goodwill and joy, and the friendship was deepened. This reconciliation is such a breakthrough, because Thais find such face-to-face talks too confrontational. I am so pleased that this can now be a biblical model to sort out other simmering conflicts in the cell group.

Jane Lee, Thailand

Lord, may we be instruments of reconciliation, spreading peace and hope wherever we are. Amen.

ORDINARY TIME – DAY 44
ALL IN NEED OF RECONCILIATION

Matthew 7.1–5

Burundi has many similarities to southern Sudan, as the inhabitants have experienced many years of tribal disputes and displacements. The country, a few degrees cooler than Sudan, is very picturesque and fertile, but is extremely poor with few children going to school.

I travelled with Archbishop Bernard Ntahouri, who emphasized that the Church is the only body in the community that can, through the gospel message, unite deep-seated tribal divisions. We need to stop focusing on tribal differences he said, as we are all Burundians, all need to repent, all need to receive forgiveness and all need to be reconciled with God and with each other.

Garry Ion

Are we prepared to recognize and acknowledge our own sin before focusing on the sin of others?

Lord – let peace begin with me. Amen.

ORDINARY TIME – DAY 45
LOVING ENEMIES

Luke 23.32–34

The perfection of brotherly love lies in the love of one's enemies. We can find no greater inspiration for this than grateful remembrance of the wonderful patience of Christ. He who is *more fair than all the sons of men* offered his fair face to be spat upon by sinful men; he allowed those eyes that rule the universe to be blindfolded by wicked men; he bared his back to the scourges; he submitted that head which strikes terror in principalities and powers to the sharpness of the thorns; he gave himself up to be mocked and reviled, and at the end endured the cross, the nails, the lance, the gall, the vinegar, remaining always gentle, meek and full of peace.

In short, *he was led like a sheep to the slaughter, and like a lamb before the shearers he kept silent, and did not open his mouth.*

Who could listen to that wonderful prayer, so full of warmth, of love, of unshakeable serenity – *Father, forgive them* – and hesitate to embrace his enemies with overflowing love? *Father*, he says, *forgive them.* Is any gentleness, any love, lacking in this prayer?

Yet he put into it something more. It was not enough to pray for them: he wanted also to make excuses for them. *Father, forgive them, for they do not know what they are doing.* They are great sinners, yes, but they have little judgement; therefore, *Father, forgive them.* They are nailing me to the cross, but they do not know who it is that they are nailing to the cross: *if they had known, they would never have crucified the Lord of glory;* therefore, *Father, forgive them.* They think it is a lawbreaker, an impostor claiming to be God, a seducer of the people. I have hidden my face from them, and they do not recognize my glory; therefore, *Father, forgive them, for they do not know what they are doing.*

If someone wishes to love himself he must not allow himself to be corrupted by indulging his sinful nature. If he wishes to resist the promptings of his sinful nature he must enlarge the whole horizon of his love to contemplate the loving gentleness of the humanity of the Lord, must extend even to his enemies the embrace of true love.

But if he wishes to prevent this fire of divine love from growing cold because of injuries received, let him keep the eyes of his soul always fixed on the serene patience of his beloved Lord and Saviour.

Aelred of Rievaulx (1110–67)

Father – fill us, we pray, with your gentleness,
that we may learn what it means to love and to forgive. Amen.

ORDINARY TIME – DAY 46
REMAKING DISCIPLES OF ALL NATIONS

1 John 1.5 – 2.2

Jesus died so we might be forgiven. 'He is the atoning sacrifice . . . for the sins of the whole world.'

But he expects us to confess our sins to him and to those we sin against. How hard! At Spring Harvest recently, an alarmingly large number of Christ's followers responded to Steve Chalke's appeal to write down their grievances against others and place them in a box for burning. So if the Church has so many grievances . . .

We take communion often. We need to remind ourselves even more often that his blood of the new covenant was poured out for many for the forgiveness of sins. Finding peace with God through that, we're in a position to find peace with others.

And then we can be peacemakers, which is what Christ's mission is all about.

The Spanish-speaking (non-Indian) church of a small town in northern Argentina is Anglican in name only! It's also the largest church in the area, trenchantly planted by a missionary in the 1960s and lovingly tended by its Argentine pastor and his family ever since. Founded on gatherings for prayer, worship, and the word of God, it's an attractive place to spend an evening.

Public testimony plays its part in the meetings. How I came to Christ. Or, more often, how I abandoned Christ and he called me back. Tears flow.

But sometimes public testimony is deeds. A few years ago one of the steadfast members was bemoaning his Christian wife's affair with another man. 'She denies it, but it's true!' Folk felt for this loyal man of no great standing yet great faith, suddenly held up to the public scrutiny of a small town.

News from there tells how the man and his wife now lead a successful evangelistic thrust in the community where she grew up, nearly 100 miles away. How come?

Long ago there was repentance, forgiveness, and acceptance from husband and church. Now there's renewed service and good fruit from it. And their son helps them when home from university, and dreams of being a pastor.

CMS mission partner, Argentina

Lord, finding peace with you, may we find peace with others. Amen.

ORDINARY TIME – DAY 47
RECONCILIATION: SHARING THE PAIN

Colossians 1.21–23

One activity of Musalaha is to organize desert encounter trips for mixed groups of Israeli and Palestinian young people. The aim of these trips is to bring about greater understanding through listening and sharing experiences. One of the young people shared their experience of one such trip:

> I was touched at the sincerity and genuineness with which people shared their pain of the conflict with one another. One Israeli shared that one of her friends was killed in the conflict, and as a result she used to hate Arabs. A Palestinian from the West Bank shared some of the humiliations he endured at the hands of Israeli soldiers, even as recently as a few days leading up to the trip. The sheer cruelty he endured brought tears to many eyes. Another Israeli expressed that as a result of this Palestinian's sharing, as well as the stories of others, did he finally realize the suffering that the Palestinians endure under the occupation. A Palestinian participant commented that she had never heard an Israeli listen and feel sympathy for the pain of her people.

The point of this trip was to listen . . . By opening ourselves to one another, through our vulnerability, we sat side by side and shared each other's pain. And we ended our trip with hearts a little heavier at hearing and knowing the suffering (not of a Palestinian or Israeli) of our friends, but also with our hearts a little lighter for having shared an unforgettable experience, and knowing that our parting was only the beginning.

Andy and Suzie Hart

Lord, as you suffered on the cross and shared our pain,
may we also share one another's pain,
that through it, together, we may find life. Amen.

ORDINARY TIME – DAY 48
RECONCILING CREATION

Isaiah 11.1–9

I was in the act of throwing away my family's rubbish while holidaying on a beautiful island, when I heard God speak: 'How do you think I feel about what you are doing to my world?'

We often think of reconciliation in terms of our relationship with God, and with our fellow human beings, but there is another often overlooked dimension to reconciliation in the Bible – the restoration of broken relationships with and within creation. Human beings are earthy creatures, 'made from the dust of the earth', Adam (earthling) created from *adamah* (soil or earth). We are created to relate harmoniously not only to God and each other but to the land and its creatures. Yet turning away from God has destroyed these good relationships. Adam is told that the land is now cursed because of him, and thereafter the Bible often describes how human sin causes nature to mourn, suffer, waste away and groan. That's why today's ecological crisis is a deeply relational crisis.

Jesus' work on the cross puts all these ancient wrongs to right, and makes it possible for 'all things in heaven and on earth' (including wildlife and the land itself) to be reconciled to God (Col. 1.19–20). That is why the Bible's images of God's ultimate future are of a kingdom of righteousness where snakes, wolves, children and the land are in harmony with each other – reconciled together in God's kingdom of peace.

Dave Bookless, Southall

How is Christ involved in this work of reconciliation? How does the cross display this ministry of reconciliation? What is the cost of reconciliation? Where have you seen God's work of reconciliation take place? How should we be involved in reconciliation?

Look out for news stories about conflict between nations, groups and individuals and pray for reconciliation among those involved.

ORDINARY TIME – DAY 49
REDEMPTION: MAKING NEW

Romans 5.1–8

To look at the children suffering from HIV you'd not know anything was wrong as the majority look healthy and have energy; however, their lives are complex, and they live daily with the need for strong medication that can make them feel terrible, and the knowledge that there is no cure for their disease and no idea how long they might be able to live for. Add to that the problems at home and at school of being 'different', or of multiple bereavements, and we wind up in a very different place. I long for them to feel the clinic is their safe place, where they feel they belong, where people care, where they are free to share whatever they like without judgement or fear, and for them to build friendships with those who share the same issues and problems. And we are getting there!

Rather than promising a way of escape from our problems, the New Testament speaks about finding hope in the midst of those troubles. This sense of hope is firmly located in the activity of God (see vv. 2, 4 and 5) and brings about renewal of our relationship with him and with each other.

Alison Fletcher, CMS mission partner working as a
physiotherapist at Kiwoko Hospital in Uganda

Why does such hope never disappoint (v. 5)? On what do we base God's promise of hope? Where do you see signs of hope in the world around us? How can we bring a message of hope to a hurting world? How can hope motivate us to bring about change and transformation in the world?

Praise God for the promise of hope.
Pray that we may walk in this hope today.

ORDINARY TIME – DAY 50
TAKING A LONG VIEW

Philippians 1.6

It helps, now and then, to step back and take a long view.

The kingdom is not only beyond our efforts,
it is even beyond our vision.

We accomplish in our lifetime only a tiny fraction
of the magnificent enterprise that is God's work.

Nothing we do is complete, which is a way of saying
that the kingdom always lies beyond us.
No statement says all that could be said.
No prayer fully expresses our faith.
No confession brings perfection.
No pastoral visit brings wholeness.
No programme accomplishes the church's mission.
No set of goals and objectives includes everything.

This is what we are about.
We plant the seeds that one day will grow.
We water seeds already planted,
knowing that they hold future promise.
We lay foundations that will need further development.
We provide yeast that produces far beyond our capabilities.

We cannot do everything, and there is a sense of liberation
in realizing that. This enables us to do something,
and to do it very well. It may be incomplete,
but it is a beginning, a step along the way,
an opportunity for the Lord's grace to enter and do the rest.

We may never see the end results, but that is the difference
between the master builder and the worker.

We are workers, not master builders; ministers, not messiahs.
We are prophets of a future not our own.

Oscar Romero (1917–80)

Father, help us to trust in your promise of a future not our own. Amen

ORDINARY TIME – DAY 51
WILDERNESS: A PLACE OF CHANGE

Matthew 3.1–10

If change is to come, it will come from the margins . . . It was the desert, not the temple that gave us the prophets.

Wendell Berry

Throughout the Bible we see the witness of the prophets who chose to live differently – to live prophetically – and thus to challenge and question the values and practices of prevailing religion and culture.

Where are the prophets in our own culture? How might God be calling us to live prophetically and be 'change-makers'? What might prophetic living look like?

Spend time reflecting on your life. Where might God be calling you to live bravely and prophetically?

ORDINARY TIME – DAY 52
SALVATION: MAKING GOOD

Exodus 3.7–10

We were investigating the case of a boy on the streets when we were told that there were three young girls (8, 10 and 13), all of them involved in prostitution on the streets. The older girl had actually been held for a few days tied up in a guy's room, where she was raped several times. These girls are normally linked to larger prostitution rings, which can be potentially dangerous, and so we had to tread carefully. We had to tread even more carefully, when we discovered that these girls live just down the road from the project . . . We couldn't risk being seen around the girls or their house and risk being recognized. So we had to go 'undercover' a few times – we met the girls' aunt who had already reported the girls and their mum to local authorities, but, when interviewed, the mum and the girls denied all the accusations – the local authorities couldn't do any more. Jefferson and I took the aunt to a higher power (the state prosecutor's office) who would be able to send an official order to the local child welfare department authorizing them to go in, with police backup, and remove the girls from this dangerous and abusive situation. The order is with the local authority and so hopefully these girls should be in safety within a few days.

Andy and Rose Roberts, CMS mission partners working with
street children in Olinda, north east Brazil

We thank you, Lord God,
that you are a God who hears the cry of the oppressed,
who longs to rescue those who are trapped in abusive and dangerous
    lives.
As you sent Moses to be your instrument of freedom, send us.
Give us eyes to see, a heart to feel for the oppressed
and the grace and courage to take risks. Amen.

ORDINARY TIME – DAY 53
LIFE RESTORED

Luke 8.40–42, 49–56

I was recently privileged to hear an amazing testimony of God's power in the life of a man and his family who come to our church. Khasi Ram was a highly esteemed Hindu tailor, who often officiated as a priest at local Hindu festivals. He read the Bible occasionally, but only to use it to argue with Christians.

Several Christian ex-pat missionaries befriended him and offered to pray for his wife, Nirmala, who was sick with an ovarian/uterine cyst. Khasi took his wife to hospital, but due to complications, caused by previous abdominal TB, the surgeons were unable to operate and sent her home with just some analgesia! Nirmala became sicker and sicker until one day Khasi arrived home to find her lying on the floor, unconscious with absolutely no palpable pulse! He immediately called his family for help and his brother and sister-in-law (both Christians) came and prayed for her. Khasi, at that time, did not like people praying, so the brother and sister-in-law had to do so in another room. While they were doing so, Nirmala came back to life, sat up and had something to eat and drink!

Everyone was obviously totally amazed (as was I when I heard the story), and from that day Khasi and his family started to believe in, and accept, Jesus as their Saviour.

Jason and Tracy Day, Nepal

Thank God for the many miracles that bring hope in our world – miracles of medicine, unexplainable miracles, acts of salvation. Pray that through them, many may come to know and to love Christ.

ORDINARY TIME – DAY 54
HOPE RESTORED

Psalm 34

Recently I visited two health centres up near the Sudanese border, Rumu and Kumuru. Rumu Health Centre has had a bit of a chequered history over the past few years . . . a hopeless health centre committee . . . were detrimental in what they did, and a not very dynamic nurse in charge there who, I guess, lost interest and felt discouraged . . . All in all, the health centre was in a mess and certainly not viable . . . the District health authorities . . . recognized that the nearest hospital was too far away for folk realistically to travel to, so there were many unnecessary deaths in the area that could be avoided if emergency surgery and transfusion facilities were available nearby.

We felt in a bit of a dilemma at the time, as we'd have loved the health centre to have been upgraded but knew that in reality it was in a mess. However, God was in control and with a change in personnel, including a new dynamic young nurse in charge together with a change in the health centre committee with a strong president, the health centre has completely changed in the past nine months or so. Now it is thriving with lots of patients and the committee has got the local community involved in building a new inpatient unit. With a bit of outside help from some friends, it should soon be usable.

Francesca Elloway, Democratic Republic of Congo

Lord God, we thank you that you are in control,
that you hear our cry in the midst of despair
and new life can spring from seemingly impossible situations.
We bring to you our own fears, challenges and concerns,
asking you to hear and to have mercy.
Help us Lord God, to work for your glory and to never lose hope.
Amen.

ORDINARY TIME – DAY 55
A NEW WORLD VIEW

Luke 15.1–7

For the hearers of Jesus, salvation was political. It meant deliverance from the enemies of Israel and economic prosperity. Jesus' vision of salvation was much broader, involving God's desire to reach out to all people, including tax-collectors and sinners. The parables in Luke 15 are told in order to show that salvation is about reaching out to the lost. Who are the lost today?

How can we be sensitive to proclaiming a gospel of salvation to people of other faiths? Salvation and healing share the same root word. What do salvation and healing have in common? What are the apparent differences?

What experience have you had of receiving God's healing? Do you think about salvation in terms of being saved from something or for something? How will our answers affect our approach to mission?

Today and throughout the week learn to cultivate the habit of praying for the stranger. See what strangers God brings into your life (such as a delivery person, a council employee, a shopkeeper, a traffic warden, a passing jogger or dog walker, the person standing next to you in a queue). Ask for God's blessing on that person. Ask that God will show himself to that person in some way. Ask that they might experience something of God's love for them or have an opportunity to hear about Jesus.

Start a conversation with a stranger this week – see what happens and where it leads.

ORDINARY TIME – DAY 56
CHANGING ATTITUDES

Isaiah 25.6–9

Neema Crafts Centre continues to make an impact on . . . prejudices towards disabled people in the local community. The centre sits beacon-like in the centre of town, in full view of the townsfolk – who continue to be astonished that such a lovely building was erected for people with disabilities, who would traditionally be hidden away at home, or left to fend for themselves begging on street corners. The cafe in particular has been a great help in drawing in more local people to see what goes on inside the building, and our customers continue to be amazed by the deaf chefs' cooking.

Before the cafe opened, deaf people in Iringa were routinely shooed out of local shops, because in local culture they were considered to be mentally unstable. Local people were either actively afraid of them or suspected that they wanted to steal from the shop, assuming that they wouldn't have any money to pay for their purchases. Now those same shopkeepers welcome our deaf people into their shops, and some of them will even move their other customers aside and beckon the deaf person to the front of the queue, so that they can show off their newly learned sign language greetings to the rest of their customers!

It's wonderful to see this change in local attitudes, as the work of Neema Crafts has always been not just about reaching out to people on the margins and bringing them back to the centre of the community, it's also about bringing the local community back into communion with those people who they had previously rejected.

Andy and Susie Hart, Tanzania

Neema Crafts involves barriers being broken down and bridges being built. What barriers do you believe need to be broken down in our society and where do we need bridges to be built?

Lord, we look forward to the day,
when all people will enjoy a rich feast together,
when disgrace will be removed from the earth,
when death will be swallowed up for ever.
We look forward to it –
and we pray that we may experience a foretaste
in our lives, in our communities, in our hope. Amen.

ORDINARY TIME – DAY 57
CLOTHED WITH COMPASSION

Colossians 3.12–15

Forgiveness is not an occasional act, it is a permanent attitude.

Martin Luther King (1929–68)

Today and in the coming days, examine your own life and consider whether you need to demonstrate or receive forgiveness towards someone else. Ask yourself:

- Do I constantly dwell upon a particular incident or experience in my life?
- Do I bring up a particular incident or experience to use against another person?
- Do I find it difficult to speak openly about such an incident or experience?
- Does this incident or experience prevent me from developing a better relationship with a particular person?

If you can answer 'Yes' to any of these questions, then you may need to receive or demonstrate forgiveness towards someone else.

Jesus, Lamb of God,
have mercy upon me.
Jesus, bearer of my sins,
have mercy upon me.
Jesus, redeemer of the world,
grant me, your peace.

ORDINARY TIME – DAY 58
SEEKING SHALOM

Jeremiah 29.4–7

It was summer 1991 that Dave was ordained to a curacy at St John's . . . and Southall can't get rid of us! Actually, in the midst of all our changes this year we have a renewed sense of recommitting ourselves locally – to our church, community and place – praying and working for the peace and well-being of the city to which God has called us (Jer. 29.4–7).

Southall has changed greatly in 20 years – from being 'Little India' to now having massive communities from Somalia, Sri Lanka and Afghanistan as well as India and Pakistan, and many groups from other places, too. It has become more overcrowded as landlords illegally subdivide terraced houses or put whole families in glorified garden sheds. There is terrible exploitation of those who are newly arrived, often escaping situations of conflict or terror and now lost without the language or knowledge to get by. Drugs are widely sold on our street, especially as children pour out of the secondary school on the next road. Alcohol abuse, gambling and prostitution are booming, and there is a seedy underworld of serious crime: people smuggling, illegal copying of DVDs and other consumer goods. Homelessness has also become a serious issue, especially among young men who either arrive illegally or innocently on student visas for courses that don't really exist. The *London Evening Standard* recently ran a front-page story on dozens of young Asian men sleeping rough in the communal bins on a local housing estate – finding some warmth amid rotting food and nappies. We've recently been featured as a national hotspot for both crime and terrorism. Yet Southall is a great place to live and bring up a family, and it's a place we passionately believe God loves.

Anne and Dave Bookless, Southall

Lord, may we seek shalom – wholeness and peace – in the places you have placed us to live, to serve, to bless. May we seek shalom so that no one is hungry and homeless, so that injustice is challenged, so that creation is renewed by your mercy and grace. Amen.

ORDINARY TIME – DAY 59
THE FEAR OF THE LORD

Psalm 111.10

While it is true that we have one of the lowest average Sunday attendances in the country, God is as much here at the heart of the new town as he is in any leafy suburban Bible-belt. There is a growing section of the community for whom church is either a distant memory or something that never played a part in their lives; yet they have some sense of their own spirituality and openness to the possibility of God. As one 20-something lady said recently, 'I think, I believe in who God was before the Church called him "God".'

Mark Berry

The fear of the Lord is the beginning of wisdom.

Lord, may we learn
not head knowledge and facts,
not religious language and concepts
but true fear of you, which is the beginning of wisdom.
Give us grace to see you in all places and all people
whatever language they use to express you. Amen.

ORDINARY TIME – DAY 60
HOLISTIC MISSION

2 Timothy 3.14–15

In one south-west Uganda community we are now busy constructing a new primary school. The site is located in a vast banana plantation. Despite the abundance of food and cash crops, it's hard to understand why there is poverty and even malnutrition. The local church sees education as the key; apparently many of the children are caught up in child labour with only a few large landowners benefiting from the profits of the harvest. Although the gospel has been proclaimed in the area for many years, the young pastor, Robert, once a street kid himself, explains, 'We need a holistic approach; without education, people remain oppressed, vulnerable and faith remains shallow.'

Garry Ion, Uganda

We praise you, Lord God, for the gift of education –
of asking questions, listening and growing together.
We pray that gift may bless all who search for knowledge and truth
and for all who seek to provide education and hope. Amen.

ORDINARY TIME – DAY 61
MEETING WITH THE MASAI

2 Samuel 22.29–30

A recent highlight for us was worshipping in a remote Masai village. The church had only been in existence for about two years but had grown significantly in this time. Their pastor had only heard the night before that we would be visiting. He was far away from home, but immediately set out so that he could be with us the next day. Unfortunately, the *dala dala* (people carrier) was only able to take him so far and then he had to walk some 30 miles through the night to reach the church in time for our service!

The worship was exuberant with the congregation jumping to the songs they sang, so pulsating with energy. During the service, I went outside the building for some fresh air and was asked by a man if I would pray for his sick child. I went back into the church at a point in the service when the pastor asked if anyone had anything to share, and at this point I called the man and his son forward for prayer. This sparked off a number of people coming forward for prayer and ministry.

The church had its beginnings when two Anglican pastors visited the village at a time when they had an outbreak of anthrax. One of the pastors was offered infected meat to eat but the Masai assured him that they had treated it with certain herbs and he would have no ill effects. He ate what they put before him and suffered no harm. They were so impressed by this that they hailed him as a 'man of faith' and declared that they would now believe in the Jesus he had been preaching to them about, and so began this wonderful church.

Adrian and Ruth Whitehall, Tanzania

You, Lord, are my lamp.
The Lord turns my darkness into light.
With your help I can advance against a troop.
With my God I can scale a wall.

ORDINARY TIME – DAY 62
GOD'S GRACE IN TIME OF DANGER

Isaiah 40.5

Isaiah speaks of comfort for God's people, but it seems to be in the context of great upheaval. Where I work, along with so many countries of the world, seems to be experiencing increasing upheaval. We are shocked when we read of killings of people. The following testimony illustrates how God provides comfort, revealing his power and glory as glimpses of the coming kingdom.

In January, B's brother was kidnapped. The kidnappers demanded a big ransom for his release. As B's brother was a widower, his children asked B to do something for the release of their father. He didn't involve the police in the issue initially as it is very hard to register a case in the police station and also because the kidnappers warned him not to do so. In answer to prayer, after one week, the local authorities helped B to register the case in the police station and the landlord, for whom his brother was working, provided financial help for his children. The police made a swift enquiry into the case and were able to arrest two people. Finally, after one month they conducted a raid on the place where his brother was being held. B takes up the story . . .

> I was with the police during that raid and was shocked to see that my brother was not there. But after just half an hour, I received one of the unforgettable calls from my little brother that my elder brother had reached home safely. The kidnappers released him before the raid and they escaped from the spot. They even gave some money to my brother to travel back to his home. My family and I were almost in tears and praising God who did that amazing miracle in our lives and especially in the life of my brother. My brother who once was never interested in listening to God's word is now a completely changed man and God is at the centre of his life. These difficult times brought my whole family closer to God and further strengthened our faith.

A CMS mission partner

Reflect on your own experience. Where has God rescued you and revealed his glory in times of trouble?

ORDINARY TIME – DAY 63
STREAMS OF LIVING WATER

John 7.38

The whole community has known Vanda for many years. She used to be a very angry person. She was always getting into fights, sometimes with a knife. She held the Living Waters Church in contempt. She did not know why, but could not stand those believers. She also drank heavily. Her whole family was very much the same and very disunited. There were 12 siblings, each with more difficult problems than the last – drinking, drugs, trafficking, weapons – all hidden inside the local garbage tip, where even the police didn't dare enter. Vanda was bringing up her children in the same way. She only came near the church when there was some benefit – a food parcel, a trip out for her children, or a party, but nothing more.

Yet, when she was sick, or a child was very ill, she called Pastor Siméa to come and pray in her house. That was the only contact Vanda wanted with the church, when there seemed no other solution to a problem.

But with the death of Vanda's believing mother, Pastor Siméa was called to the funeral and afterwards a thanksgiving service was held in church. Before the service, Pastor Siméa gathered the whole family together to talk about death, life and eternity. Siméa tried to treat them like a mother caring for children who were desperately lost. That was when Vanda grew to respect the pastor and the church. Gradually she entered into the life of our church family.

When a nephew was arrested for drug trafficking, or there was a quarrel in the family, the church was there to help sort things out. Vanda said, 'Slowly the love of God was touching my heart, so I gave my life to Jesus and was confirmed.' She then began to seek spiritual growth, because, in her words, 'I wanted to see my husband and my children changed.'

When Vanda's husband lost his job, he began meeting more with Siméa, and he and Vanda were amazed how quickly he found a new job.

He has given his life to Jesus but is still struggling to overcome drugs and alcohol. Vanda said she wanted to see her husband changed immediately, 'but I felt the Holy Spirit telling me not to worry because he'll complete the job he has begun. God is working. I did not believe in Jesus before, but now I see Jesus in my home.'

Ian and Siméa Meldrum, working in Living Waters Church in a
deprived area in Olinda, Brazil

Pray for all those battling addiction and facing unemployment. Pray that they may discover the living water of Jesus in their homes and their lives.

ORDINARY TIME – DAY 64
A DEEPER REALITY

Psalm 56.8–13

Pat Gilmer writes of her time in Uganda under the Idi Amin regime:

> I saw people killed, I saw dead bodies on the road, I picked up people who died in my car after beatings, I found patients who had had their backs beaten raw. I even nearly got shot once. I heard some terrible screaming near where I was working, and I ran out. They were dislocating a man's shoulders, and they'd put another man on the ground, and they were pegging him out for the sun to make him blind. I screamed at them, I really screamed at them, 'You stop it! You're not allowed to torture!' Perhaps stunned, the soldiers stopped what they were doing. But the constant strain of travelling through barrier after barrier, maintained by troops looking for bribes or just on a power trip, never knowing when things might turn nasty, took its toll.
>
> It broke me, it really broke me to live in that situation, where everybody was frightened, where we'd had public executions. But I found something happening inside myself, which made me hunger to know God. I said, 'Father, I need a reality with you, deeper than even I've got now, to live in a world like this.'

So after carrying the leprosy programme for 19 years, and describing herself as 'absolutely flaked', Pat came back to the UK. But she describes her lowest ebb as a real gift.

> God met me at a great depth then and my whole prayer life changed. I became much more contemplative in my praying and my thinking.

Pat describes this experience as 'far, far deeper' than 'baptism in the Holy Spirit'. 'You just know God in some way has taken you in his arms and given you such a hug – and changed your mindset.' She came to understand how different prayer can be from the 'shopping lists' we so often make. 'There were nights when I wept for the country, and my own inner pain was my prayer.'

Do we see our inner pain as gift of prayer to God? Where does God touch you with the pain of the world? Spend time praying for that place of pain.

ORDINARY TIME – DAY 65
THE BLESSING OF DISCOMFORT

Luke 19.41–44

May God bless you with a restless discomfort
about easy answers, half-truths and superficial relationships,
so that you may seek truth boldly and love deep within
your heart.

May God bless you with holy anger at injustice, oppression,
and exploitation of people, so that you may tirelessly work for
justice, freedom, and peace among all people.

May God bless you with the gift of tears to shed with those
who suffer from pain, rejection, starvation, or the loss of all
that they cherish, so that you may reach out your hand to
comfort them and transform their pain into joy.

May God bless you with enough foolishness to believe that
you really can make a difference in this world, so that you are
able, with God's grace, to do what others claim cannot be done.

And the blessing of God the Supreme Majesty and our
Creator, Jesus Christ the Incarnate Word who is our brother
and Saviour, and the Holy Spirit, our Advocate and Guide, be
with you and remain with you, this day and for evermore. Amen.

A fourfold Franciscan blessing

*Pray the blessing for yourself, allowing the words to sink in and impact
you.*

ORDINARY TIME – DAY 66
SPACE TO REST

John 4.4–6

I was recently given a book to read by a colleague on the topic of 'rest',
with particular reference to Christian ministry whether full time or part
time. The book uses the story of Jesus resting by the well (John 4) as its
anchor, reflecting on parts of the story: the journey Jesus was making,
the need for a rest, and the refreshing water he drank while he rested.
Reading this book is a timely reminder to me of the need to stop, to rest
and reflect, and it is somewhat ironic, therefore, that I am writing this on
my supposed 'day off', as I haven't had time during the week.

Alison Fletcher, Uganda

Lord, inspire in us a deeper awareness of our needs –
our need to reflect and rest,
our need to drink deep of the life-giving waters you provide in abundance.
Give us grace to stop, as you did,
and to be refreshed and restored. Amen.

ORDINARY TIME – DAY 67
SPACE TO REFLECT

Mark 6.31–32

We choose to be busy, because it facilitates our consumerist lifestyle that requires us to work harder and harder and to fulfil our consumerist ambitions. It distracts us from the deeper realities of life. When given space for stillness and silence, we prefer to rationalize our discomfort rather than face the sources of our restlessness. Communities who build in contemplation as a regular practice can begin to address these sources of restlessness. It is a gift we can offer non-Christians as they search for ways to de-stress and become less anxious in what has been described as 'the general mayhem' of modern life.

Christopher Jamieson

Is taking time regularly to review your prayer life, your mission, your commitment to social justice, part of your Christian journey? How has it benefitted you in the past? How might it benefit you in the future?

Servant Christ,
help us to follow you
into the place of quiet
to intercede for the confused, the despairing
the anxiety-driven,
to prepare ourselves for costly service with you;
Servant Christ, help us to follow you. Amen.

Litany of the Disciples of Christ the Servant, India

ORDINARY TIME – DAY 68
REST IS GOOD

Matthew 11.28–30

Resting has been a bit of a theme in my Christian journey, and I write as a recovering workaholic. It was the invitation of Jesus to come to him and rest that I first found irresistible as a young student, but some years ago I realized that I had relapsed rather badly and become a prime example of that living contradiction – the busy Christian. I was always looking out for my next job for God and it was a shock when, at the end of a conference week on the theme of 'calling', I heard again the call of Jesus to rest.

In Leviticus 25.4 we read that the land given by God to the Israelites must itself observe a Sabbath rest before the Lord every seventh year. It sounds as if the land has a worship life all of its own, that in order to work properly, everything that is created needs to be in a right relationship with its Creator.

In the case of the Israelites, they care for each other as they care for the land – letting the land rest *is* going to pay off in terms of increased productivity, but also in providing for people who don't own land of their own – who are to get food from it during the Sabbath year.

In Matthew's Gospel (11—12), Jesus' invitation to come to him and rest is immediately followed by the account of his attitude towards the Sabbath.

The Pharisees want to give the disciples the equivalent of a speeding fine for picking grain on the Sabbath, but Jesus tells them they're missing the point and that he is Lord of the Sabbath. When Jesus heals a man's shrivelled hand on the Sabbath, it acts as a trigger for the Pharisees to plot his murder.

In Jesus the legalists had found a rule-breaker. The world is given to us to enjoy, and the need for rest is built into creation. Jesus doesn't cancel the Sabbath, but takes it over and gives it back to those who will receive it from him.

As ministers of Christ, we help others to recognize that the earth belongs to him because he made it. Perhaps that recognition is exactly what Sabbath is.

As lovers of Christ, we help ourselves by coming to him for rest and allowing him to be our God – and that takes time.

Pippa Soundy

Send down, O God, O Gentle and Compassionate One, into my heart faith and tranquillity and stillness, that I may be one of those whose hearts are tranquillized by the mention of God.

Ibn-al-Arabi

ORDINARY TIME – DAY 69
THE WIDER VIEW

Hebrews 4.9–11

Over the summer, we spent a few weeks staying on a farm, on top of a hill above the Aire Valley. From there, we had a wonderful view of the moors and hills, and a real sense of being on holiday (which was actually the case for the children, but not so much for us!). We were struck by the privilege of living in a place where we could see the wider view. Just five minutes away, down in the town in the valley, life was hectic and busy and full of work and shops and businesses and people living their everyday lives. What a privilege to be able to literally withdraw from all that and come away to a quiet place, where we could see the big picture beyond the workaday life of the valley.

In some ways, this is a picture of how our lives are, being for much of the time in the midst of the workaday reality of everything we do . . . yet having the privilege of being able to come away from all that and see the wider view.

We continue to be struck by the importance of each of us resting in who God has made us to be, in the place he has put us, and letting God do his work through us. As society changes so quickly, we both know that ultimately only Christ is worthy of our allegiance and pray that each of us, as his followers, will shed his light wherever we are.

Martin and Pam Lawson

O God, our hearts are homesick until they rest in thee, for thou hast made them for thyself.

Augustine of Hippo (354–430)

ORDINARY TIME – DAY 70
STILLNESS AND ACTION

Luke 4.42–44

Jesus' daily way of life is revealing. In the Gospels we find him practising a repeated cycle of prayer in solitude – often in the open air, sometimes at night – energizing him for action and conversation in the day. Both are connected; the flow from stillness into action and back again are part of a seamless whole, a connected life.

    As you go into prayer, choose a place, find a time and adopt a posture that you know may help you to be still. When the time comes to move into action, imagine this to be an extension of your prayer, repeating to yourself 'this too is prayer'.

Ian Adams

A simple prayer you can use to accompany this exercise:

Praying Jesus
be with me in stillness – this is prayer.
Engaging Jesus
be with me in action – this too is prayer.

ORDINARY TIME – DAY 71
IN THE BEGINNING

John 1.1–2

A friend of mine, a Japanese Christian missionary in Thailand, has among his acquaintances a few deeply religious Buddhist monks. On one occasion they decided to enter into theological discussion, and as part of the process resolved to study together their respective scriptures. One of the books they chose was John's Gospel. So, one day, they began the study of John, and started with the first verse of the first chapter, 'In the beginning was the Word.' 'My,' said one of the Buddhist monks, 'even in the beginning you Christians didn't have a little time for silence!'

There is no doubt about it that those of other faiths often find us Christians a noisy and boisterous people, with no great depth to us, and little time for quiet.

T. K. Thomas, South Indian editorial secretary of the
Christian Literature Society of Madras

Oh, make my heart so still, so still,
   When I am deep in prayer,
That I may hear the white mist-wreaths
   Losing themselves in air.

Utsonomiya: a Japanese leprosy patient

ORDINARY TIME – DAY 72
BREATHING LIFE INTO PRAYER

Matthew 6.7

Before the missionaries came, my people used to sit outside their temples for a long time meditating and preparing themselves before entering. Then they would virtually creep to the altar and offer their petition and afterwards would again sit a long time outside, this time – as they put it – to 'breathe life' into their prayers. The Christians, when they came, just got up, uttered a few sentences, said 'Amen' and were done. For that reason, my people called them Haolis – 'without breath', meaning, those who failed to breathe life into their prayers.

James Michener

Lord, I just don't know what to say when I am asked to make a prayer. It is like being asked to breathe.

Young Indian Christian participant in School on Worship, South India

ORDINARY TIME – DAY 73
PLANNED NEGLECT

Luke 10.38–42

In order to live a fully rounded life, life as God intends it to be, we must include things other than our work. This almost inevitably means leaving something undone. For us, planned neglect will mean deliberately choosing which things we will leave undone or postpone, so that instead of being oppressed by a clutter of unfinished jobs, we think out our priorities under God and then accept without guilt or resentment the fact that much that we had thought we ought to do we must leave.

We shall often be tempted into guilty feelings when we do take time off. But we should then remind ourselves that such guilt is a sin against the generosity of the Spirit, and also extremely infectious.

The Companions of Brother Lawrence: Rule of Life

Lord, in the midst of busyness and demands, may we remember the better – and needful – things and be wise in setting priorities. Amen.

ORDINARY TIME – DAY 74
GOING SLOW

Genesis 1.31 – 2.3

Are you a fast person or a slow person?
Do you want to slow down or speed up?
Is your life already fast or slow?
Are you in a fast place or a slow place –
    spiritually, mentally, physically?
Do you want to be in a fast place or a slower place?
How fast or slow do you want to get there?

Do you seek slow love and fast food? or vice versa?
Is work too fast and travel too slow? or vice versa?
Are you a contemplative trapped inside a commuter?
If the motorway is empty do you slow down or speed up?
Is your computer too slow or too fast?

O God, you are slow to anger and swift to have mercy,
Forgive us when we treat time as a commodity
Or an enemy
When we abuse your gift of time.

In our fastness and our slowness,
Help us to keep pace with you.

Free us to live in your time, a new time,
In which there is a time for everything under heaven,
And slow is not too slow, and fast is not too fast.

Transform us into people who see time as a gift
And a friend
Who live as if we have time,
Because we know that your time will never cease. Amen.

Mike Rose and Anna Poulson

ORDINARY TIME – DAY 75
WORDS AND SILENCE

Romans 8.26

We continue a series exploring some apparent paradoxes in prayer wondering about the connection between words and silence.

Prayer is often, of course, our activity. We find a space to pray, we look for words to give shape to our prayer, and we even seem to decide when the praying is over. But there's also a strong Christian tradition that sees prayer as primarily God's activity within us. God the Father drawing us into the divine life, Jesus the Son praying in and through us, and the Holy Spirit making prayer within us when we do not know how to pray.

When you go into prayer today write your words on a piece of paper. When you are ready, put down your pen, and put the paper to one side. Take out a blank sheet of paper. Let this open space symbolize the way in which God may be praying in you.

Ian Adams

A simple prayer you can use to accompany this exercise:
God take me from my words, to your prayer.

ORDINARY TIME – DAY 76
ANCIENT AND NEW

Luke 18.9–13

There can be great vitality in the prayers and prayerful actions that we create ourselves, in our own language, in our own style, in our own setting. There's also great strength in the prayers and prayerful actions of the Church, prayers that have been prayed and actions that have been made for centuries.

So when you pray today, begin with a prayer in your own words, accompanied by your own instinctive prayerful action. Then pray an ancient prayer and take an ancient stance. You could kneel, and use this ancient prayer from the Orthodox Church, often called the 'Jesus Prayer'. Repeat the prayer slowly, let it carry all your hopes and yearnings . . .

Ian Adams

Lord Jesus Christ, Son of God, have mercy on me, a sinner . . .

ORDINARY TIME – DAY 77
SETTLEMENT AND MOVEMENT

2 Samuel 6.14

There's something very strong about being rooted in one place. To stand still, to be settled, our feet firmly connected to one piece of ground, gives an earthy sense of connection to all of creation.

There's also something life-giving in movement. Walking, running, cycling and swimming can all sharpen our sense of being alive.

So try to pray today when you are moving. Let the rhythm of your movement shape and carry your prayers. You might like to use this prayer as you go . . .

Ian Adams

Holy Trinity, God of place, flow and movement
Hold me, shape me, move me . . .

ORDINARY TIME – DAY 78
PRE-PRE-EVANGELISM

Matthew 13.1–9

I have come up with a new word. Pre-pre-evangelism means what you do before you consider pre-evangelism.

You see, pre-evangelism is described as 'preaching a message to the unconverted and unsaved people of the world that they can understand and will lead them first and foremost into the knowledge that God exists, created all things, and is in ultimate control of all things'.

There are two aspects that disturb me as I reflect on this definition; one, how do you preach to people who are not exposed to any concept resembling God, and without presenting verbose arguments suited only for the literate? Is the gospel reserved for the schooled? We have found it almost impossible to 'preach' on Harpurhey streets and pubs.

Second, the definition above seems not to address the society or community that surrounds the individual. Human beings were made to function not as individuals but as part of a community. The community that surrounds an individual determines what they give consideration to and how they engage with 'new thinking'. Christianity is a community concept. It can hardly be understood by the individualistic mind, made worse if that mind has been hurt in prior years by all they know as church.

Church on the streets has been evolving within its six-year life, as we have translated and reflected on these difficulties. The best way to articulate the vision of church on the streets is now 'Rediscovering, Inspiring and Enabling the development of shared values among the peoples of Harpurhey, with the express goal of Community cohesion'. This vision stands in hope that faith thrives in community, and that in the future, when evangelism is done in Harpurhey, there will be success.

Cyprian and Jayne Yobera, Manchester

Father, give us grace and imagination as
   we prepare the soil for planting,
as we build community,
as we discover shared values,
as we sow seeds. Amen.

ORDINARY TIME – DAY 79
COMMUNITY IN CHRIST

Galatians 3.26–30

Christianity means community through Jesus Christ and in Jesus Christ. No Christian community is more or less than this. Whether it be a brief single encounter or the daily fellowship of years, Christian community is only this. We belong to one another only in and through Jesus Christ.

Dietrich Bonhoeffer (1906–45)

Thank God for the gift of community that we enjoy as Christians – whether in brief encounters or lasting fellowship.

O Lord and Master, who are yourself the truth and the way, we thank you for the fellowship of your people in which the unknown are well known, and the stranger is at home. Make our hearts and minds so welcome your words that in us they may richly dwell and from us any surely pass in their way into all the world. Amen.

ORDINARY TIME – DAY 80
FRIENDSHIP AND THE GOSPEL

James 5.7

The overlap with parents at school and the gospel message was a real excitement to me this year as, for the first time, I felt it was the right time to invite children of four friends, one of whom is Muslim, to join the Easter Christian club. And in fact all of the families allowed their children to come! It was a huge reassurance after many hours spent being friends over the school gate or at coffee time – that until now has shown nothing in terms of 'mission' – that it has all been part of God's patient timing of trust and friendship, which leads to doors opening in people's lives to glimpse Jesus. In particular, one mother who isn't a churchgoer responded to my invitation saying she 'just really wants her kids to go somewhere they can learn about what Easter means and who Jesus is'!

David and Amy Roche, France

Lord – give us grace to persevere in building friendships and to trust in your timing. Amen.

ORDINARY TIME – DAY 81
THE POWER OF PRAYER

1 Thessalonians 5.16–18

Alf Cooper writes of the experience of the Chilean miners who were trapped underground and then dramatically rescued:

The engineer, André Sougarret, the brains behind the rescue but not a believer himself, said publicly: 'In the drilling process, things happened

that held no logic with engineering. I believe that something happened.'
He attributed it to an energy generated through prayer and goodwill.

Several have expressed the wish to give all the glory to God. The reason is that they share very simply how their spiritual awakening began under the landslide. They say that during the first moments of the accident, the younger miners panicked greatly. The older more experienced miners also felt that they were going to die but tried not to show it. José Herniquez told me that that was the moment he heard God's voice: 'Call them together.' He did so and said: 'We may seem to have lost everything at present, brothers, but we still have prayer.' So they held hands and he prayed. They sensed then the living presence and power of God as well as being given a renewed sense of hope. They were almost a kilometre underground but God was with them! They prayed from then onwards at noon and at 6 pm every day and were often aware of God's real presence.

Jose told me that only five had descended the mines with a close relationship with God, but 22 received Christ underground. All 33 came to the surface speaking of the reality of God's help in their extreme time of need.

May we learn to pray at all times, whatever circumstances we face, and may we learn to see your hand and your presence in the midst of our lives. Amen.

ORDINARY TIME – DAY 82
OPENLY THANKFUL

Luke 17.11–19

We have been inspired here in Bangladesh by the public and corporate way of thanking God for his gifts to us. What often strikes us is that following an answer to prayer, God is so clearly and publicly thanked. Sometimes at the office *mishit* (sweets) or lunch is provided by a staff member, to celebrate and thank God for answered prayers such as a new grandchild or good exam results. Bishu, the office cook, cooked lunch one day for all the office staff on the church compound. It was her way of thanking God that she had finally been able to put a tin roof on her village house where one day she will go back and live. It was a real privilege to share in that with her.

David and Sarah Hall, Bangladesh

Today, and in the coming week, consciously look for opportunities to show thankfulness to God and to share it with others.

ORDINARY TIME – DAY 83
INSPIRING COURAGE, CHANGING LIVES

Isaiah 61.1–3

On 10 April 1911, a doctor, a linguist/pastor and an explorer arrived at the sugar plantation of Leach Bros in northern Argentina with the intention of meeting Indian migrant workers from the Chaco forest. The three men had previously been involved in similar missions in Paraguay and Patagonia. Their peaceful encounter led to the establishment of missionary work in the area, which 100 years later has led to an Indian-led church of some 20,000 members in over 120 towns and villages, and several cities.

Over the decades it has helped bring survival, dignity, spiritual life, health, education, development and justice to the peoples in whose communities it exists. There are many stories of God's work in people's lives and of the outstanding ministries of missionaries and Indian leaders alike. Unlike parts of the British Empire where the arrival of Christianity was some-times too closely associated with commerce and civilization, the Chaco missions tended to shun these despite their original contacts through the sugar harvest. However, there will certainly be some debate this year about the successes and failings of the development of the church in this century. Celebrations are underway, which start at Easter with a meeting in Misión Chaqueña, and continue all year in different places, including conferences, church services, publication of a book, and t-shirts with a commemorative logo. This will give an opportunity for the older people to remember what difference the gospel made to their lives, and also for the younger genera-tion to visualize what changes it can bring to their future.

Today we need to ask in what ways this church can still be a bearer of good news. In some places it has become part of the social fabric of Indian society, and faces a totally different set of challenges. In others it is one of many options. Let us pray that the unchanging gospel will continue to inspire courage and change lives.

Nick and Catherine Drayson, Argentina

Reflect on how the Church today can still be a bearer of good news.

ORDINARY TIME – DAY 84
FROM THE MOUTHS OF CHILDREN . . .

Matthew 21.15–16

After taking the Listening to Children module of Viva's Celebrating Children course, caregivers at a World Vision project in Uganda organized a committee of 12 children to give their opinions and ideas on the running of the project. Immediately the children declared that they wanted to start their own garden at the school. World Vision provides seeds and tools for adults to farm their own land, but the children wanted to learn these skills for themselves. The seeds World Vision gave the children not only provided enough maize to feed the 210 children attending the project's school, but the cost of the school lunch was lowered so much that 90 new students were able to attend school who couldn't afford to before. Now the students have also been given orange trees and cassava to plant in the school garden.

A proud caregiver says: 'Through their own doing, the children secured their own nutritional well-being and enabled others to receive an education.' Listening to children helped these adults learn the value of children's ideas, and the result has been both nutritious and educational for hundreds of children.

Isabel Booth-Clibborn

Are we prepared to listen to children and respect their creativity and ideas? Do we see children as engaged in mission just as much as adults are? How might our churches be different if children were key players?

Father of all, may we learn to listen to children and to learn from them, as we serve and worship you together. Amen.

ORDINARY TIME – DAY 85
'WE DID IT OURSELVES'

1 Thessalonians 5.11

Go to the people
Live among them
Learn from them
Love them
Start with what they know
Build on what they have
But of all the best leaders
When their task is done
The people will remark
'We have done it ourselves.'

A Chinese proverb

Think of a person who has encouraged and built you up in faith, perhaps as a child, perhaps over many years, perhaps recently. Thank God for that person.

Pray that we may become real encouragers of one another, learning from, loving, and building on each other's gifts.

ORDINARY TIME – DAY 86
PLANTING FOR GROWTH

Mark 4.30–32

This is a perfect picture to describe Jigsaw. God sent Tim and myself as the sowers. We took with us a seed, which in our case was a belief that children are important and need places they can go to that share God's love and salvation. Places where there is security, self-esteem, community, creativity, boundaries and grace. Places where they are the focus. Places where love can grow.

We planted that seed in the lives of the staff and communities that Jigsaw worked in. The roots of the seed grew by working alongside people, modelling good children's work, implementing boundaries of accountability, justice, management and leadership systems.

Today, a new phase in our life and Jigsaw's life has started. These are exciting times but also heartbreaking times. In September of last year both myself and Tim knew that God was asking us to take a step of faith in our trust of him for our life and Jigsaw's.

The staff at Jigsaw have over the years received a fair amount of training in kids' work, management, welfare and Bible study. The Jigsaw team is now a strong one, united in their goal to see their own communities changed and children's lives transformed through knowing Jesus. The team have again and again proved their capabilities in planning, preparing and delivering excellent programmes while also being flexible in dealing with various crises and problems.

So in many ways the job that Tim and I came to do is now nearly done. Our focus over the six years has been on empowerment, training and encouragement, and the results of this are now evident. It's painful as no one likes to feel that they are no longer needed but the truth has become more and more apparent. We feel like parents who have nurtured their child and now need to accept the fact that they need to leave and let them grow up. It's hard and painful but we know it's the right thing.

Jigsaw would not have existed had we not been placed in Manila by God, but God never intended us to build an organization that relies on us to stay for years and years to run it.

Kate Lee, Jigsaw Children's Project in Manila, Philippines

Pray for Jigsaw and similar projects where people are being empowered to lead and develop.

ORDINARY TIME – DAY 87
TENDING THE SHOOT

Hosea 14.5–6

At Jigsaw we really believe that all people are created by God to be equal – equally valued, loved and significant. This belief extends to how Jigsaw is run, who is employed and what we do. As the foreigner here, we cannot change the Philippines – it has to be done by Filipinos for Filipinos.

We want Jigsaw to be seen as a light in dark communities, showing that in God there is a different reality. We also want to show that Filipinos can run something for themselves that is worthwhile. Right now, the longer that Tim and I are a visible presence here the more we reinforce the idea that projects can only successfully be run and administered by foreigners. So we propose to continue to dedicate our life and energy to Jigsaw but behind the scenes.

Right now Jigsaw is a large shoot, but the vision is that it will grow into a big strong tree within the community, a tree that provides places of refuge and safety for the urban poor and street children who live nearby. Although the tree will have characteristics of the original seed (that is what Tim and I brought to it), it must grow to be a wholly Filipino tree that is developed within the culture and context of urban poor life. If not, how can the birds of that place – the kids – live in a tree that is not familiar to them?

The shoot of Jigsaw at the moment is the family centres, with kids clubs, literacy programmes and school sponsorship. These places are so vital and so desperately needed for bringing change, as the poverty and abuse are horrendous. Where there is a Jigsaw centre, change is happening, but this shoot now needs to be tended and given space for God to grow it.

So the next stage for us is the tending, supporting, watering and protecting of the shoot. It is the responsibility of the sower (that is us) to do this. If not, it will be eaten or destroyed, or lost in a storm. So this next stage of growth in Jigsaw is just as vital as the six years we have spent sowing the seed, putting down roots and growing the shoot.

Tim and Kate Lee, Philippines

Lord, give us grace to tend, support, water and protect the shoots we
plant –
But to know that you are the one who brings life and growth
To let go, and to trust your providence. Amen.

ORDINARY TIME – DAY 88
BROKENHEARTED

Zechariah 9.16 –17a

You have broken my heart.
I cannot stop thinking about you.
I love you even though I have met you only once.
I looked at you through tear-filled eyes.
Others may have given up on you, not realizing your
potential but I see something in you.
You made me cry but you have helped me to realize
what is important in life.
You have been someone who has begun
to change something in my life.
You sparked something in me; a desire to change lives,
beginning with you.
We have not spoken to each other.
You did not even hold my hand.
You have not looked at me or even acknowledged me,
but I still love you.

Amy Dawkins, Ecuador

We thank you, Lord, for your promises, that all who are downtrod-
den will one day sparkle in your land like jewels in a crown. May we
see in one another your beauty and honour one another by our love.
Amen.

ORDINARY TIME – DAY 89
WHAT DO YOU DO?

John 17.6–19

What do you do? . . . What do you do when the people on your street (the street you love) are in such dire need? What do you do when your neighbour (a fantastic family man, helpful in the community and very handy – selflessly so) is picked up by the police and 'thrown in', leaving his family struggling for sheer survival? What do you do when your other neighbour (whom you have grown to trust as a friend) is a 'distributor' and uses the teenage children of your other friend as runners? What do you do when your newest street dweller is robbed twice in the same month and consequently moves off the street? What do you do when a good member of the residents association has her door kicked in while her partner is at work, while she is looking after her one-year-old and four-year-old in the house? And by four hooded men who had obviously mistaken her house for a den?

These are just a few things that have happened in the last six months on my street. The question is: What do you do? What does one do to be effective in a community like this? Leaving is not an option.

Cyprian and Jayne Yobera, Manchester

What do you do? What do you do in the midst of the pain and suffering of the world? How might we respond together as a community of Christians?

Lord,
there are no easy answers,
no quick-fix solutions to the pain and suffering of this world.
And yet, we trust.
We trust that you are with us.
We trust that you will always be with us.
You did not choose to take us out of the world,

but you promise to protect us from the evil one.
Lord, consecrate us again in your truth.
Send us out again to share your gospel,
to respond with grace and love and mercy,
even when we cannot know what to do,
so that lives may be transformed.
Consecrate us, Lord and unite us as your people –
a people of mission, a people of light, a people of love. Amen.

ORDINARY TIME – DAY 90
SETTING CAPTIVES FREE

Isaiah 58.6–8

A Vineyard church in Southampton challenged members to live at the level of welfare recipients for a period of time and to give the surplus money to the Jubilee 2009 Fund. This small congregation managed to release an amazing £24,000.

Tom Sine

How can we use all we have (however little that may be) to bring freedom and transformation?

Come, Holy Spirit, grant us the gospel of Jubilee, the good news of liberation, freedom and unity; proclaim the release of the prisoners of division; recover the sight of those blinded by hatred, jealousy, greed and power; grant peace and freedom for the poor, oppressed, and lost. Amen.

Korea: Prayers for 1995 as a Year of Jubilee for Unification

ORDINARY TIME – DAY 91
THE PEARL OF GREAT PRICE

Matthew 13.45–46

In addition to developing a crèche for the children of sex workers in Pune, India's red light district, CMS co-mission partner Dr Lalita Edwards also has a special ministry to the local *hijra* or *kinnar* (eunuchs), whom she calls 'my special people'. She befriends them and serves them however she can. They call her *uma* (Mum or Aunty).

On a recent visit, I met Penna, Koelli and Keralla; all three have come out of the sex trade. In her small one-room flat over a cuppa chai, Penna showed me pictures of her dancing days. With all her make up, she looked like Greta Garbo. Then, she earned 10,000 rupees a night dancing. But she wouldn't go back. Now she has a sense of peace and purpose. At one point she sang me a song: *Koi bhi chore mujhe, Jesus kebhi nehin chorega* ('Even if others leave me, Jesus will never leave me').

Phil Simpson, India

We praise you, Lord, that life in you is the pearl of great price,
that you promise us new life and riches beyond all else we have known,
that you promise never to leave us. Amen.

ORDINARY TIME – DAY 92
PASSION FOR SERVICE

Luke 9.12–17

Tango (Together As Neighbours Giving Out) was spawned by a small group of people led by Avril, who was moved and motivated by the deprivation that dominates whole sections of our community. Under her leadership, they built up a thriving ministry, connecting with scores of families, opening a common meeting place, and providing clothing, food and furniture on a huge scale. Again, the emphasis was on 'what we have in common' (in this case a common concern for the disadvantaged), and again the building blocks of church were put in place, with cell groups, pastoral care, and a worship gathering. As it developed, the feeling had emerged that our own church building would quite frankly feel too 'posh' for many of the Tango clientele, so an alternative venue was set up. Fascinatingly, both church and Tango offer lunches each day, situated on opposite sides of the same road, both consistently busy, yet offering startlingly different menus, prices and approach. Each of them is working with 'what we have in common', but with two very different cultures that exist on opposite sides of the same parish fence.

They are also operating out of the gifts and vision of one person, who happens to have a passion for hospitality, a lifelong connection with the church and community, and an even bigger heart for the poor.

Phil Potter

Jesus says (v. 13), 'Give them something to eat yourselves.' Where do your passions, or the passions of your local church, connect with the differing needs of your community? How might your church building be used (or not!) to welcome people?

Pray that our churches may receive all guests as they would receive Christ himself.

From Rwanda

ORDINARY TIME – DAY 93
MAKING THE MOST OF OUR LIVES

Ephesians 5.15

I would never expect to find happy people living among rubbish but for many Christians who live in that very poor community, they are some of the happiest people I have ever met because they really can see the difference Jesus makes in people's lives. In the Western world we often source our happiness from materialistic things, but these people, who are very materialistically poor, are spiritually very rich.

Andy and Rose Roberts, Brazil

Andy and his Brazilian wife Rose work as mission partners at the My Father's House project for vulnerable boys, which works in partnership with the Living Waters Church in a bid to reach out to the surrounding community – a particularly dangerous area – to support people both physically and spiritually through faith in Jesus Christ. The couple are also youth leaders at Living Waters – which was set up beside the rubbish dump back in 1993 by CMS mission partners Ian and Siméa Meldrum.

Andy first met Rose when he was in short-term mission, working at the Living Waters Church during his gap year, aged 18, in 2004. This was Rose's home church; her family are from the area around the church and she was brought up in the shanty town. Through the dance ministry of Living Waters Church, Rose became a Christian in 2001, and she's been a leader of the dance group, called MISART, ever since.

Andy's placement in Brazil shaped the rest of his life. 'I thought I would be in Brazil for just six months, but God had other plans.' Working with the street children on the shanty town, Andy says his eyes were 'opened' and he was challenged about his role in the world. 'I realized that in the short time we have on this earth we need to use that for God's glory and make the most of our lives.'

May we use the short time we have on earth to your glory – starting today. Amen.

ORDINARY TIME – DAY 94
I'D RATHER HAVE JESUS . . .

Matthew 6.24

This world and that to come are enemies. We cannot therefore be friends of both but must resolve which to forsake and which to enjoy.

Clement of Rome

This quotation has stayed with me ever since I came upon it a few months ago, subconsciously influencing several sermons and talks that I have given recently. It fits well with one of the hymns in our chapel hymnbook, which also persistently runs around in my head, and which I seem to choose to sing every time I preach:

> I'd rather have Jesus, than silver or gold,
> I'd rather be his, than have riches untold;
> I'd rather have Jesus than houses or lands,
> I'd rather be led by his nail-pierced hands.

It is easy enough to sing this, but I have to keep asking whether this is really true for me. Which kingdom am I really in love with – this one or the one to come? Many people assume that for mission partners this question has been clearly settled, but this is not true. Often our lives here are very comfortable and it is not such a great sacrifice – apart from being separated from family and friends . . . and perhaps missing out on a few, small, creature comforts. Nor are we particularly 'spiritual' people, doing amazing things.

Hugh Skeil

> I'd rather have Jesus, than silver or gold,
> I'd rather be his, than have riches untold;
> I'd rather have Jesus than houses or lands,
> I'd rather be led by his nail-pierced hands.

Rhea F. Miller

ORDINARY TIME – DAY 95
BE AVAILABLE

Romans 12.13

On 6 May 1980, I arrived in Bunia for the first time, feeling that I had arrived 'home'. Now as I look back over 30 years, I am so grateful to the Lord for his calling on my life. I knew nothing about the Congo, and yet as I look back I am amazed how wonderfully he has planned my life. As Westerners, what we do is always important to who we are and where we find our identity. But to the Congolese, it is through relationships, sharing oneself with others, even the vulnerable, weak parts that one discovers who one truly is. To them relationships are more important than the work done.

When I first went out and lived in a village called Komanda with Bridget Lane, a CMS mission partner, I was grateful for the way she shared her life so openly and freely with the Congolese. Through her example I learned how to live, to be available, to put people before work and to share my home with others. I think the record of how many stayed in Bunia was when I had every bedroom full and at least 20 sleeping on the floor in the sitting room, during the celebrations for the inauguration of our Province! It was not always easy and yet this has been a tremendous richness over the years because as I have related to others, so others have freely related to me and we have built up long-lasting deep relationships.

Judy Acheson, Democratic Republic of Congo

O God, our heavenly Father, your son Jesus Christ enjoyed rest and refreshment in the home of Martha and Mary of Bethany; give us the will to love you, open our hearts to hear you, and strengthen our hearts to serve you in others for his sake; who lives and reigns with you and the Holy Spirit, one God, now and for ever. Amen.

From the USA

ORDINARY TIME – DAY 96

BE HOSPITABLE

1 Peter 4.12

In 1 Peter 4, we read about the suffering of Jesus, and the suffering his followers go through as they walk the narrow way. We go through difficulties too, maybe in the form of rejection, abandonment or unfaithfulness, from society, family, friends, colleagues. I have known this; I'm sure you have too.

Peter says that if we want to survive and even thrive in these times, we need to forgive the offender, focus on God, face the future, and find supportive relationships. One aspect of this support is hospitality. When I looked up 'hospitality' on Wikipedia I read that it refers to the relationship process between a guest and a host, and it also refers to the act or practice of being hospitable, that is, the reception and entertainment of guests, visitors, or strangers, with liberality and goodwill.

In 1976, I went with two friends to visit Christians in Hungary. Our purpose was to be an encouragement to them, because at that time, there was a lot of persecution for Christians in Eastern Europe, and the people we met were no exception. Their faithfulness to Jesus meant they were unable to travel outside the country and were banned from worshipping openly; in addition, some could not get jobs, those in work were frequently denied promotion, and consequently money was in short supply. Here were people who really were suffering for Jesus, and it was humbling to be there.

One day we went to a house for tea, a little uncomfortable that we were putting anyone out for us, for after all, we were there to encourage – not to take the little they had. We were met by a very elderly lady who opened a door to her tiny lounge and the sight that greeted us was incredible, for she had laid out a banquet that was truly fit for heaven. What amazing hospitality! We were invited to take our seats and feast, while our hostess delighted in our joy.

Peter, when describing the tough times the people of God go through, advises us to serve, encourage and help those in need, to practise hospitality. He knows that one of the best responses to suffering is to focus away from yourself and focus on others by serving and blessing them. St Francis knew this, it is a loud and clear message from his famous prayer, the Prayer of St Francis.

Paul Morris

Pray this as you reflect on our call to be hospitable to one another:

Lord, make me an instrument of thy peace; where there is hatred, let me sow love; where there is injury, pardon; where there is doubt, faith; where there is despair, hope; where there is darkness, light; and where there is sadness, joy. O Divine Master, grant that I may not so much seek to be consoled as to console; to be understood, as to understand; to be loved, as to love; for it is in giving that we receive, it is in pardoning that we are pardoned, and it is in dying that we are born to Eternal Life. Amen.

ORDINARY TIME – DAY 97
THE GIFT OF HOSPITALITY

Genesis 18.1–8

There is, indeed, a sitting ritual we have had to learn. There is a special mud-walled, grass-roofed round building in most compounds called a Payotte. This is the place to receive guests and talk. We have to remember to bend as we enter because the opening is usually very low. The attractive cane chairs are locally made, and would fit in well with the 'Country Living' lifestyle, at £50 each. Here they cost 50p (1,500 Ugandan shillings = 50p . . . there is no Sudanese currency in circulation yet).

We are hospitably shown to the biggest chairs, and a prayer is said to bless the visit. Conversation is always polite and gracious. While it proceeds, the women and children living on the compound are summoned and come shyly to meet the strange Khowodger (white people) and shake hands. Water is brought to drink, and we now appreciate the women's labour behind this, as we have seen the work of walking to the bore hole, queuing for a turn, pumping up the water into a jerry can, and returning with it balanced on the head. The sitting and talking is expected to be protracted, and indeed the guest should ask the permission of the host when planning to go. It is possible that the women are hustling to prepare tea or even have just killed one of their precious chickens in your honour, and it would be the height of rudeness to walk away from this generous sharing, or, indeed, to show impatience during the time taken to pluck the bird, light the charcoal stove, cook and serve the food.

The Sudanese are a warmly hospitable people who believe that visitors bless their home, and have not got into fast-track Western living which can ration unannounced visitors into convenient short slots. We are learning to work the purposes of our visits into these sleepy sitting times. Listening properly to people is a knack not always compatible with action plans, timed deliveries and other Western modes of relating.

Mike and Sue Hawthorne, Sudan

Like Abraham and Sarah, who were blessed by the visitors they received,
may we learn what it is to be a blessing to one another –
in giving and receiving. Amen.

ORDINARY TIME – DAY 98
LEARNING TO 'BE'

Isaiah 43.4

'So what are you doing here exactly?' people ask. Well, again in Crooks' book, they said: 'it really doesn't matter much what you do here. What matters to us is that friends . . . chose to send you, and that you have come to be with us.' So I am concentrating on being for now and we will see what happens.

Marjorie Gourlay, Lebanon

We need the fellowship of the West, but neither its protection nor its paternalism . . . fellowship in the sense of solidarity, prayer and sharing . . . in the renewal movement that has already started doing this you could be a great service to this part of the world.

The Catholicos

Reflect on the call to BE rather than to do or to define our identity through being needed or through status. Pray that we may discover our true worth as precious and honoured in God's sight. Pray that will set us free to establish real friendship and fellowship with our brothers and sisters in Christ.

ORDINARY TIME – DAY 99
BREAD OF LIFE

John 6.32–35

A few days ago, Hilary got talking to one of the local bakers. El Escorial has three bread shops. There is obviously fierce competition between them. The nearest one to our flat is usually a bustle of activity. Recently the owner of this bakery has opened another tiny shop on the main street. He is in there on his own every day. Hilary went in the other day for our usual bread and just to make a little conversation asked him what he felt about being on his own in this little shop, since it seemed such a contrast. It's amazing, sometimes, what a casual question can start. The man described how he was alone at work and alone at home. He has been a widower for years and although his two sons work in the business they have their own lives when not at the bakery. He said how hard it was for him to go home after work and be alone and face all the jobs to be done alone. We have had various chats as a family as to why we go to church, what we expect to give and receive when we are there. One of the reasons is that Christians meet together so that they are not alone in their faith. Our church building is now situated in the same main street as the new bakers. There are several events organized for this month and it would be great if the baker could come along and find enjoyment being with other people.

Jonathan and Hilary Rowe, Spain

What is the spiritual hunger of those in our local communities – even our own families? How might we share our experience of Christ as the true and living bread? How can we build relationships with those who live and work in our neighbourhood?

> Lord, we pray for all who are hungry,
> hungry for food,
> hungry for companionship,
> hungry for warmth,
> hungry for acceptance and love.
> May they find in you, the true and living bread,
> the grace and nourishment they need. Amen.

ORDINARY TIME – DAY 100
RECEIVING MORE THAN GIVING

Mark 10.29–30

Soon after we returned, we had a visit of 12 church members with a crate of Fanta and gifts of food for the family. We were extremely touched by this, especially as they had included four expensive imported apples – our British fruit! In his thanks during a sermon the next Sunday, Richard was able to read Mark 10.29–30 (NIV): "'I tell you the truth,' Jesus replied, "no one who has left home or brothers or sisters or mother or father or fields for me and the gospel will fail to receive a hundred times as much in this present age (homes, brothers, sisters, mothers, children and fields – and with them, persecutions) and in the age to come, eternal life.'"

Richard and Sue Kellow, Rwanda

We praise you, Lord God, for blessing us with gifts to share,
for enabling us to both give and receive,
as we rejoice in our fellowship together. Amen.

ORDINARY TIME – DAY 101
TRANSFORMING COMMUNITIES

Matthew 5.14–15

One British family decided they would arrange for one of their children regularly to invite a different family from their street in for a meal. They report that after a few months there was a discernible change in the neighbourhood. There is a change, too, in the children of that family. They are more outwardly focused and have concern for the needs of others rather than just wanting more, bigger and better for themselves. How can we be salt in our communities – salt that seasons and transforms the world? How can we better encourage young people within our community to be shaped and transformed by their encounter with Jesus and their encounter with others?

Tom Sine

Lord God, in community we are drawn together,
different ages, different experiences, different needs, different gifts,
and yet the same calling – to be salt and light, leaven and love.
Help us to appreciate one another,
to learn from one another,
to recognize our need of each other,
as we share together in the call to mission. Amen.

ORDINARY TIME – DAY 102
ENTERTAINING ANGELS

Hebrews 13.2, 16

Just married, my wife and I moved into a new area of London, and the housewarming party six weeks later was our deadline for clearing the boxes. At least, enough boxes so we could have people round. Our new place is in a cul-de-sac, and we decided to invite all the neighbours in the street – maybe about 14 houses. We'd been thinking about our new life together and had said that we wanted our house to be open and hospitable. But on the evening we'd designated for knocking on our neighbours' doors, we spent at least an hour trying to think of reasons why we shouldn't: some of our friends and family would be coming from quite a distance – would it make them uncomfortable to have strangers round the place? What if the one person that turned up was smelly, socially awkward, and just planted themselves on the sofa for three hours? Both of us had spent time volunteering in other countries, but nothing we'd experienced there seemed quite as daunting as knocking on a stranger's door in London. We finally convinced ourselves to stick to our original vision, said a little prayer for courage and hit the street, only to find out that it was full of delightful people who were mainly very pleased to see us – and pleased we'd taken the initiative to get to know them. About four sets of neighbours showed up at the party, and another household, who were struck down with colds, sent round a pre-chilled bottle of bubbly even though they couldn't come. We were really touched by people's goodwill. It feels good to have started our life here by opening up to others instead of hiding away.

Anonymous

Reflect on these words from a Christian in Polynesia:

Lord, you made us known to friends we did not know, and you have given us seats in homes which are not our own. You have brought the distant near, and made a brother/sister of a stranger. Forgive us, Lord . . . We did not introduce you.

Give thanks to God for the opportunities to befriend others – pray that he may use us and give us courage to share his grace with wisdom, compassion and sensitivity.

O God our Father,
give us a passion for your word
and boldness in telling our neighbour about your grace.
May the Holy Spirit convict the lost
and draw them to the Saviour, Christ our Lord. Amen.

From Kenya

ORDINARY TIME – DAY 103
A GOSPEL RHYTHM

Acts 2.46–47

Tom Sine recounts a life-changing experience during work on a project in rural Haiti; the people among whom he laboured had a 'gospel-rhythm' to their lives, always having time to stop and talk with passers-by: 'On many warm Haitian evenings during my sojourn we would visit the homes of friends. They would open up their homes to us and serve us food and drinks. We would spend a whole evening telling stories, laughing, singing, and playing with the children to the flicker of kerosene lamps . . . I thank my Haitian friends for helping me discover a more biblical approach to my time.'

Tom Sine, Haiti

Do we have a 'biblical approach to time'? How might developing a gospel rhythm of life help us to live in a more balanced, open-hearted way?

Bless our home, Father,
that we cherish the bread before there is none,
discover each other before we leave,
and enjoy each other for what we are,
while we have time. Amen.

ORDINARY TIME – DAY 104
SEVEN HABITS: BE PROACTIVE

Seven reflections based on Stephen Covey's book, "Seven Habits of Highly Effective People".

Psalm 25.1–7

Be proactive – to do this it means that I've had to focus on the things that I can actually do something about and distinguish these from the things that I can only pray about. I've also been challenged as to what belongs on each list, sometimes preferring not to do anything about something over which I could have some control, but didn't want to for fear of upsetting someone. It's best not to waste time worrying about the things over which you have no control, and getting bogged down by things that you actually can do something about! This has meant that I've had to focus on what it is about me that needs to change, how I relate to others, and asking God to change my heart and thoughts, so that they more closely echo his. I'd like to say at the end of ten years that I had it sorted, but unfortunately that's not entirely accurate.

Sian Hawkins

God, give us grace to accept with serenity
the things that cannot be changed,
Courage to change the things
which should be changed,
and the wisdom to distinguish
the one from the other.

Living one day at a time,
Enjoying one moment at a time,
Accepting hardship as a pathway to peace,
Taking, as Jesus did,
This sinful world as it is,
Not as I would have it,
Trusting that you will make all things right,
If I surrender to your will,

So that I may be reasonably happy in this life,
And supremely happy with you forever in the next. Amen.

Reinhold Niebuhr (1892–1971)

ORDINARY TIME – DAY 105
SEVEN HABITS: START WITH THE END IN MIND

Luke 14.28–30

Start with the end in mind – how does God want me to have lived my life at the end of my days, and so how do I live each day trying to head towards that goal? What are the values that are important to me? How do I demonstrate these to other people? And can anyone else tell me what those values are from how I live my life? This means taking time to do the important things, which often get pushed aside in the rush to do the urgent things. For me, interfaith dialogue has become a very important value over these last ten years.

Sian Hawkins

Lord, as we follow your leading,
may we be ready to take up our cross,
to accept the cost of following and serving,
and to always keep the end in mind. Amen.

ORDINARY TIME – DAY 106
SEVEN HABITS: PUT FIRST THINGS FIRST

Galatians 2.20

Put first things first – who is the person God wants me to be in this place? What do I prioritize, so that I can be this? Both in Afghanistan and in the UK, I have believed that my key role has been in empowering others and trying to help people reach their potential. This relational aspect within the team that I'm working with has meant that I haven't always been able to focus on wider community and sometimes that has been frustrating. However, it has been rewarding to see people growing in their abilities.

Sian Hawkins

Lord – as we engage in mission, help us to be the people you call us to be in the place you call us to be and to keep the 'main thing' the main thing. Amen.

ORDINARY TIME – DAY 107
SEVEN HABITS: WIN/WIN

Matthew 20.1–16

Win/Win – we have a God with abundant resources. We can ask for his provision with regard to our work and mission. All of our work is important in the mission of God, so how can we work together so that we all get what we need to do the work we need to do? This is probably one of the hardest things to achieve, as people often embed themselves into their positions of 'this is what I have to have'; it may be that the basic need can be met in some other way. The trick is finding it!

Sian Hawkins

Lord, we praise you for your generosity and abundant resources,
that you are always ready to give beyond what we are confident
 to ask.
May we live in your economy of grace,
where there is enough for all,
as we work for the coming of your kingdom. Amen.

ORDINARY TIME – DAY 108
SEVEN HABITS: UNDERSTAND BEFORE BEING UNDERSTOOD

Romans 14.13

Understand before being understood – this has been key in working in cross-cultural situations both in Afghanistan and in Southall. How can I expect people to understand my position if I haven't taken the time to understand their position and treat it with respect? In doing this it means that I may even be influenced by what they have said, and if I can be influenced then we might influence each other! I have needed to understand issues of faith, issues of context, and in being understood I have needed to be clear on my relationship with God, Father, Son and Holy Spirit. I have also been challenged as to whether we are offering a 'conditional friendship' that depends on someone's response to Jesus. We must love people for their own sakes.

Sian Hawkins

God, may we place no stumbling blocks in the way of others,
nor make assumptions about their values and beliefs.
May we become people of graciousness and respect,
open to share and to learn.
We ask this for the sake of Jesus, your Son. Amen.

ORDINARY TIME – DAY 109
SEVEN HABITS: SYNERGY

Ecclesiastes 4.9–12

Synergy – this is when two people working together can produce ideas that are three times better than either one could have come up with on their own. This is a potential between all people, but I have had to learn to appreciate and try to value the differences between another person and myself to enable this to work. It's hard when you don't get on with the person, and particularly if their way of working is very different from your own.

Sian Hawkins

Spend time praying for, and giving thanks for, those with whom you work or have worked in the past – especially for those who are very different from us.

ORDINARY TIME – DAY 110
SEVEN HABITS: SHARPENING THE SAW

Proverbs 27.17

Sharpening the saw – taking care of all that God has given me – that is my mind, my emotions, my body and my spiritual relationship with him. Generally we have focused on one over the other, but all are important and if we care for and nurture each aspect of what God has given us in this bodily form, then we will work better, and enjoy ourselves more in the mission of God.

Sian Hawkins

As tools come to be sharpened by the blacksmith, so may we come, O Lord. As sharpened tools go back with their owner, so may we go back to our everyday life and work, to be used by thee, O Lord.

Prayer of Zande Christians

ORDINARY TIME – DAY III
WAVING ACROSS THE WASHING!

Colossians 4.5–6

For me, God has been reminding me again about the importance of making time for relationships, and putting people above projects. Recently, I was struck one morning by one of the readings in the CMS *40 days of Yes* booklet, which posed the questions, 'Do you have a biblical approach to time?' and 'Do you have a gospel rhythm to your life?'

Later that day I felt God challenging me to stop and talk to the children on the opposite balcony who love to call out banter while I'm hanging out the washing! (A few months ago wonderful huge shady trees overhung our balcony blocking out the flats behind; you wouldn't believe how furious I was when they were savagely cut down one day, removing our privacy!) Anyway, after just a few words to the children their mother came out to chat. The following day, I was on the balcony again and I heard the children inside shouting to their mum: 'Quick, Mum, the foreigner is on the balcony!' and a good friendship is now blossoming with this Muslim lady and her family. A few hours after our first chat, she texted me this message: 'Maybe God wants us to meet a few wrong people before meeting the right one, so that when we finally meet the right one we know how to be grateful for that gift.'

Angela Chorlton

Lord, help us to step from the security and privilege of privacy
to a new place of encounter and opportunity.
May we have wisdom to know
how to respond to those whom we meet. Amen.

ORDINARY TIME – DAY 112
PRAY WITHOUT CEASING

1 Chronicles 16.11

In a time of change and crisis, we need to be much in prayer, not only on our knees, but in that sweet form of inward prayer in which the spirit is constantly offering itself up to God, asking to be shown his will. One good form of prayer at such a juncture is to ask that doors may be shut, that the way be closed, and that all enterprises that are not according to God's will may be arrested at their very beginning.

Frederick Brotherton Meyer

Seven whole days, not one in seven,
I will praise thee;
in my heart though not in heaven,
I can raise thee.
Small it is, in this poor sort to enrol thee:
e'en eternity's too short to extol thee.

George Herbert (1593–1633)

ORDINARY TIME – DAY 113
PRAYER AND LOVE

Matthew 5.43–45

God never gives us discernment in order that we may criticize, but that we may intercede.

Oswald Chambers

There is nothing that makes us love someone so much as praying for them.

William Law

Loving God, help me make your love the foundation of my life.
Teach me to be truly thankful for your gifts in others.
Give me grace: to build up, not tear down; to encourage not criticize;
to forgive not harbour hurts or disappointments.
Knowing that you are faithful and just and ever-ready to forgive whenever I fail or fall. Amen.

John Martin

ORDINARY TIME – DAY 114
PRAYER IS CO-OPERATION

Matthew 6.7–13

Prayer is not just communication. It is co-operation. It is the means by which we receive divine instruction from God for us to build a ministry according to his blueprint and design. E. M. Bounds says, 'Prayer is not preparation for the battle. It is the battle.' A healthy personal prayer life is an indispensable discipline.

Set aside set times each day to meet with God. Recruit a team of intercessors to be praying for you. Prayer keeps your eyes on the one who called you and helps you close your eyes to the one who is trying to stop you.

Here are seven things to pray for every day:
1 Pray for every member of your family.
2 Pray for wisdom.
3 Pray for faith.
4 Pray for courage.
5 Pray for favour.
6 Pray for a discerning heart.
7 Pray for specific needs.

Clifton Clark

O Master, teach me to pray, and thus help me bore a hole through which I may see you. Amen.

From New Guinea

ORDINARY TIME – DAY 115
GOD BE IN MY HEAD

Matthew 5.8, 6.22–24

The cleansing of the heart is, we might say, the cleansing of the 'eye' by which we see God. In keeping that eye 'single' we must take the kind of extreme care that is demanded by the great dignity of the one we behold with such an eye. Yet even when the eye is cleansed, it is difficult to prevent a certain dust from creeping over it without our awareness, arising from those things that tend to accompany even good actions, for example the praise of others. If those among whom you live won't praise you when you live uprightly, then they are of course in error. But if they will praise you, you're actually in danger. You can avoid this danger only if you have a heart so single and pure that, when you act uprightly, you aren't doing so because of the praises of others.

Augustine of Hippo (354–430)

God be in my head
And in my understanding
God be in my eyes
And in my looking
God be in my mouth
And in my speaking
God be in my heart
And in my thinking . . .

Walford Davies (1869–1941)

ORDINARY TIME – DAY 116
PRAYER – HELPING OTHERS

John 14.13–14

Most of the families who attend San Mateo Church in Río Verde regularly are very poor. Doña María is one of a large family (12 in all), and her mother, a very dynamic woman, lives next door. She spends a lot of her time travelling round the different children and looking after the grandchildren. They have a small plot of land and among them a herd of about ten cows, which the grandchildren take in turns to pasture along the side of the road. This is how they managed to get through the drought. Most of the adult members of the family have work either in Río Verde or on ranches and so they are able to pay the fees in the local Adventist school.

In January María decided to build a rainwater cistern. This is the best way to prepare for the dry months, but it is not cheap to build. We didn't want to interfere or take away their initiative, but were keen to try and encourage them. But, how could it be done without appearing paternalistic?

So I prayed about it and then, two weeks ago, María rang to ask if I would be prepared to use my truck to bring them some bags of cement to finish the job. At the time there was a cement shortage, making it much more expensive and especially so in the Chaco. But being in Asunción I was able to follow up a contact that María gave me and get her five bags of cement at a reasonable price. What a joy to hear María and her husband Dario giving thanks to God for his provision the following Sunday in church.

Ed and Marie Brice, Paraguay

'I will do whatever you ask in my name, so that the Son may bring glory to the Father.' Lord, teach us to ask in your name. Amen.

ORDINARY TIME – DAY 117
FIVE MARKS OF MISSION: PROCLAIM

Romans 10.13–15

Evangelism involves a subtle process of human interaction. Through it, men and women experience God's love, expressed in his people, and come to hear and understand the truth of the gospel. The Holy Spirit is at work in all this, often in ways we do not understand. As a result, people start to follow Christ and join his Church.

John Clarke

The promises of God are 'Yes' in Christ.
We speak the 'Amen' to the glory of God.
Glory to you for the incomprehensible life-giving glory of grace.
Glory to you who raised up your Church as a quiet harbour for a tormented world.
Glory to you for renewing us with the life-giving waters of baptism.
Glory to you, inexhaustible depths of forgiveness.
Glory to you for the cup of life,
for the bread of eternal joy.
Glory to you who is leading us out to heaven.
Glory to you for everything. Amen.

Archpriest Gregory Petrov, from Akathist of Thanksgiving, c. 1947

ORDINARY TIME – DAY 118
FIVE MARKS OF MISSION: TEACH, BAPTIZE AND NURTURE

Matthew 28.19–20

We wish to shake our baptized people out of habits that threaten to make them practically baptized pagans, idolaters of their money and power. What sort of baptized persons are these? Those who want to bear the mark of the Spirit and the fire that Christ baptizes with must take the risk of renouncing everything and seeking only God's reign and his justice.

Oscar Romero (1917–80)

Are we prepared to renounce everything and seek only God's reign and his justice?

Send me Jesus; send me Jesus; send me Lord.
Lead me Jesus; lead me Jesus; lead me Lord.
Fill me Jesus; fill me Jesus; fill me Lord.

From South Africa

ORDINARY TIME – DAY 119
FIVE MARKS OF MISSION: RESPOND TO HUMAN NEED

Luke 10.36–37

The human progress that Christ wants to promote is that of whole persons – in their transcendent dimension, and their historical dimension, in their spiritual dimension and their bodily dimension. Whole persons must be saved persons in their social relationships, who won't consider some people more human than others, but will view all as brothers and sisters and give preference to the weakest and neediest. This is the integral human salvation that the church wants to bring about – a hard mission! Often the Church will be catalogued with communistic or revolutionary subversives. But the Church knows what its revolution is: the revolution of Christ's love.

Oscar Romero (1917–80)

Teach us, Good Lord,
to serve you as you deserve,
to give and not to count the cost,
to fight and not to heed the wounds,
to toil and not to seek for rest,
to labour and not to ask for any reward,
save that of knowing that we do your will.
Though Jesus Christ our Lord.

Ignatius of Loyola (1491–1556)

ORDINARY TIME – DAY 120
FIVE MARKS OF MISSION: TRANSFORM UNJUST STRUCTURES

Leviticus 19.1–18, 30–37

John is just the right man for the job,
which is, after all,
one of justice and righteousness.
Savile Row clothes aren't suitable,
nor is aftershave;
the dust and smell of the desert
hang about him;
so do the people.
The word of the Lord, silent for so long.
At last is heard again:
'It's time to change!'
Not a polite call, in this waste land,

of 'Time, gentlemen, please';
Not 'Time to leave for tomorrow is another day'
– for it probably isn't!
But 'The crisis has come. This is it.
Here is he who comes after me.'
Not 'You can't change the world,
that's just the way it is.'
But the specific question 'Is it just, the way it is?'
The health of the poor in Britain rots
– improve housing and benefits;
The hunger and debt of the world mounts
– trade fairly and justly;
The inside of the stock market collapses
– deal honestly and openly;
Star wars astronomically cost the earth
– be content with present defence.
His shout demands, 'Time to change,
turn around, you can't go on.'
Not a casual 'Take it or leave it'
But a crucial 'Take it or be left – like the chaff.
And don't you try the old school tie;
Trees are judged by fruits, not roots.'

Graham Kings

Spend time reflecting on the poem. Where does God call you to speak the words: 'It's time for us to change'?

ORDINARY TIME – DAY 121
FIVE MARKS OF MISSION: SUSTAIN AND RENEW THE EARTH

Genesis 1.26–28

The Christian doctrine of creation gives you a far more robust, resilient way of demonstrating that nature is special than any secular argument. Four biblical foundations for a Christian ecology are:

1 The natural order, including humanity, was created by God and belongs to God. A plaque in St Paul's Cathedral about Sir Christopher Wren says: 'If you are looking for his memorial, look around you'. Similarly, creation points to the greater beauty of God.

2 Humanity is distinguished from the remainder of creation by being made in the 'image of God'. This is God delegating responsibility, not conferring privilege. There is no excuse for environmental exploitation – we are accountable to the Creator and Owner.

3 Humanity is charged with tending creation (as Adam was entrusted with the care of Eden – Genesis 2.15), knowing that creation is God's cherished possession. 'It is God's and he loves it . . . we must think before we act.'

4 There is no theological ground for humanity having the 'right' to do what it pleases with the natural order. Humanity is creation's steward, not its exploiter.

Alister McGrath

If you look for God's memorial, look around you. Today spend time looking at creation – stopping to look at intricate detail we so often miss. Praise God for the wonder around us.

ORDINARY TIME – DAY 122
THE BEST THERE IS

Genesis 1.28–31

We believe that God is both creator and sustainer of the earth – he established the earth and it endures. In the search for a sustainable future for this planet, there is a real missiological opening within today's environmental movement, torn between the inefficacy of an anthropocentric world view, and the paralysis of an ecocentric world view. Humanity has caused the environmental crisis, but it seems that humanity neither can, nor, according to some, should be trying to, solve it – yet who else is there? Bill Bryson, in his entertaining and wide-ranging *A Short History of Nearly Everything*, concludes:

If you were designing an organism to look after life in our lonely cosmos, to monitor where it is going, and keep a record of where it has been, you wouldn't choose human beings for the job. But here's an extremely salient point – we have been chosen, by fate or providence or whatever you wish to call it. As far as we can tell, we are the best there is.

Creating God, you give light and life,
and express delight in your creation.
You gave the command to till and care for your garden,
but we have abused the beauty of creation and the keeping of your
    word.
We confess the plundering of finite resources.
We confess to stealing our descendants' birthright to life.
We confess the flagrant pollution of land, sea and air.
We confess the churches' lack of concern for the well-being of
    creation.
We confess the excesses within our own lifestyle.
Creating God, we have desecrated your creation and darkened your
    light.
In a moment of quiet we confess our profligate lifestyle and
    human greed.

God of life and God of light, as we seek a new relationship with your created order, may we sense the grace and peace of a new relationship with you. Amen.

Celebrating Creation, www.ecocongregation.org

In the dawn of the day lead us to the garden of life that we might . . .
Prune the excess,
Root out injustice,
Water the wilting,
Nourish the withered,
Empty the potting shed of poison,
And at the eve of the day, rest, and wonder at God's garden. Amen.

Celebrating Creation, www.ecocongregation.org

ORDINARY TIME – DAY 123
EVERYDAY HOLINESS

Romans 12.1–2

Why is this a common statement? 'I teach Sunday school 45 minutes a week, and they haul me up to the front, and the whole church prays for me. I teach school 45 hours a week, and no one ever prays for me.' Would that be true for you and your job? The answer, of course, is that the secular–sacred divide is well and truly entrenched in church culture. The 'really spiritual' is divorced from the real world. True worship has to do with how we live the whole of our lives, not just the part that we take along to church on Sundays. Worship has to do with getting involved in God's world precisely because that is where he is involved.

Graham Buxton

Reflect on the secular–sacred divide in your own life. Do you allow your faith, your commitment to mission, to spill over and bring life to every-thing you do – even the most ordinary things? How might the world be different if we all did that?

Earth's crammed with heaven,
And every common bush afire with God:
But only he who sees takes off his shoes.

Elizabeth Barrett Browning (1806–61)

Lord – teach us to see. Amen.

ORDINARY TIME – DAY 124
CHURCH: PLAYING A PART

1 Corinthians 12.12–22

Many people who are now church refugees have been burnt out. As in many kinds of organizations, it is the people who are perceived as talented or gifted who are embraced into the core. Once there, there may be no end to the 'opportunities' to utilize these talents. In the context of Christian community and ministry there is a tricky tension between burying your treasure in the sand (along with your head), and bleeding it away to nothing. We need to set sustainable limits on our involvement.

Cathy Kirkpatrick

Lord, may we truly be the body of Christ,
each knowing our place and playing our part,
for the health and vitality of the whole. Amen.

ORDINARY TIME – DAY 125
CHURCH: RECOGNIZING LIMITATIONS

1 Peter 2.9–10

Life–Community, as the community of the Spirit or the body of Christ, does not . . .'divinize' the church. It is aware of its weakness and its vulnerability. Therefore, it is 'an ever-reforming body', constantly needing to submit to God's word, to repent and to change. It is truly *ecclesia semper reformanda*. Consequently, authority must be checked and constantly submit itself to God's word, ready to change when it is needed.

Titré Andre

Father, we thank you for your calling to be a holy people,
a people who declare your praise.
Father, we know our frailty and our failure to live up to our calling.
We pray for humility, for grace to repent and be changed
to the honour and glory of your name. Amen.

ORDINARY TIME – DAY 126
CHURCH – A WHOLE PEOPLE

1 Corinthians 12.27–30

As the *laos* is the whole people, Life–Community does not make a
distinction between the laity and the clergy. Life–Community is a
chosen people, a people with a special status and dignity because of
their relationship with God. Life–Community is a congregation that
is to be fashioned into the image of Christ and called to proclaim the
mighty acts of God. It transcends the unity based on identity derived
from citizenship in a nation, or from being of the same race, sharing a certain occupation, and participating in a certain social class.
Life–Community is the people of God because of now being found in
Christ.

Titré Andre

Lord, in your body there are many gifts:
apostles, teachers, prophets, helpers, miracles workers . . .
May we learn to value all your gifts,
so that the *laos* – the WHOLE people of God – may be
empowered to serve. Amen.

ORDINARY TIME – DAY 127
CHURCH – MEETING A NEED

Galatians 5.16–26

Every Christian group or cell should look for some way in which it can meet a genuine human need in the situation in which it is placed. If all group study and reflection should swing between the two poles of the Bible and the immediate environment or sphere of responsibility, it is bound to point to a particular line of action which the group is being called to take up in service to the world. Failure to go into action at that point is the first step to sterility.

John V. Taylor

> O gracious and holy Father,
> Give us wisdom to perceive you,
> Intelligence to understand you,
> Diligence to seek you,
> Patience to wait for you,
> Eyes to see you,
> A heart to meditate on you,
> And a life to proclaim you,
> Through the power of the spirit of Jesus Christ our Lord. Amen.

St Benedict (480–547)

ORDINARY TIME – DAY 128
CHURCH: JOINING IN THE MISSION

Romans 1.11–12

How different is the missional approach to the 'rhetoric of exclusion' that worked so well in modernity: 'There are blessings to being on the inside. You're on the outside and so can't enjoy them. Want to be a blessed insider like us?' In contrast, missional Christianity says, 'God is expressing his love to all outsiders through our acts of kindness and service. You're invited to leave your life of accumulation and competition and self-centredness to join us in this mission of love, blessing, and peace. Want to join in the mission?

Brian McLaren

O God, we are one with you, help us to realize that there can be no understanding where there is mutual rejection.

O God, in accepting one another wholeheartedly, fully, completely, we accept you, and we thank you, and we adore you; and we love you with our whole being, because our being is in your being, our spirit is rooted in your spirit.

Fill us then with your love, and let us be bound together with love as we go our diverse ways, united in this one spirit, which makes you present to the world, and which makes you witness to the ultimate reality that is love.

Love has overcome.

Love is victorious. Amen.

ORDINARY TIME – DAY 129
CHURCH: JOURNEYING TOGETHER

Matthew 9.20–22

When we begin to make ourselves vulnerable; to share with others from our own brokenness; to dig deep and reveal our own real struggles, needs, doubts and dreams . . . we begin to stand together. When we conspire to create, we begin to travel alongside one another. When we seek to make a space, a place, a time of gathering for one another, we avoid the danger of controlling the show from a position of safety where we/I do something *to* you. Let us move towards mutuality in our struggles; and form a culture of vulnerability, safety, honesty and valuing as we encourage each other along the road of life and faith.

Cathy Kirkpatrick

Take time to reflect on the courage and vulnerability of the woman in reaching out for healing. Are we prepared to reach out and receive the healing and wholeness of Christ through one another?

Lord – may we have the courage to reach out for wholeness and healing. Amen.

ORDINARY TIME – DAY 130
CHURCH: KNOWING OURSELVES

2 Timothy 1.6–7

Self-revelation, Benedict says, is necessary to growth. Going through the motions of religion is simply not sufficient. The Benedictine heart, the spiritual heart, is a heart that has exposed itself and all its weaknesses and all of its pain and all of its struggles to the one who has the insight, the discernment, the care to call us out of our worst selves to the heights to which we aspire. The struggles we hide, psychologists tell us, are the struggles that consume us. Benedict's instruction, centuries before an entire body of research arose to confirm it, is that we must cease to wear our masks, stop pretending to be perfect and accept the graces of growth that can come to us from the wise and gentle hearts of people of quality around us.

Sr Joan Chittister OSB

Father, may we stir into flame the gift that is given to us. May we know your spirit inspiring power, love and self-discipline within us. Give, we pray, the courage to face and name our struggles and bless us with wise friends and counsellors to walk beside us. Amen.

ORDINARY TIME – DAY 131
COURAGE TO FACE THE DARKNESS

Romans 7.15–24

If we are honest, we find this (honesty) very, very hard to sustain, for we are all naturally afraid of the unresolved opposites in ourselves. In John V. Taylor's words, 'we find it very painful to include and accept the dark self along with the light, the destroyer as well as the creator in us, both the male and the female element in our personality, both the child and the parent which we are'. We want a simple unity when in fact we are a mass of contradictions. It follows that it takes a high degree of maturity to respect an opinion that conflicts with my own without itching to bring about a premature and naïve accommodation. Being really present to one another, persisting in dialogue, John V. Taylor suggests – no doubt with one of his secret smiles – is actually about loving one's enemies! All jokes aside, however, he never allows us to forget that mission is an act of love-making.

David Wood

Refect on Paul's words 'What I do is not what I want to do.' Where in your life do you find yourself echoing that sentiment?

Paul says – 'Who will rescue me from this body of death? Thanks be to God through Jesus Christ our Lord' (vv. 24–25).
 Thanks be to you, O God, through Jesus Christ. Amen.

ORDINARY TIME – DAY 132
BECOMING A 'ROUNDER PEG'

2 Peter 1.3–8

It tells me that I have a wonderful God who is able to mould me from a square peg trying to fit into a round hole, into a rounder peg, so that eventually I will hopefully fit to his purpose. I tell you, though, knocking some of those corners off is not easy and I do get self-indulgent, feeling that I have rights too and why can't I get cross and rant and rave (which I can assure you I do at times, but manage to restrain them to private moments, or with other ex-pats who can relate to the frustrations). Actually the dog-walking at the end of the day is often very therapeutic, time to think and assimilate the day as well as providing some exercise – a very good time of unwinding on the whole.

I hope this doesn't come over as being too negative. I really don't want you to think that, but it is a taster of some of the day-to-day frustrations. It is very rewarding to spend time with a student, particularly when a blank face turns into one of enlightenment as they understand what it is you are getting at and see its relevance. One also gets very good at laughing at oneself and one's reactions to situations, which seem so trivial after the event.

Life has plenty of fun moments and moments of awe and wonder. Around the hospital, there are views out over endless countryside over which we often see fantastic sunsets, usually when you haven't got the camera with you! At the moment it is very hot, dry and dusty, resulting in bright blood-red sunsets due to the dust in the atmosphere. Alternatively there are those days where the rays of sun splay out, broken by the cloud, which remind me of those pictures of Christ with rays splaying out around his head. It does remind you of the glory of God and his power and that he can certainly take control of each little situation that arises.

Liz Hosegood, Zambia

We praise you, Lord God, that you give us all that is needful for us to grow actively and effectively in you. Help us to use all the circumstances of life as teachers of faith, that we may reflect your image more and more, to the glory of your name. Amen.

ORDINARY TIME – DAY 133
SUFFERING THAT WE MAY OVERCOME

Romans 5.1–5

As salaam alaykum (Peace be upon you). It's not been an easy year. Suffering is not something that comes easy to us, especially us in the West, and many Christians try and claim that suffering is not part of Christian life. Strange then that time and time again the Bible points to suffering as part of Christian life, but suffering that we may overcome. This in turn produces patience, another commodity in short supply in our modern world. Yet this is a sign to those around us of the hope, the expectation, that we have of the glory of God and to us also, and in that again we can rejoice.

Michael Green, Jordan

Praise God for the hope we have in him – however painful life can be at times.

ORDINARY TIME – DAY 134
GOD'S SUFFERING

Isaiah 53.3–9

There are days
When the storms of life
Rampage
Pushing the meek
To the side of the page;
They target the voiceless
The poor and betrayed
Flooding their homes
And chasing out orphans

Into this wayward and
Startling world.
Like a broken cup
No offering you bear;
With a face of sadness
You stand and stare
At God's suffering.
There are days
When the love of God
Overflows
Pouring through the cracks
And hidden sorrows
Sharing your secrets
Wiping your tears
Renewing your spirit
And chasing your fears
From this aching yet
Fantastic world.
The Father's hands
Silently rest on your head
And your needs are met
Through the wine and bread
Of God's suffering.

Jon and Lyn Gregson, Nepal

Thank you, Lord God, for the days when your love overflows and pours through the cracks of our suffering. Thank you that, in you, all our needs are met through the gift of your suffering for the world. Amen.

ORDINARY TIME – DAY 135
MISSION SPIRITUALITY

1 Timothy 2.1–2

Any kind of spirituality involves the practice of regular prayer. That goes without saying. A mission spirituality, however, would make sure that the content of that prayer is one that reaches out to all the world. It might be one that uses the newspaper as a basic prayerbook.

It is also a prayer that constantly calls to mind the people who are served, with all their cultural richness. It will be a prayer of *kenosis* or self-emptying. It will be a prayer that, where appropriate, will use the forms and content of the other faiths among whom missionaries work.

A mission spirituality will practise a simplicity of life, in solidarity with the poor of the world. This may be a real challenge to those of us from more affluent countries, but it is essential.

Steve Bevans

How might our prayer be different – and more challenging to our affluent lifestyles – if we used the newspaper as a basic prayerbook?

Spend time praying with a newspaper or news programme for the needs of our world.

ORDINARY TIME – DAY 136
CHURCH WITH OTHERS

Ephesians 4.16

Roland Allen started the process of change. Eventually 'the church-for-others was slowly turning into the church-with-others'. . . Mission could no longer be viewed as one-way traffic, from the West to the Third World; every church, everywhere, was understood to be in a state of mission.

David J. Bosch

Alone a youth runs fast, with an elder slow, but together they go far.

African proverb

How does the way we talk about mission reflect this new understanding of mission as a shared calling for all churches, everywhere? Pray that the language we use and the ways we relate to one another may reflect 'a new day' in mission.

Lord, we long to speak effectively in your name,
but our words come out muddled and blunted.
Give us the fresh, new-minted words
that heart may speak to heart
and a new day begin.

Christopher Lamb

ORDINARY TIME – DAY 137
LIVING IN NEWLY DISCOVERED REALITY

Romans 12.1–5

The prevailing impression I have . . . is of an ever-widening chasm between the fantasy in terms of which the media induce us to live, and the reality of existence as made in the image of God, as sojourners in time whose true habitat is eternity. The fantasy is all-encompassing; awareness of reality requires the seeing-eye that comes to those born again in Christ. It is like coming to after an anaesthetic; the mists lift, consciousness returns, everything in the world is more beautiful than ever it was, because related to a reality beyond the world – every thought clearer, love deeper, joy more abounding, hope more certain. Who could hesitate confronted with this choice between an old fantasy and a newly discovered reality?

Malcolm Muggeridge

Glory to you our Lord and our God.
In your great love, you have called us to be your people.
By your Spirit, you have endowed us with an abundance and
diversity of gifts to share in your mission.
We pray, Lord, that you will shape us to become a community of faith.
Make us instruments of peace, love and justice.
Help us to go forth boldly to tell of your saving work in Christ. Amen.

ORDINARY TIME – DAY 138
KEY VALUES: FAITHFUL

Romans 12.11–12

Pilgrimage and homelessness have been themes of my life since childhood, and still more so now, today. It is those themes that have bound
me so intimately with Kakuma Refugee Camp, a place that epitomizes
both much that I love intensely, and hate. For me there is no more para-
doxical place than Kakuma: the desert terrain, with its unremitting heat,
so similar to the San Joaquin Valley, where I grew up. The life of its
refugee populations, for their spiritual dynamism and creativity against
all odds, these I passionately love. For its malnutrition and degradation,
its unfulfilled promises, death, and dashed hopes, it is hell. It epitomizes
much of my pilgrim life with Sudan: its agony and ecstasy, its daily encounter with death and resurrection. For all it contains of homelessness
and pilgrimage, a part of me remains at Kakuma.

Marc Nikkel, Sudan

*Just six weeks before he wrote that, on 25 August 1998 Marc, a joint
CMS and ECUSA mission partner in Sudan, had been diagnosed with ex-
tensive cancer of the abdominal cavity and had two weeks to live. Marc
lived for two more years, and over that time continued his extraordinary
and faithful ministry among the Dinka and Nuer, and his writing.*

Give us, O Lord,
steadfast hearts, which no unworthy thought can drag downwards;
unconquered hearts, which no tribulation can wear out,
upright hearts, which no unworthy purpose may tempt aside.
Bestow upon us also, O Lord our God,
understanding to know thee,
diligence to seek thee,
wisdom to find thee
and a faithfulness that may finally embrace thee.

Thomas Aquinas (1225–74)

ORDINARY TIME – DAY 139
KEY VALUES: RELATIONAL

Acts 16.13–15

Our stand at the Mind Body Spirit Festival was named *Dekhomai*, a Greek word that means 'the welcoming place'. *Dekhomai* aimed to offer a place of hospitality, conversation, relaxation, respite and renewal to visitors, a space where we could share something of the spirituality of the Christian tradition, including prayers for blessing, healing and reflection. Not a single visitor turned down intercession during those Thursday and Friday mornings. The intimacy of massage, open and honest conversation, and sharing, led quite naturally to the offer of prayer. The team was very aware of, and grateful for, the cradle of protective prayer in which its work was held before and during the event. God honoured every exchange with his spirit of mutuality – and, often, fun.

Patrick Gavigan

Dear Jesus, help us to spread your fragrance everywhere we go.
Flood our souls with your spirit and life.
Penetrate and possess our whole being so utterly
that our lives may only be a radiance of yours.
Shine through us, and be so in us,
that every soul we come in contact with
may feel your presence in our soul.
Let them look up and see no longer us but only Jesus!
Stay with us, and then we shall begin to shine as you shine;
so to shine as to be a light to others;
the light O Jesus, will be all from you, none of it will be ours;
it will be you, shining on others through us.
Let us thus praise you in the way you love best
by shining on those around us.
Let us preach you without preaching, not by words
but by our example, by the catching force,
the sympathetic influence of what we do.
The evident fullness of the love our hearts bear to you. Amen.

John Henry Newman (1801–90)

ORDINARY TIME – DAY 140
KEY VALUES: PIONEERING

Acts 11.5–18

The Greek word translated pioneer is *archegos*. This is a leader who is also a founder: someone who breaks a path and establishes a way. The *archegos* pioneers the way by becoming and living the new vision, not by 'claiming new ground' or imposing by force. We discover God revealing himself to us in Jesus only as we follow the path and way of Jesus. Wise and prudent people would not have been able to work out, without revelation from God, that it was to be through suffering that Jesus would restore the glorious destiny of humanity and all creation.

Our pioneering mission today is to discover for ourselves that humanity of God in Jesus – working together all over the world to discover Jesus and live out the new vision for life he gives. That's truly pioneering.

Tim Dakin

'How could I stand in God's way?' says Paul in verse 17.

Lord – may we not stand in your way,
but follow the leading of your Spirit,
wherever it takes us. Amen.

ORDINARY TIME – DAY 141
GOD SPEAKS

Exodus 3.1–6

Did Moses just happen to go that way with his sheep and goats? Or had he a purpose that day? Was he expecting something would happen? Was there some premonition in his mind that he was going to meet someone, hear a voice, have a revelation? We do not know.

What we do know is that Moses while in the wilderness came to the mountain of God, to a place where tradition, at least, suggested that revelation might happen. What is more he came of a race that had already proved that God spoke in the most unlikely places.

No wonder, then, that it was back to the same place, to the mountain of God in the wilderness, that Moses came a year or two later, leading this time not a flock of sheep and goats but the people of God to meet with him in the wilderness. And by that mountain of God there came to that man and his people another revelation of God as a God of holiness who expects his people to be holy, of God as a God of purpose who calls his people to share his purpose, of a God who can lead his people through the wilderness.

Max Warren

Holy God,
Awesome God,
Reveal yourself anew to me today,
I humbly pray. Amen.

ORDINARY TIME – DAY 142
KEY VALUES: EVANGELISTIC

Acts 5.42

Evangelism . . . cannot be divorced from the larger mission of the church. And even if we include recruiting of new members and offering eternal salvation in the aim of mission, the question remains: what are people becoming church members for? What are individuals being saved for? . . . to become a disciple of Jesus [primarily] means accepting a commitment to Jesus and to God's reign . . . to follow him . . . Evangelism is . . . a call to service.

Proclamation knows nothing of coercion. It always remains an invitation. Is it possible to imagine a more ardent and compelling missionary spirit?

David J. Bosch

Give me, I pray you, Lord,
in the name of Jesus Christ, your Son and my God,
that love that does not fail
so that my lantern, burning within me and giving light to others,
may be always lighted and never extinguished.

Colombanus (540–615)

ORDINARY TIME – DAY 143
EXPECT GREAT THINGS FROM GOD

Habakkuk 2.1

Faith in the Bible is not the quality of submission but of co-operation, not of acquiescence in the unpredictable but of commitment to the known. You put your trust 'into' someone, and you expect the answer, not necessarily the answer you want but the answer which will be just right for the circumstances. You know the answer will be right because you know the person who gives the answer. This, then, is the great principle of our telling, that we shall expect great things from God.

That notable missionary William Carey knew that here was the point of beginning for the 'Mission'. It is because we expect great things from God that we can attempt great things for him. The greatest thing we can expect is 'grace in the wilderness', grace to do the next thing. That is the grace–faith relationship which, working out in small things, and in big, means salvation.

From Mombasa in Kenya, a doctor writes, 'There is a railway draftsman, a leader of the "brethren". Always cheery, with his whole life a witness to the grace of God, he is consistently on the move in his spare time, linking up with other Christian groups, and being a continuing inspiration to fellow-Christians, black and white.' The back of the man's devotion is expectancy.

Another example. 'The local headmaster's wife here, who is an outstanding witness to the faith, has five small children, all with whooping cough at the moment. She herself is not well, but remains serene. "If I think only of the children I am troubled, but if I think of Jesus first and then of the children it is all right" which is typical of her.'

Max Warren

Do we expect great things from God – or try to do things in our own strength?

Holy God,
Awesome God,
we pray for grace in the wilderness
and for great things to happen in your name.
By your grace, we pray. Amen.

ORDINARY TIME – DAY 144
THE 34TH MAN

Psalm 145.3–4

It has been a glorious two days. I went up to the mine with the president and was able to preach to the assembled town of Copiapó the night the last of the miners were brought out. Later, in the hospital, the main spiritual leader José Henriquez (they now call him 'the Pastor') told me that when the mine collapsed and all the miners panicked, groaning in fear 720 metres underground, God spoke to him that they would survive. José called them together, calmed their fears and got them all praying together. Through this, they received such a sense of peace and knowledge that they would come through this ordeal. The miners despaired as they heard the drilling operations pass them by, and so prayed that they would be found!

Finally . . . the miracle!

Despite it being as unlikely as finding a needle in a haystack, the drill struck a rock, was deviated and hit their chamber. The uproar of joy was heard all over Chile, when we heard the words shouted: 'We are alive and well – all 33 of us in the shelter.'

We believe this is a miracle that will speak to the world of the love of God.

The engineer, André Sougarret, the brains behind the rescue but not a believer himself, said publicly: 'In the drilling process, things happened that held no logic with engineering. I believe that something happened.' He attributed it to an energy generated through prayer and goodwill. I was later in Copiapó for the rescue itself and there seemed to be a revival going on in the town. That night I was given the opportunity to address the jubilant crowd in the Plaza. I asked permission to get up on a stage that was in the centre of the celebration and simply explained that I was going to do what the miners would want. I got on my knees and prayed.

The whole place hushed completely and it made me think of the scenes we read about in the Wesleyan revivals. There is a new respect, even from unbelievers, for the things of God. The president himself has continually given God the glory and called the nation to pray. The one or two attempts at cynicism from the world press and/or local newsmen have crumbled rapidly before the gigantic testimonies of the miners who speak of Jesus being the 34th man down there with them.

Alf Cooper

We praise your name, O Lord! You are great and most worthy of praise; your greatness is beyond our fathoming. One generation commends your work to another – together, we proclaim your mighty acts. Amen.

ORDINARY TIME – DAY 145
TRUSTING IN GOD'S
REDEEMING MERCIES

Psalm 68.19–20

God pulled Luka back from the brink, and found him worthy to be pulled back – not only from death (as he should have died in that fall) but also from permanent paralysis: an African boy with development delay, socially outcast because of both this and his epilepsy, and also unlikely to become socially or politically 'relevant', the least of the least by the world's reckoning. But if God can and *will* do that for Luka, can not you and I be also sure of his redeeming mercies, his miraculous powers and his will/ready love to relieve us and set us free as well?

Ruth Hulser, Tanzania

Praise God for stories like Luka's, and for the hope and confidence they offer to us in our stumbling faith.

ORDINARY TIME – DAY 146
ALL HAVE FALLEN SHORT

Romans 3.23

It falls to my lot very frequently to travel by road from Blackheath to Blackfriars. I am quite familiar with that bit of the wilderness of South London! In the course of various journeys I have travelled by road from Freetown to Port Loko, from Kano to Lagos, from Onitsha to Port Harcourt, from Dar-es-Salaam to Morogoro and Dodoma. I know the road from Nairobi to Kisumu over the Rift Valley. I have driven from Kampala to Gulu, from Juba to Yambio. I know the road from Cairo to Menouf, the road from Kowloon to the border of China, and even some of the roads round Shanghai and Hangchow and Nanjing, to say nothing of the American throughways and the German autobahns.

I can only testify from my own experience that the people who live beside the road from Blackheath to Blackfriars are very like the people who frequent other roads. To begin with, I've found them all likable, all about equally suspicious of strangers, all equally ready to join in a joke and to share a smile, all of them children of God. But I've not gone about with my eyes shut. I've seen where they lived, studied something of their problems, seen a little below the surface of their lives, and found there, in every case, the same common needs.

When we really get down below our superficial differences we know with St Paul that the truth about us is that 'there is no distinction; since all have sinned and fall short of the glory of God' (Rom. 3.23). We are all in the wilderness without exception. But that isn't the last word. St Paul goes on to say that 'they [that is all of us] are justified by his grace through the redemption which is in Jesus Christ' (v. 24). In the wilderness is the sign of the cross.

Max Warren

We thank you, Father God, that we are justified by grace, that in the wilderness we find the cross of Christ. Amen.

ORDINARY TIME – DAY 147
PRAYER FOR THE DAY

Psalm 51.10–13

O God, give me strength to live another day. Let me not turn coward before its difficulties or prove recreant to its duties. Let me not lose faith in my fellow men, keep me sweet and sound of heart, in spite of ingratitude, treachery and meanness. Preserve me from minding little stings or giving them. Help me to keep my heart clean and live so honestly and fearlessly that no coward failure can dishearten me or take away the joys of conscious integrity. Open wide the eyes of my soul that I may see good in all things. Grant me this day some new vision of thyself, inspire me with thy spirit of joy and gladness, and make me the cup of strength to suffering souls in the name of the strong deliverer, our only Lord and Saviour Jesus Christ. Amen.

Prayer of Bishop Kimber Den of Chekiang, which he used daily in prison

Write your own prayer for the day.

ORDINARY TIME – DAY 148
MISSIOLOGY OF THE CROSS

Matthew 10.5–14

Francis of Assisi joined the Fifth Crusade, but, instead of fighting, he went into the enemy camp armed with nothing but a single companion and spoke to the sultan, al-Kamil, about Jesus.

Francis's missiology was effective, because it was Christ's own, lived out in incarnation and crucifixion, and explained to his disciples in Matthew 10. Go with nothing. Go into communities. Greet people with peace. Accept their hospitality. Eat their food.

Francis's monastic First Rule lays this out, and chapter 16 addresses the Islamic context, instructing: go when the Holy Spirit leads; do not argue; live under their rules, but be clear about your Christian identity; speak about the gospel only when God shows you that the time is right; and be ready for martyrdom. The motivation is love for Christ and the Muslims' need of him for salvation. Jesus came to us with nothing but himself and the greeting of peace – his missiology took him to the cross, and to the five wounds that mark him in glory. I do not think that we can improve on Matthew 10: any missiology without this foundation will distort the image of the Master.

Ida Glaser

O Christ, light of the Father in heaven, Who didst come in thy mercy to the world to save humankind, cause thy light of thy wisdom and knowledge to shine in the souls of those who seek after thee; that they may walk in the path of thy radiance, until at last they find rest in thy home in glory. There shall they see thee in thine effulgence.

O thou who didst ascend to heaven, and who art our advocate before the Father, lift up our thoughts unto the place where thou art and give us to know thy wisdom.

O Star who dost shine in every pure heart, give me to shine with thy beauty, and make me worthy to adore thee in spirit and in truth.

Glory of the Father, Wisdom from on high, O Word of God, who didst open for us the gate of the kingdom and reveal unto us the secrets thereof, do thou make us fit to partake of the joy of thy goodness.

Thou who art our only good, our only goal, O sole guardian of all saints in their quest of life and felicity, hear us. Amen.

Eastern Orthodox prayer

ORDINARY TIME – DAY 149
HUNGER FOR GOD

Psalm 42.1–2

One dimension of Andrew Wheeler's life in Sudan was the encounter with Islam. He recounts coming across an informal Sufi gathering where men rocked to and fro on their heels repeating the name of God, Allah, Allah, Allah. 'I just remember the repetition of the word Allah, over and over, and the intensity, the hunger, as it seemed to me, with which it was said . . . What struck me was the hunger for God, the dedication to prayer, the focus and desire. And in those I found a challenge. I had left a successful career in teaching to live among and serve the people of Sudan. To that I was deeply devoted. Was there also a hunger for God himself, the intent to seek him with my own being?

Andrew Wheeler

Am I hungry for God? Do I want to seek him with my own being?

I hunger and thirst for you – the living God. Amen.

ORDINARY TIME – DAY 150
RICH IN GOOD DEEDS

1 Timothy 6.17–19

Christians who reject the idea of involvement in issues of social and economic justice may appeal to scripture in order to support their arguments. A much more difficult task, however, is to marshal biblical evidence to provide a rationale in favour of what may be the strongest factor disabling many Christians all over the world to express love for justice in practical ways, namely, a massive accommodation of the Church to the consumer society. As Sklair has put it, 'Without consumerism, the rationale for continuous capitalist accumulation dissolves. It is the capacity to commercialize and commodify all ideas and the products in which they adhere, television programmes, advertisements, newsprint, books, tapes, CDs, videos, films, the Internet, and so on, that global capitalism strives to appropriate.' Habermas . . . pointedly termed this 'the colonization of the lifeworld'.

Sad to say, all too often it is this 'colonization of the lifeworld' by consumerism, effectively promoted by the mass media, that prevents us from putting into practice the Pauline injunction to Christians not to be conformed to this world but to be transformed by the renewing of their minds, so that they can discern 'what is the will of God – what is good and acceptable and perfect' (Rom. 12.2).

C. René Padilla

O Lord Jesus Christ,
High Priest and Victim,
You are the lamb who was slain and has risen again.
By your most Precious Blood save your people
trapped in selfishness and sin.
To you who trampled death by your death we cry,
Jesus, convert our nation!
From the culture of death to your gospel of life,
Jesus, convert our nation!
From the culture of fear and addiction
to the freedom of your children,
Jesus, convert our nation!

From the culture of disbelief, despair and greed
to the civilization of faith, hope and love,
Jesus convert our nation!

Franciscan Friars of the Renewal

ORDINARY TIME – DAY 151
KINGDOM ECONOMY

Luke 14.15–24

Two billion people live on less than £1.30 a day. Fifty per cent of the
world's population is under the age of 24. In the next 20 years, three
billion young people will enter the marketplace looking for employment.
Thus we can never meet some of the most dire needs of the world, unless
we address the area of economic development. If we want to preach the
whole gospel in a way that is 'good news' to the world, we must be seen
as meeting real needs and influencing the whole of society. Therefore we
will increasingly need to emphasize economic and business development
intentionally with a kingdom point of view.

Mats Tunehag

Lord, we long for a day when all will sit down and eat together at the
table of your kingdom. Lord, may that day come quickly and may we do
all we can to work to see its dawning. Amen.

ORDINARY TIME – DAY 152
LIVING AS CITIZENS OF HEAVEN

Hebrews 12.1–2

For the Christians are distinguished from others neither by country, nor
language, nor the customs that they observe. For they neither inhabit

cities of their own, nor employ a peculiar form of speech, nor lead a life which is marked out by any singularity. The course of conduct that they follow has not been devised by any speculation or deliberation of inquisitive people; nor do they, like some, proclaim themselves the advocates of any merely human doctrines. But, inhabiting Greek as well as barbarian cities, according as the lot of each of them has determined, and following the customs of the natives in respect to clothing, food, and the rest of their ordinary conduct, they display to us their wonderful and confessedly striking method of life. They dwell in their own countries, but simply as sojourners. As citizens, they share in all things with others, and yet endure all things as if foreigners. Every foreign land is to them as their native country, and every land of their birth as a land of strangers. They marry, as do all [others]; they beget children; but they do not destroy their offspring. They have a common table, but not a common bed. They are in the flesh, but they do not live after the flesh. They pass their days on earth, but they are citizens of heaven. They obey the prescribed laws, and at the same time surpass the laws by their lives. They love all people, and are persecuted by all. They are unknown and condemned; they are put to death, and restored to life. They are poor, yet make many rich; they are in lack of all things, and yet abound in all; they are dishonoured, and yet in their very dishonour are glorified. They are evil spoken of, and yet are justified; they are reviled, and bless; they are insulted, and repay the insult with honour; they do good, yet are punished as evil-doers. When punished, they rejoice as if quickened into life; they are assailed by the Jews as foreigners, and are persecuted by the Greeks; yet those who hate them are unable to assign any reason for their hatred.

The Epistle of Mathetes to Diognetus 5

O Lord, Jesus Christ,
the Way, the Truth and the Life,
we pray that you will not let us stray from you, the Way;
nor distrust you, the Truth;
nor rest in anything other than you – the Life.
Teach us by your Holy Spirit, what to believe, what to do,
and how to take our rest. Amen.

Erasmus of Rotterdam (1466–1536)

ORDINARY TIME – DAY 153
THE PATH OF LIFE

Psalm 16.11

The most satisfying thing about my job is seeing my trainers grow in stature and competence as they travel all over the country, training teachers. The thing I love most about my job, though, is actually doing the teaching myself . . . it is a real joy to see those folk who are committed to the children and are keen to learn because of that commitment. So many of the teachers here are volunteers . . . in other words: no salary! But why am I a mission partner? God only knows . . . and I mean that reverently! I have been one since 1978, and it has been one long adventure, which has seen me working for the church in one capacity or another in eight countries. He knows me better than I know myself (Ps. 139), so at the moment I guess this is what he wants for me.

Robbie Langford, Sudan

We ask the God of our Master, Jesus Christ,
that we will be good apprentices in our manner of life;
in our direction, faith, and steadiness;
in our love and patience;
in troubles and in sufferings.
And as the scriptures train God's servants
to do all kinds of good deeds
we ask the glorious Father to give us his Spirit,
to make us intelligent and discerning in knowing him personally
and knowing how to serve.

Based on 2 Timothy 3.10,11,16 and Ephesians 1.17

ORDINARY TIME – DAY 154
KNOWING OUR PATH

Psalm 142.3

I am working with children who have been rescued, helping children to work though trauma, assessing whether it is safe to return to their families or not and supporting a child (where possible) with rehabilitation to their family/community. Also, if it is not possible for a child to return to their family, then looking at where they will stay.

I will also be working with the children of those in the sex industry to help prevent this cycle of abuse and in the future I would hope to be involved in preventative work. The path to healing. Obviously when a child is rescued, this is only the beginning of the journey to healing and for some it may be a very long journey. Some of the work that I have done before is to use art and play as a way of helping children communicate when they find it hard to articulate things verbally. Sometimes a child needs someone just to be with them while they say how awful it feels and without hearing the words, 'it's ok now' – for someone to be with them in their pain and not to rush it away but to work through it at their pace.

Psalm 142.3 (NKJV) says: 'When my spirit was overwhelmed within me, then you knew my path . . .' God's healing is deeper than any other that can ever be experienced and his healing goes to our very core as he created us.

As you can imagine, there are huge issues of forgiveness to deal with, against both those who have wronged them and those who have walked past and done nothing . . . Sometimes a child may hold a grudge against God himself and need to work through that, and some may need to forgive themselves, as many will have a false sense of guilt believing that it is their fault or that they could have stopped it.

Kylie Duncan

Lord, we thank you that you are our refuge,
our portion in the land of the living,
that you watch our steps,
that your healing mercy touches our innermost being. Amen.

ORDINARY TIME – DAY 155
NOT TRUSTING IN WEALTH

2 Corinthians 8.11a–15

The river swells with the contribution of small streams.

African proverb

Those among us who have sufficient capital to invest . . . should opt for the kingdom of God not only with ourselves, but also with our goods. 'Those who trust in their wealth behave like fools; they will not redeem themselves and will leave their fortunes to others' (Ps. 49.6,11).

Joseph G. Donders

> Lord of grace and peace,
> it is not we who have a mission to the world;
> the mission is yours through Christ.
> I acknowledge that all I am and all I have come from you;
> and that your mission of love through Christ for all the world
>   includes me.
> Today I dedicate myself, committing
> all that I am and all that I have to you Lord,
> with thanksgiving, and for your glory. Amen.

ORDINARY TIME – DAY 156
FAITH TO MOVE MOUNTAINS

Mark 11.22–24

I guess it isn't the usual way to start a party. Nancy Njagi, who heads up all our informal training at the Centre for Urban Mission, had been meeting with third-year students for their leaving party which, as every year, they chose to hold in Kibera. 'Before we began I had them all out in the road pushing the rubbish piled up in the drain.' Nancy pressed on: 'We have to deal with this one and get the local government involved.' She went on to remind me that if our advocacy agenda is to have real credibility we have to model it ourselves and one step could be getting the rubbish problem sorted.

We had just held an excellent conference on 'Building Just Communities'. The event was partly sponsored by a small grant from CMS. We had hoped for 200 people, but found ourselves with 300 and had to cope with delegates sitting outside the door. The head of Kenya's Anti-Corruption Commission (not the most comfortable of positions!) was our opening speaker. A keen Christian, he provided a rallying call to Church and nation, articulating a vision of what a just community might look like. Through three days of speakers, a series of workshop tracks and some great video testimonies, we explored what it means for the Church to work for justice at grassroots.

This was our third conference and perhaps our most successful, and yet I fear Nancy is right. Hosting a good conference was important and the video testimonies of churches we work with provided a powerful and much-needed reminder that change is possible. But in our own front yard, at the very door of CUM, we must demonstrate those possibilities. Jesus reminds us that faith can move a mountain, but right now we must find the faith that shifts rubbish, gets pit latrines emptied, finds children in school and lets a young person find a paid outlet for their God-given gifts and skills.

Colin and Anita Smith, Kenya

Lord, give us the faith that shifts rubbish,
that gets pit latrines emptied,
that finds children in school and young people in jobs,
faith that moves mountains. Amen.

ORDINARY TIME – DAY 157
RECONCILIATION BEFORE JUSTICE

Matthew 5.43–48

We take the view that there can (indeed must) be reconciliation *before* justice has been achieved where believers are involved. In Israel there are believers on both sides of the conflict as there are 1.2 million Arabs in Israel alongside the four to five million Jews.

As an evangelical ministry Musalaha has affinity with Arab evangelical Christians and with Messianics, and engages with and brings together both these communities because of the unique partnership between Salim and Evan and their leadership role in their communities.

Musalaha takes very seriously the gospel message that we must love our enemies. They do not blench to admit that believers share their cultural and historical identities with non-believers, and see the other side as the enemy. The challenge that Musalaha can make is that as Christians this won't do. It's not a question of waiting until better times before seeking out and making peace with the other side.

The message I keep hearing is that in the land there is less intolerance of the other side than outside it. So in Israel, Israelis whether Arab or Jewish can overcome the natural barriers more readily than those in the West who eagerly take one side or the other. [. . .] It is one thing to be an activist and to have a strong opinion from a distance, it is another to be faced with the day-to-day reality and to struggle with it. But this is of course how we all live our lives in a world that is not black and white.

Martin Clay, Southborough

Father, may there be no limit to our goodness, just as your goodness knows no bounds. Amen.

ORDINARY TIME – DAY 158
A SPINNING TOP

1 Corinthians 1.18

The Spinning-top

Lord, we are so top-heavy; our whole structure –
In Session, Synod, Council and Assembly –
The whole thing topples, and to keep from falling,
We, top-like, spin and spin on our own axis,
Self-centred, humming, whipped to static fury;
And so gyrating, pride ourselves on action.

Lord, knock us sideways, send us spinning outwards;
Uncentre us from self, and make our axis
That transverse axle-tree. The cross, that turning
On Christ alone we may roll forward, steady,
To that great day, when, every creature gospelled,
The end shall come, and nations see the glory.

Robin Boyd, Gujarat, North India

Lord – may we 'turn' not on our own axis but on the cross alone. Amen.

ORDINARY TIME – DAY 159
OPPORTUNITIES TO SHARE

Romans 1.16

On opportunities to share the gospel . . . 'Sometimes those opportunities come
in such unexpected and natural ways, that I marvel at why I bother to search

for them. For instance, back in October, I received a mobile phone message asking me if I could attend a Hallowe'en party at a local university. My response naturally was to decline, stating what I believed and why Hallowe'en was in opposition to that belief. The result was a deeply apologetic reply from the sender and an opportunity for me to present the gospel. Fantastic! It's not every day that you get to share the gospel through SMS . . .'

Reflect prayerfully on opportunities to share the gospel in the last week. Pray that God will enable us to use every opportunity we're given to share the good news.

CMS mission partners

ORDINARY TIME – DAY 160
FREE FROM FEAR

Psalm 27.1

Fifty of the new first-year students here at St John's University have signed up for my English Bible class. I am writing this on the first day of the eighth lunar month, which means that Ghost month finally finished yesterday, and life can begin to return to normal. For four weeks the whole country, with the exception of the Christian community, has lived in fear and trepidation of these ghosts. They are 'allowed out' for a month to roam around the world, and in order to persuade the ghosts not to enter a home or a place of work, vast feasts are prepared each day and placed outside the main door – in the hope that the ghosts will eat and be satisfied before leaving and going elsewhere. It really looks quite bizarre to see uniformed office workers, town hall staff in their suits, banks, companies, shopping malls, fancy boutiques and, of course, homes all busily preparing huge offerings of food and drink for the ghosts. And for a whole month, no one dares get married, travel, move house, open a business . . . unthinkable! Thank God that Christians are free from all such fear! Now we are looking forward to the Moon festival when the moon is apparently at its best for the whole year and we have a day off to celebrate. It's also a sign that the heat and humidity of the summer are finally on their way out.

Catherine Lee, Taiwan

ORDINARY TIME – DAY 161
EYES FIXED ON JESUS

Matthew 14.22–33

I am very grateful to Jesus for leading me back into a closer more prayerful relationship. The business and demands in my outer life can very easily hide emptiness in my most important relationship, which is with God the Father, Jesus the Son and the Holy Spirit. This does not mean I have automatically solved all my problems and am smiling only. But it means that my eyes are more fixed on *him* again, and I am more ready and willing to 'take the next step out of the boat'. (Guess what I have been reading . . .)

The funny thing about these steps is that they are not a 'one off event' in reality (like one could think from Peter's story), but they appear to be a lifetime's *daily* work. I certainly sometimes have the feeling I go under more then I walk . . . but his hand keeps me every time, and the honour goes all to him.

Ruth Hulser, Tanzania

How is God calling me to take the next step out of the boat today?

Lord, may we keep our eyes fixed on you, as we step out in faith today. Amen.

ORDINARY TIME – DAY 162
A PRE-FORGIVEN UNIVERSE

2 Timothy 1.8–10

This is a pre-forgiven universe. God had chosen in eternity to take upon himself the risk and the cost of creating this kind of world. As a precondition of creation, he took upon himself the judgement and death of the sinner. Being forgiven is therefore a more primary condition for us than being a sinner. Being in Christ is a more essential human state than being in ignorance of Christ. So any and every movement of the human mind and will that can properly be called a response of faith is truly faith in Christ to some degree even though Christ is still only the invisible magnetic pole that draws us on.

So, with our minds open to recognize the reality of the experience of divine grace and salvation within all the faiths of mankind, we can say that what God did through Jesus Christ is the one act which it was always necessary that he should accomplish in time and at the right time if he was to be the God who throughout time is accessible and present to every human being in judgement and mercy, grace and truth. Wherever we see people enjoying a living relationship with God and experiencing his grace we see the fruits of Calvary though this may be neither acknowledged nor known. It still makes a vast difference to people when they have seen the cross of Jesus as the indicator of the inner nature of God, and that remains the theme of the Christian witness. But in bearing that witness we do not have to deny the reality of the experiences of grace and salvation that are found, because of Christ, in all the faiths of mankind.

John V. Taylor

We praise you, Lord God,
for taking on the risk and cost of creating our world,
for your grace, which is from all eternity.
Let us be in Christ, as fully human and fully alive. Amen.

ORDINARY TIME – DAY 163
AMBASSADORS FOR CHRIST

2 Corinthians 5.20

The freedom and the protest of Jesus of Nazareth, his dying for us all and his resurrection, are both history and eternal reality. They happened, and they are the way things always happen. And we can be transformed, not only by relating to that past life and death and resurrection, in which the pattern was made plain once and for all, but also by relating to that true pattern wherever it emerges in the tissue of our contemporary experience.

Why then, look for more? Why seek conscious allegiance to Jesus Christ rather than let people live by the light they already enjoy? Not, John V. Taylor answers firmly, because there are no degrees of salvation apart from naming the Name, and certainly not because Christ is greedy for the credit. We seek conscious allegiance to Christ in order that everyone may rise to their full stature as adult daughters and sons of God, through attachment to him who was and is and ever shall be the fully human being because he is the perfect son. And if that perfect sonship could not be complete without the cross, then no one's salvation is complete until we become cross-bearers.

The common approach to salvation is to think of wholeness – atonement where there is now estrangement, restoration of lost harmony. Suppose, however, that we are so constituted as only to be truly human when we are bearing one another's burdens? If this is so, then the happy pagan has not yet in fact been made whole. Making love is not enough; one must actually say the words 'I love you.' To be a Christian within this or that particular furrow is not enough; one must perform the duties and obligations of being an ambassador. This is not so that anyone will switch from one religion to another. It is that men and women, all of us without exception, should experience the miraculous newness to be found in Christ and start living here and now as citizens of heaven.

David Wood

Lord, may we rise to our full stature in you,
learning what it means to bear one another's burdens,
to be your ambassadors,
to lead others to experience the miraculous newness of life in you. Amen.

ORDINARY TIME – DAY 164
THE EASTER EVIDENCE

2 Corinthians 3.18

The end is in God's hands, but meanwhile we ourselves are the Easter evidence. Mission for us is following the incarnate Lord, giving the Spirit our hearts and hands and lips, again and again becoming Christ's body now in the world. Cradled in Mary's arms, when we look with the eyes of faith, we see ourselves. As we might say, we see our real selves, human becomings in the process of transfiguration, on the way to resurrection after the pattern of the only true human being, the pioneer and perfector of our faith.

Let not my humble presence affront and stumble
your hardened hearts that have not known my ways
nor seen my tracks converge to this uniqueness.
Mine is the strength of the hills that endure and crumble,
bleeding slow fertile dust to the valley floor.
I am the fire in the leaf that crisps and falls
and rots into the roots of the rioting trees.
I am the mystery, rising, surfacing
out of the seas into these infant eyes
that offer openness only and the unfocusing
search for an answering gaze. O recognize,
I am the undefeated heart of weakness.
Kneel and adore, fall down to pour your praise:
you cannot lie so low as I have been always.

John V. Taylor

Holy Spirit, take us, take our hearts and hands and lips and transform us,
That we may become your body in the world. Amen.

ORDINARY TIME – DAY 165
THE GIFT OF TODAY

1 Corinthians 9.24

I have always been looking to the future for opportunities to glorify thee. I live in the future and not in this day that thou hast made. A life of dedication I want to have, but I am longing to have it only in the future. I want to make my relations pure only in the future. I am a Christian, in a dream, living in an unreal future world, neglecting the marvellous opportunities thou offerest me today. Lord, give me the strength to rise above the weakness of 'postponement' and continuously create in me a feeling of 'life is today', for tomorrow I may never be.

Meditation of a Christian from India

This day I will praise thee, O Lord:
This day I will thank thee, O Lord:
This day I will love thee, O Lord:
This day I will serve thee, O Lord.

Prayer suggested for use by an Indian theological college

ORDINARY TIME – DAY 166
SORROW AND JOY

2 Corinthians 1.3–4

Everyone has stories of amazing hardships, sacrificial sharing of resources that no one actually talks about and is taken for granted by them. Life here is a struggle beyond what we really know and expect. That is even before unemployment, illness or death happens. The cheerfulness, songs, laughter and prayer are one side of reality. There is another side that is equally deep and is filled with often exhausting struggles in everyday life. Both sides are as real, but the culture here does not permit to share easily any of your struggles.

Ruth Hulser, Tanzania

Thanks be to God – the God whose consolation never fails.
We thank you, Lord God, that you are within every sphere of reality, laughter, songs, illness, struggle – even death itself.
May we share together in the challenges of joys of life,
and in the consolation that you hold out to us. Amen.

ORDINARY TIME – DAY 167
A DIET OF TEARS

Psalm 51.16–17

A diet of tears is not savoury. O spirit of midnight, collect thou my tears in the bamboo tube. As my mass before God I will bring the tears of melancholy. I have now nothing else to offer on God's altar. Instead of the oil of the festival season I will bring before God my bamboo tube of tears. In it are stored tears of repentance, tears of gratitude for favours granted, tears in acknowledgement of blessings received, tears that flowed when emotions ran high, and tears of ecstasy. Created a child of tears, I am ashamed to advance into God's presence in the full light of day. Alone, in secret, in the midnight hour, I seek his face.

Melt, O pupil of my eyes! Let their very lenses stream forth. Shall I not offer up to God the very marrow of my soul. I yearn that these tears for the altar shall emit the sweetest fragrance. I want them to be as clear as crystal.

Tears! O tears! Tears wrung out of the soul's very marrow. Tears of ecstasy in drawing nigh to God! Tears of horror in not being able to enter into his presence. Tears that cause a plaintive melody as they alternate and intermingle! Come, O tears! Come without hesitation before God.

Toyohiko Kagawa, Japan (1888–1960)

No single teardrop lies hidden
From you
My God, my Creator, my Deliverer,
No, nor any part thereof.

Syria, Orthodox Church, St Simeon the Graceful

ORDINARY TIME – DAY 168
THOU ART OUR NEED

Philippians 4.19

Thou art our need and to thee we come, a song of thanksgiving in our hearts sweeter than the song of harvesting women, more eternal than the earth. For thy gifts are of thee, and thou art God, thou art Creator, thou art Giver, thou art Father, *thou art our need.*

Give us strength to multiply our love as a grain of rice multiplies its seed, as the rivers spread throughout the land, as the sound of drums reaches mountain crests. Give us strength to open our arms to those who hate us, to embrace thy son's 'seventy times seven', to make the words of our mouth as gentle as our Lord's 'Peace be unto you', to see no colour but thy forgiveness. O God, *thou art our need.*

From thy immeasurable love send the rain to our fields, send the sun and gentle it, give sweetness to the hands of those who make our harvesting tools, shield our fruit-bearing trees from barrenness, steady our bodies and make keen our eyes as we stalk game in the forest. Make our work in village and city, in field and office, fruitful to others and to ourselves and in thy sight.

O God, *thou art our need.* Strip fear from us as the hunter strips skin from his game. Let us in nothing be anxious. Let our courage be as steady as the giant cottonwood, as penetrating as the harmattan wind, as contagious as a child's laugh, for *thou art our need.*

From Africa

Lord – thou art our need.
Help us to trust your promise –
the riches of your grace.
May our love for others and for all creation
spring from your boundless love. Amen.

ORDINARY TIME – DAY 169
MEETING GOD

Mark 2.15–17

God dwells among the lowliest of men. He sits on the dust-heap among the prison convicts. With the juvenile delinquents he stands at the door, begging bread. He throngs with the beggars at the place of alms. He is among the sick. He stands in line with the unemployed in front of the free employment bureau.

Therefore, let him who would meet God visit the prison cell before going to the temple. Before he goes to church let him visit the hospital. Before he reads his Bible let him help the beggar standing at his door.

If he visits the prison after going to the temple, does he not by so much delay his meeting with God? If he goes first to the church and then to the hospital, does he not by so much postpone beholding God? If he fails to help the beggar at his door and indulges himself in Bible reading, there is a danger lest God, who lives among the mean, will go elsewhere. In truth, he who forgets the unemployed forgets God.

Toyohiko Kagawa, Japan (1888–1960)

When did you last encounter God in an unexpected person or place? Are you missing opportunities to meet with God?

Lord – remind us afresh that your presence is to be found in unexpected places. May we not confine you to religious buildings and rituals but discover you in one another and in the poorest of the poor. Amen.

ORDINARY TIME – DAY 170
SAILING TOO CLOSE TO THE SHORE

Luke 5.1–11

Disturb us, Lord, when we are too well pleased with ourselves,
When our dreams have come true
Because we have dreamed too little,
When we arrived safely
Because we sailed too close to the shore.
Disturb us, Lord, when
With the abundance of things we possess
We have lost our thirst
For the waters of life;
Having fallen in love with life,
We have ceased to dream of eternity
And in our efforts to build a new earth,
We have allowed our vision
Of the new heaven to dim.

Francis Drake (1540–96)

Like the disciples, do we fail to be fruitful in mission:

Because we are sailing too close to the shore, valuing comfort and safety above all else?

Because we are failing to listen and trust the words of Jesus, trusting in our own strength and self-confidence?

Because we are trying to 'go solo', when we're called to work together towards a shared vision?

Spend time reflecting on the Bible passage and questions – ask God to disturb any complacency that is holding you back.

ORDINARY TIME – DAY 171
ALL THE ENDS OF THE EARTH

Psalm 22.27–28

The other evening the whole family watched the sun go down over the magnificent mountainous skyline across from Suva harbour. 'Just think,' said my wife, 'as that sun is sinking here behind those hills it is rising in England.' That seemed to be a parable, somehow, of the presence of the Lord with us always, binding his people together across the world.

Letter from Fiji

> The sun that bids us rest is waking
> Our brethren 'neath the western sky
> And hour by hour fresh hymns are making
> Thy wondrous doings heard on high.
>
> So be it, Lord, thy throne shall never
> Like earth's proud empires, pass away;
> Thy kingdom stands and grows forever
> Till all thy creatures own thy sway.

John Ellerton (1826–93)

ORDINARY TIME – DAY 172
AS THE NIGHT WATCH LOOKS FOR YOU . . .

Psalm 130

> Come,
> Lord,
> And cover me with the night.

Spread your grace over us
As you assured us you would do.

Your promises are more
Than all the stars in the sky;
Your mercy is deeper than the night.
Lord,
It will be cold.
The night comes with its breath of death.
Night comes,
The end comes,
But Jesus Christ comes also.

Lord,
We wait for him
Day and night.
Amen.

A young Christian from Ghana

Lord, we wait for you
Day and night. Amen.

ORDINARY TIME – DAY 173
THE HONEYCOMB GOSPEL

John 5.1–6

Traditionally, we've been encouraged to see the gospel as a set of simple truths that follow on from each other. We start at the top and end at the bottom and whoever we are talking to has then had the whole gospel. However, there are lots of different ways of explaining the gospel, and lots of different places that we can start. We could start with 'sin' – all of us are sinful and separated from God; Jesus died for our sins on the cross; to get right with God we need to repent of our sin and receive his forgiveness. Or we could start with 'creation' – God created a beautiful world for us to inhabit in relationship with him; the whole creation, including our relationship with God, has been spoilt by us going our own way; Jesus died to reconcile us to God and to restore the whole creation.

Those two explanations don't contradict each other, but they start at two very different places.

Pete Ward, in his book *Youthwork and the Mission of God*, suggests that a more helpful understanding of the gospel 'might be to see theological truth as a 3D honeycomb or cluster of ideas. Any one of the key ideas within the honeycomb can act as an entry point or doorway to understanding the gospel. This model enables understanding of the gospel to develop in a more organic way, from one cell of the honeycomb to another in any order. When someone has understood all the key cells of the honeycomb and incorporated them into their lives, then they will be a disciple of Christ; the point at which they started is not important. This approach enables us to relate to people where they are and with the issues that concern them.

CMS Publication

Lord – help us today to meet people where they are,
at their point of need –
in need of companionship, healing, encouragement, challenge.
Help us to meet with them,
and through us may they encounter you. Amen.

ORDINARY TIME – DAY 174
A DOUBLE-EDGED SWORD

Hebrews 4.12

The Lumko method of action – reflection using the Bible
The method presented here was developed for neighbourhood gospel groups by the Lumko Institute, South Africa. From there, it has spread into many African countries and has been well received in other countries as well. It deals with a method of communal, prayerful approach to the sacred scripture which may help us to encounter God and one

another and to help us open our eyes to the presence and to the working of God in our everyday life. The Bible contains, is and imparts the word of God. It is a book that concerns us personally and likewise can make us concerned. This method provides the opportunity for allowing the Bible to speak to oneself first and, out of this perplexity, to share with one another (rather than just 'talk about' the Bible).

On the other hand, the Bible is a book that renders the faith experiences and faith testimonies of peoples from different times and cultures. We are standing in the living tradition of the people of God who have heard the word of God since Abraham and lived because of it. The Bible is therefore at times a strange and disturbing book. Hence, the meditative prayerful approach directed towards life is not the only one; rather it should be supplemented by biblical study.

Bible discussion and Bible meditation groups should not be too large. The ideal size is four to eight participants so that everyone may have the opportunity to talk. An atmosphere of quiet and calm is necessary. Just as important is an attitude of openness, of reciprocal listening in addition to the readiness to talk about oneself, that is, one's life and one's faith. The function of the facilitator consists only of this – that he or she announces the individual steps of the method.

The seven steps look very simple and indeed they are. Our experience in the dioceses of South Africa and elsewhere has shown us, however, that these 'simple' steps may also lead up to an encounter with God and our fellow humans.

Steps 1–4 help us to 'persevere' with God, to 'listen' to participate in the biblical action, 'to surrender ourselves to God'. **Step 5** brings us together as brothers and sisters, because we risk sharing our experience with God with one another. This is not the most important step, but it gives great joy to all those who want to build and experience a deeply human community in God. In **step 6** we confront our life with the word of God. It is often the case that in this atmosphere of prayer, individuals discuss problems that they wish to resolve as a neighbourhood group. In **step 7** all are invited to share in spontaneous prayer.

Rose Uchem

Reflect on how you have allowed the word of God to challenge you in the last week.

ORDINARY TIME – DAY 175
INVITING THE LORD

Jeremiah 33.3

First step: we invite the Lord
Once the group settles down, the facilitator asks someone to volunteer
'to invite the Lord'. The belief in the living presence of the risen Christ in
our midst is the presupposition and basis of our meditation.

We want to meet the Word who became flesh and dwells among us.
We remember Jesus' promise: 'Where two or three are gathered in my
name, I am there among them' (Matt. 18.20).

*Do we believe that when we gather to study God's word with fellow
Christians we are truly in the presence of the living Lord? How might our
lives today be different if we invited Jesus into every aspect?*

> Come among us, Lord Jesus,
> be in our meetings and our partings
> in our words and in our silence.
> Come among us
> and dwell in us today. Amen.

ORDINARY TIME – DAY 176
DWELLING ON THE WORD

Psalm 121

Second step: we read the text
The facilitator announces the chosen text. First the book, then the chapter. He/she waits until everyone has found the chapter and only then

announces the verse. When everyone has found the passage, the facilitator invites someone to volunteer to read the text. A moment of silence follows.

Third step: we dwell on the text
The facilitator continues: 'We dwell on the text. Which words strike you in a special way?'

In doing so, almost the entire text is listened to again. The participants spontaneously read aloud the word or words that have impressed them. Whole verses are not read, only short phrases or individual words.

The participants are encouraged to repeat those words silently to themselves three or four times. It is extremely important that a moment of silence be kept after each person has spoken, allowing the message to 'soak in'. As a result of this step, 'simple' words often take on new meaning.

What words strike you in a special way from the verses read in Psalm 121? Take time to reflect on those words, allowing them and their meaning to 'soak in'.

ORDINARY TIME – DAY 177
GOD IS NOT FAR FROM US

Psalm 145.17–18

Fourth step: we are quiet
After spending time on the individual word, the entire passage is read again slowly. Then the facilitator announces a time of silence, giving the exact length of time, for example, three minutes.

We advise the people to spend this time in silence before God. 'We are open to God.' 'We allow ourselves to be loved by him.' 'We let God look at us.' A helpful practice during this silence is to repeat a specific word.

Read Psalm 121 again.

Meditation: Simply to be open to God, to wait for him, to be with him, 'indeed he is not far from each one of us' (Acts 17.27).

ORDINARY TIME – DAY 178
SHARING FROM THE HEART

James 5.16

Fifth step: we share what we have heard in our hearts
After the time of quiet, the facilitator announces the next step: 'We share with each other what we have heard in our hearts.'

We do this to share with one another our faith experience and to help each other to grow in the faith. The entire sacred scripture is nothing less than a God experience which the people of Israel and Jesus 'share' with us.

It is somewhat strange that we can talk to friends about almost every aspect of our lives, yet when it comes to sharing with others our experience with God, we become shy. In this Bible meditation method, however, anyone can learn 'to risk' this sharing in a very natural and unpressured way.

Lord, give us grace, we pray,
to take risks in sharing with one another,
to confess to one another,
to acknowledge our needs to one another
and to pray for one another
In the name of Christ. Amen.

ORDINARY TIME – DAY 179
SEARCHING TOGETHER

1 Peter 5.6–7

Sixth step: we search together
The facilitator announces: 'We search together.'

Now the time has come for the participants to examine their lives in the light of the gospel. At this stage, a basic community might discuss everyday problems such as:

- Someone needs help in the neighbourhood . . .
- Children need instruction in the faith . . .
- Who will lead the Service of the Word next Sunday, since the priest will not be there? . . .
- How can we settle a discord that has arisen? . . .
- What can we do about getting the street lamp repaired? . . .

None of these problems needs to have a direct connection to the Bible passage that had been read and shared. However, they emerge and can be resolved because of the mutual confidence that now exists in an atmosphere of the presence of God. Things look different when God is allowed to be present.

Do we bring the most practical issues and problems we face to God, or do we consider them unworthy of his attention? Reflect on the practical issues that are troubling you or concerning you today. Bring them – however small – to God, allowing him to be present in the midst of our lives.

ORDINARY TIME – DAY 180
THE POWER OF PRAYER

1 John 5.14–15

Seventh step: we pray together
The facilitator now invites everyone to pray.

The words of scripture, the various experiences of God's word, the daily problems – these all become fuel for prayer. Some find this form of sharing in prayer the easiest way to communicate with others.

The participants are encouraged to incorporate in their personal prayer whatever has been of special importance to them during the meditation.

Only at the end is a formal prayer known to everyone recited.

Lumko Institute, shared by Rose Uchem

O Lord, we beseech thee to deliver us from the fear of the unknown future; from fear of failure; from fear of poverty; from fear of bereavement; from fear of loneliness; from fear of sickness and pain; from fear of age;

and from fear of death. Help us, O Father, by thy grace to love and fear thee only, fill our hearts with cheerful courage and loving trust in thee; through our Lord and Master Jesus Christ.

Akanu Ibiam, Nigeria

ORDINARY TIME – DAY 181
LORD OVER NATURE

Mark 4.35–41

Take time to reflect on the image of Jesus below. Is it an image that appeals to you? Does it reflect the Jesus you read about in the Bible? How does it challenge you to think differently about Jesus?

Who are you, O Lord, that even the winds and waves obey you?

ORDINARY TIME – DAY 182
FAITH IN THE ORDINARY

2 Corinthians 5.17

This is a painted wooden cross, made in memory of Maria Cristina Gomez, a Baptist woman in El Salvador. She was a primary school teacher and an active member of her church. She used to join with others in small groups to discuss the meaning of their faith in a country where violence and injustice are rife. In April 1989, Maria was kidnapped leaving school one day and brutally killed. People who knew her commissioned this cross to celebrate her life and faith. She was an ordinary woman; the painting shows her at work as a teacher, at home with her family, tending her animals. Her faith showed itself in the ordinary and everyday.

Spend time reflecting on what images would be painted on a cross celebrating your life and faith. Where is the cross reflected in your day-to-day living?

ORDINARY TIME – DAY 183
GENTLE JESUS MEEK AND MILD?

Luke 11.37–44

Take time to reflect on the image of Jesus below. Is it an image that appeals to you? Does it reflect the Jesus you read about in the Bible? How does it challenge you to think differently about Jesus?

Lord Jesus,
we thank you for your gentleness and compassion.
Forgive us when we domesticate you,
when we overlook your challenging words,
your claim on our lives.
Help us, Lord Jesus,
to see the whole of your life,
not just the parts we are comfortable with. Amen.

ORDINARY TIME – DAY 184
DEEPLY ROOTED

Luke 22.31–34

Powerfully
I am drawn to that which has grown slowly
And driven its roots deeply
Which has permanence
And knows the pains of growth.

To grow is my wish
But am I prepared to receive the wounds of life?
To let any weather pass over me?
Am I ready to give shelter to many?
Yet to seek shelter only with you?

I want to be radiant from the inside
I want to stand firm and to mature
To grow into you
To draw my roots deeply
To live through you
But I know
That the price is high.

Ulrich Schaffer

Henceforth, let me burn out for God. Amen.

Henry Martyn (1781–1812)

ORDINARY TIME – DAY 185
THE POWER OF A SMILE

Nehemiah 8.8–10

Did you know that there are 13 different acknowledged types of Thai smiles? Here they are: 'I'm-so-happy-I-am-crying' smile/ the polite smile for someone you barely know/the 'I-admire-you' smile/the stiff . . . 'I-should-laugh-at-the-joke-though-it's-not-funny' smile/the smile that masks something wicked in your mind/the teasing or 'I-told-you-so' smile/the 'I-know-things-look-pretty-bad-but-there's-no-point-in-crying-over-spilt-milk' smile/the sad smile/the dry 'I-know-I-owe-you-money-but-I-don't-have-it' smile/the 'I-disagree-with-you' smile, also known as the 'You-can-go-ahead-and-propose-it-but-your-idea's-no-good' smile/ the 'I-am-the-winner' smile/the smile in the face of an impossible struggle/and the 'I'm-trying-to-smile-but-cannot'.

The authors [Holmes/Tangtongtavy in *Working with the Thais*] explain that smiles '. . . *are intended to relieve tension, in an effort to preserve the relationship, social harmony on which people depend*'. In each culture where I have lived, I have tried to assess whether or not a smile is appropriate. Here all types are! Are we not all guilty at times of wearing one outside when we feel the opposite inside?

Curiously enough, the word 'smile' is not in my concordance. Apparently, in the European Middle Ages, Christians did not smile or laugh, as there is no scriptural reference to Christ doing either of these. Joy, encouragement and happiness are listed, but not how they were facially expressed! I am glad to be living in this era where the smiles of Jesus' followers should reflect genuine friendliness. More than one Buddhist monk has looked surprised when I smiled at them on the street.

The prophet Nehemiah says in 8.10: '. . . the joy of the Lord is my strength'. May this be true of us, and may we be aware of how our facial features are affecting others!

Shelagh Wynne, Thailand

Am I filled with joy and ready to smile whenever I have opportunity?

Father,
today, as I go about my daily life,
may I know your joy welling up within me
and even in the midst of difficulty and challenge,
may I bless others with a smile that speaks of your love. Amen.

ORDINARY TIME – DAY 186
A SCRIPTURAL FOUNDATION

John 2.1–11

Every spirituality needs to be rooted in scripture, and mission spirituality is no exception. One needs to ask the question, therefore, what passage(s), books, or themes of scripture are those that ground one's missionary life.

There may, of course, be some passages that figure large at certain times of one's missionary service. One may take strength and inspiration, for example, from some of the great vocation passages like Isaiah 6.1–8, Jeremiah 1.4–10, Matthew 4.18–22 (the call of Peter and Andrew, James and John), or Jesus' invitation to Andrew and Peter to 'come and see' in John 1.35–39. One may also be buoyed up in difficulty by Jeremiah's sufferings in Jeremiah 38, by Jesus' passion as a consequence of his own faithful missionary witness to the reign of God, or by Paul's being suspect by fellow Christians (Acts 9.23–30) or those whom he had tried to evangelize (for example, Acts 9.19b–25 or 13.50–52).

There may also be passages, however, that can provide basic guidance, inspiration and direction to one's work of crossing a culture, struggling with a language, being accepted by a people, bonding with the people among whom one works. Paul's passionate statement that he had become a slave to all so that he could win more of them to Christ – indeed, that he had become 'all things to all people', so that he might 'by all means save some' (see 1 Cor. 9.19–23) might serve as the anchor and beacon for missionaries in a very different culture from their own.

One of my own inspiring passages is that of John 10.10 – the reason for my ministry, the reason for witnessing to and proclaiming Christ, is to bring, like Jesus, abundant life to the world. One missionary in a course on missionary spirituality, my colleague Larry Nemer relates, chose as a foundational passage the story of the wedding at Cana in the second chapter of John's Gospel: the missionary, this person explained, is like water, but at the word of Jesus and in his hands he or she can be transformed into rich, joy-giving wine. The movement of the Acts of the Apostles has always struck me as a marvellous story of missionary spirituality. It is the Spirit who challenges, calls, pushes the Church beyond the boundaries of their understanding of the gospel to include all peoples and all cultures in the plan of salvation. It is precisely this move of the Spirit that calls the Jesus community to be church.

Steve Bevans

What passages of scripture are the ground of your calling to mission?

> Lord, we thank you for the inspiration and nourishment of your word.
> We pray that it may renew our call to mission,
> our call to follow,
> our call to stand firm in suffering,
> our call to bring fullness of life,
> to be water which will be transformed, by your hands,
> into rich, joy-giving wine.

ORDINARY TIME – DAY 187
MAKING SCRIPTURE LIVE

Romans 10.13–17

Along with other dioceses, Manchester promotes a shoe shine on Maundy Thursday as a modern take on foot washing. The cathedral clergy thought about this and decided to do it in the Arndale, which is Manchester's biggest city-centre shopping mall.

So in our red cassocks we went over to the centre and set up our stall in the Halle Square at the heart of the Arndale. We had four chairs, shoe shining equipment, and some leaflets explaining about Maundy Thursday and inviting people to church on Sunday. Despite the fact that it was a hot day and many were wearing sandals, we had a steady stream of 'customers', who were rather surprised by our free offer.

Shoe shining is a fairly intimate task and so you have five minutes to talk with your customer, explain about Maundy Thursday and Easter and listen to their story. One of my customers was a businessman who had come down from Glasgow; he shared how his sister had lost a baby at seven months the previous day; we were able to share in his pain and to offer our prayers and concern.

We had over 30 customers in the hour we had been allocated and had many conversations, even with those who didn't want their shoes shined.

The whole thing was possible because the dean of our cathedral spends time each week visiting the centre, being available for pastoral talks and building up relationships with the management there; his hard graft week by week now pays dividends in allowing us to be in the public square sharing our faith. And it was great fun!

Mark Ashcroft

How might we 'make scripture live'?

> Lord, give us creativity, we pray
> as we read what Jesus did
> and seek to live it out today.
> May we make scripture live,
> so that faith may come through seeing and hearing. Amen.

ORDINARY TIME – DAY 188
WEEPING FOR THE WORLD

Jeremiah 3.21

We live in a broken world full of need, some of which we see around us, and some of which we experience ourselves. Find a newspaper and tear out images and stories about brokenness in the world that needs God's love and intervention. Try to find stories that connect with your own life, as well as huge global issues – brokenness in families, neighbourhood, church, country and the world.

What does God want to do about this brokenness? What has he done already? How might he intervene in these situations to bring healing to the world? Like Jesus, we are called to have compassion on – to weep for – the world around us. God works through his people – he calls us to be involved in his mission. Look particularly at the stories that are local, Christ calls us first of all to where we are.

Place the newspaper cuttings around you and spend time praying for God's intervention in these situations of pain and need.

ORDINARY TIME – DAY 189
NEW EVERY MORNING

Lamentations 3.22–24

Every morning, when I draw back the curtains, the first thing that I see is a fresh array of the beautiful blue flowers of the plant called 'morning glory' that climbs over our garden fence. Perhaps the struggle to get it to grow has made success feel even sweeter. The special feature of this creeper is the fact that by the end of the day all the flowers, which I will always associate with Uganda, have died and every morning fresh ones are blooming, nudging the first words of a hymn into my mind. I will only quote the first verse but the other verses are well worth reading.

Rosalind Arnold, Uganda

New every morning is the love
Our wakening and uprising prove;
Through sleep and darkness safely brought
Restored to life, and power, and thought.

Spend some time praising God for the gift of a new day.

Father God, it is hard to hope each morning, to look forward to new treasures and mercies, discovered when we are alive to your presence in all that we encounter.
Open our minds to the endless possibilities of life and power and thought.

Help us to meet you in our everyday life, in our anxieties and difficulties, for you are there with us in our pain and sorrow.
Lift us from despair to new hope.
Restore and renew us each returning day, so that we may find joy in our journey with you. Amen.

From the Mozarabic Sacramentary (tenth century)

ORDINARY TIME – DAY 190
A MILLION MINOR MIRACLES

John 6.5–13

I'm standing at night in this subterranean place of prayer, and perhaps it's the coffee, or the music, or the Spirit, but the darkness doesn't seem too strong. I'm praying for miracles in the city where I live – for healings, and salvations, and justice, and revival, and all those usual kingdom kind of things. But tonight, as I do so, I find myself suddenly startled – like a boy blinking at fireworks – bewildered by how many miracles there already are.

It occurs to me that here in my city today, doctors dispensed healing – can you imagine anything more wonderful? Neighbours did favours. Dog-walkers in the park silently admired the shape of trees. Jokes were told in nursing homes. For a moment or two, thousands and thousands of people prayed, or wished, or merely unwittingly wanted what God wanted.

Chances are that somewhere today a young man and a young woman began to fall in love (although they don't yet know it). A teenager picked up trash she had not dropped. A single mother decided, just for once, to buy herself a slice of chocolate cake and to celebrate the moment in long, slow, mouthfuls of happiness. A painter-decorator stepped back from a wall he'd just painted the colour of claret, and maybe at that moment the sunlight broke through the window, and he saw that it was a good piece of work. A man resisted the temptation to click the link he wouldn't want his wife to see. Maybe he failed yesterday. Maybe he'll click it tomorrow. But today he overcame. In the hospital perhaps a surgeon pinned a broken arm with immaculate skill. Delicious food was prepared and cooked and served in thousands of homes joyously. A pastor's words, so carefully crafted, brought a little comfort to grieving relatives. People cried, but a check-out girl smiled at a lonely old lady. People died, of course, but babies were also born. From time to time today, I was born too. We all were. A million, minor miracles.

We do not pray *ex nihilo*. We pray for more of whatever it is we see. Nothing comes from nothing – certainly not faith like this. Tonight I'm blessing the evidence of miracles; the pre-existing goodness, the presence of Christ in these streets, these surgeries, these schools, these art galleries, these pubs, these homes, these wards. Witnessing so many minor miracles I applaud the world. If all of this is happening all around me, what might not happen next?

And so I stand here now in this subterranean place of prayer and it seems self-evident that there is more light in the night than darkness in the day. There is goodness breaking through, everywhere I look. And I'm praying for miracles tonight with greater faith than frustration for once. I can see creation rising like the moon above the Fall. Ultimately, almost inevitably, benevolence wins the day quietly.

I'm climbing the stairs to my car now, stepping out of the prayer room into the darkness. I'm driving home past houses and perhaps it's the music on the stereo, or the coffee, or the Spirit, but the city seems to me to have become the place of prayer.

Pete Greig, founding member of the 24–7 movement and director of prayer for Holy Trinity Brompton in a 24–7 prayer room in Guildford

Spend some time thanking God for the small miracles in the world around us.

ORDINARY TIME – DAY 191
LOOKING UPWARDS

Isaiah 40.21–23

The honest, unpretentious use of raw materials, the expanse of windows looking out to the world, will, I hope, say something. At the heart of our activity the chapel will be a pool of silence, as far as the architect can make it. Visually it is not cut off from the rest of the building, and from most points one can look right into it. It is important also that from inside the chapel one can look right out of it, not only back into the corridors and committee rooms, but, more importantly, down into the ceaseless traffic of the Waterloo Road. 'Glory to God in the High Street!' We are, I believe, only on the threshold of a new theology of the horizontal 'here-and-now-ness'. Yet we must not simply opt for that alone, and those who too readily abandon the vertical of God's transcendence are robbing us of an essential dimension. Now I understand why the angle between the east wall and the floor of our chapel had, from the beginning, been so crucial in my thought that I had asked for the floor to slope downwards and the wall inwards, as if to intensify that that point of intersection was the place for the overflowing font. It might be that the architect must suffer an unresolved conflict between the two foci of attention as the only honest symbol of a reality we are still groping to express.

John V. Taylor about the architecture of Partnership House, Waterloo Road

Father, in our worship, in our buildings, in our lives, may we reveal your presence among us and your presence beyond us. Amen.

ORDINARY TIME – DAY 192
GOD'S MISSION NEVER ENDS

2 Kings 2.9–15

The job we have been doing for more than seven years has now come to its end. But you well know that we started not just another job but instead God's mission. *God's mission never ends.* People's mission (a specific mission at a specific location) has its end, either because of God's plan for them to move to another stage of mission or because of their inability to do mission anymore (illness, death or other unfortunate circumstances).

Valentin and Daniela Kozhuharov, Bulgaria

God of eternity, give us grace to recognize our part in the
    bigger picture of your mission.
Give us grace to seek your face and to know your plan for us.
Give us wisdom to pass on the mantle of mission to others
and to know when the time is right. Amen.

ORDINARY TIME – DAY 193
HOW MUCH IS ENOUGH?

Proverbs 30.15–16

How much is enough? If people would only ask themselves this question more often, and answer it more honestly! The author of Proverbs 30 asked this important question, and also answered it himself. He had probably observed the excesses of Solomon and how these excesses had led to his spiritual downfall. He wrote this prayer in connection with money: 'Two things I ask of you, O Lord; do not refuse me before I die: keep falsehood and lies far from me; give me neither poverty nor riches, but give me only my daily bread. Otherwise, I may have too much and disown you and say "Who is the Lord?" Or I may become poor and steal and so dishonour the name of my God.' He rightly observed that too much material wealth could lead to disowning God. It is very difficult to express dependence on God when you have all that you need and more, and never have to pray for anything. On the other hand, it is very easy to dishonour God when your very survival and that of your family is at risk. He asked for daily bread – just enough, not too much. Life is lived one day at a time: too many of us worry about tomorrow and never get to live out today. Jesus also taught us to ask for 'daily bread'.

Dennis O. Tongoi

Take my life, and let it be
consecrated, Lord, to thee;
take my moments and my days,
let them flow in ceaseless praise.

Take my hands, and let them move
at the impulse of thy love.
Take my feet, and let them be
swift and beautiful for thee.

Take my voice, and let me sing
always, only, for my King;
take my lips, and let them be
filled with messages from thee.

Take my silver and my gold;
not a mite would I withhold.
Take my intellect, and use
every power as thou shalt choose.

Take my will, and make it thine:
it shall be no longer mine.
Take my heart: it is thine own;
it shall be thy royal throne.

Take my love; my Lord, I pour
at thy feet its treasure-store.
Take myself, and I will be
ever, only, all for thee.

Frances R. Havergal (1836–79)

ORDINARY TIME – DAY 194
PROPHETIC WORLD VIEW

Micah 6.6–8

At the heart of the evangelical movement in the London area was a group of laymen who lived in Clapham, then a large village separated from the city by three miles of meadow and common. All held important positions in public life, and happened to be neighbours in the parish of John Venn, the rector of Clapham. Moreover, some of them had first-hand knowledge of other parts of the world such as was rare in those days. Their lives were crowded with secular activities and responsibilities.

Their religion was intensely real. It was their habit to spend three hours daily in prayer and meditation (5 to 6 am; 12 noon to 1 pm and 5 to 6 pm). Their public life reflected the spirit of these hours. When they met, which they did frequently in the home of Thornton or Venn, it was to discuss the wrongs that must be righted and their own responsibility as people of their times.

So it came about they tackled the slave traffic and for 20 years (1787–1807) struggled untiringly for its abolition. Nor were they blind to the needs of England. When Wilberforce paid a visit to a friend in Somerset and found the children of the Mendip mining villages growing up 'ignorant, profane, and vicious beyond belief', he at once set to work to get schools started, and with Thornton's help paid for schoolmistresses for every hamlet. They stirred the conscience of the nation through the printed page. Books, cheap tracts, and a cheap magazine, the first to be sold at a cheap price of 1s were produced and found a ready sale. Indeed, as one of their number put it, the religion of the Clapham Sect was 'hardy, serviceable and fruit-bearing'.

R. E. Doggett

Let us give thanks; Let us give thanks to the Lord in the
   day of devastation;
Let us give thanks in the day of contentment.
Jesus has bound the world round with the pure light of the
   Word of his Father.
When we unite our hearts and beseech the Lord, and have hope
then the bad spirit (jak) has no power.
God (Nhialic) has not forgotten us.
Evil is departing and holiness is advancing;
this is the transformation which throws the earth into convulsions.

Song of Sudanese youth during visit to Southern Sudan by the Archbishop of
Canterbury in 1993, published in a link letter by Marc Nikkel

ORDINARY TIME – DAY 195
LIVING THE LIFE

Psalm 46.1–3, 7

Living the life
This call to a renewed mindset and a deeper discipleship is not new, but in the current global and local situation it has a renewed urgency. At the global level, humanity is facing questions and pressures never before experienced, and in the local situation of our own nation and society the economic issues we are facing will demand new ways of seeing and understanding. These things will be an immense challenge to the Christian

community, but could also be a God-given *kairos* moment. It is in this moment of crisis that Christians could not only speak a word of hope, but also live that hope in the power of God's Spirit and demonstrate the power of the age to come – the reality of the kingdom.

Imagine if you dare, individual followers of Jesus, and communities of such followers, living as 'wide awake' people seeking to share the grace and love of Christ at every opportunity and in every place. No longer limited to current church structures and thinking they would be willing to cross every frontier – political, ethnic, social – to share the love of the one who calls them, living with risk and vulnerability, but enabling that to happen through the deeply communal life they share. At the very heart of these communities would be the one who down the centuries and around the world has called his disciples to follow him into that world to share his transforming love.

Chris Neal

In this *kairos* moment,
may we be people who live your hope,
people who, throughout the world, demonstrate the power
   of the age to come.
God, speak to our hearts in this time,
speak to our hearts – and give us the vision, the courage,
   and the will to respond. Amen.

ACKNOWLEDGEMENTS

Every effort has been made to trace all the copyright holders, but if any has been inadvertently overlooked, the publishers will be pleased to make the necessary arrangements at the first opportunity.

Grateful acknowledgement is made to the following sources for permission to reproduce material in this book.

Advent 1	John Carden (ed.), *A Procession of Prayers*, London: Mowbray, 1998, p. 11. © Church Publishing Inc.
Advent 6	Carden, *Procession of Prayers*, p. 8. © Church Publishing Inc.
Advent 8	John Carden (ed.), *Morning, Noon and Night: Prayers and Meditations from the Third World*, Oxford: CMS, 1976, p. 32 © CMS
Advent 9	Carden, *Procession of Prayers*, pp. 65 and 89 © Church Publishing Inc.
Advent 10	Carden, *Procession of Prayers*, p. 126. © Church Publishing Inc.
Advent 18	Carden, *Procession of Prayers*, p. 132. © Church Publishing Inc.
Advent 20	Global Ideas Bank, *500 Ways to Change the World*, London: Collins, 2005, p. 167.
Advent 21	Carden, *Procession of Prayers*, p. 222. © Church Publishing Inc.
Advent 22	By Phi Potter, from 'The Challenge of Change', BRF www.brfonline.org.uk 2009, used by permission. p. 109.
Advent 25	Carden, *Procession of Prayers*, p. 26 © Church Publishing Inc. and John V. Taylor, The Go Between God, London: SCM, 2004, p. 90
Advent 26	Carden, *Procession of Prayers*, p. 24. © Church Publishing Inc.
Advent 27	Carden, *Procession of Prayers*, p. 28. © Church Publishing Inc.
Christmas Eve	Cheryl Lawrie 'Hold This Space', Proost www.proost.co.uk, used by permission
Christmas Day	Taken from a prayer by Doug Gay, *Alternative Worship, ed Jonny Baker and Doug Gay with Jenny Brown*, SPCK 2003, p. 16, by permission of SPCK
Christmas 2	Carden, *Morning, Noon and Night*, p. 60. © CMS
Christmas 6	Story from the Eden Project, Manchester
Christmas 7	Ruth Etchells, *Safer than a Known Way*, London: SPCK, 2006, p.166–7 adapted, by permission of SPCK

Christmas 8	Esther de Waal, *Living with Contradiction: An Introduction to Benedictine Spirituality*, Norwich: Canterbury Press, 2003, p. 139
Christmas 10	By Michael Mitton, from '*A Handful of Light*', www.brfonline.org.uk, 2008, p. 151–2 adapted, used by permission
Christmas Day 11	Gold Frankincense and Myrrh Confession by Mike Rose'Grace Pocket Liturgies' p. 62, Proost www.proost.co.uk, used by permission
Christmas 12	Carden, *Procession of Prayers*, p. 53. © Church Publishing Inc.
Epiphany	Carden (ed.), *Morning, Noon and Night*, p. 64 and *Maggi Dawn, Beginnings and Endings [and what happens in between]*, pp. 166–7 adapted, www.brfonline.org.uk, 2007, pp. 151–2 adapted, used by permission
Epiphany 3	Helder Camara.
Epiphany 4	Carden (ed.), *A Procession of Prayers*, p. 116. © Church Publishing Inc.
Epiphany 7	Mark Berry, taken from 'navigatio' Proost www.proost.co.uk, p. 18 used by permission
Epiphany 8	Carden (ed.), *A Procession of Prayers*, p. 127. © Church Publishing Inc.
Epiphany 10	Martin Luther King, from http://www.mlkonline.net/promised.html.
Epiphany 11	David Wood
Epiphany 12	*Not Strangers But Pilgrims*, Jamie Wallace, Pilgrims at Prayer, p. 2
Epiphany 13	Carden (ed.), *Morning, Noon and Night*, p. 81. © CMS
Epiphany 15	*Not Strangers But Pilgrims*, Bernard Thorogood. Pilgrims at Prayer, p. 1
Epiphany 16	David Wood
Epiphany 19	C.S. Lewis, *Mere Christianity*, HarperCollins, 2011. © HarperCollins
Epiphany 20	Robert Lentz, Lion of Judah Icon, © Trinity Stores.
Epiphany 21	Laughing Christ, artist unknown
Epiphany 22	Angry Christ, © Asian Christian Art Association/Pace Publishing 1991
Epiphany 23	first published in Jane Upchurch, *Inner Wellies* (Christian Education, 2010), used by permission
Epiphany 25	Max Lucado, *Cure for the Common Life* www.maxlucado.com.
Epiphany 27	Taken from *The Purpose Driven Life: What on Earth Am I Here For?*, by Rick Warren p. 238. Copyright © by Rick Warren. Used by permission of Zondervan. www.zondervan.com.
Epiphany 28	Carden (ed.), *A Procession of Prayers*, p. 37. © Church Publishing Inc.
Epiphany 32	Carden (ed.), *Morning, Noon and Night*, p. 87. © CMS
Epiphany 41	Steve Bevans, *Towards a Mission Spirituality*, p. 2, used by permission
Epiphany 44	Pete Grieg, pp. 24–7 Prayer Movement
Epiphany 55	Carden (ed.), *Morning, Noon and Night*, p. 24. © CMS

Epiphany 56	Christ entering Jerulsaem on Palm Sunday. © USPG Archives
Epiphany 57	Simon of Cyrene helps Jesus carry the Cross © Asian Christian Art Association/Pace Publishing
Epiphany 58	The Tortured Christ. © Oikumene
Lent 1	Anthony Bloom, *Meditations on a Theme*, p. 1. Reproduced by permission of Continuum International Publishing Group, a Bloomsbury Company
Lent 3	Jonny Baker (ed.), *Grace: Pocket Liturgies*, p. 62, Proost www.proost.co.uk, used by permission
Lent 10	Prayer of Archbishop Desmond Tutu
Lent 3	Jenny Baker, *Grace: Pocket Liturgies*, Proost www.proost.co.uk, used by permission
Lent 12	Carden (ed.), *A Procession of Prayers*, p. 250. © Church Publishing Inc.
Lent 13	Carden (ed.), *A Procession of Prayers*, p. 140. © Church Publishing Inc.
Lent 15	Adam Baxter, *Grace: Pocket Liturgies*, p. 78, Proost www.proost.co.uk, used by permission
Lent 17	Carden (ed.), *A Procession of Prayers*, p. 17. © Church Publishing Inc.
Lent 22	John Pritchard, *Telling it Slant: The Need for Eccentric Mission*, Crowther Centre monographs pp. 8–10 © CMS
Lent 32	Jeavons, Thomas H. *When the Bottom Line is Faithfulness: management of Christian service organisations*, Indiana University Press 1994, pp. 114 and 205. Used by permission
Easter 5	Jocelyn Murray, *Proclaim the God News, A short history of the Church Missionary Society*, ©1985 Church Mission Society, pp. 289, 292 © CMS
Easter 17	Carden (ed.), *A Procession of Prayers*, p. 115. © Church Publishing Inc.
Easter 18	Taken from *The Irresistible Revolution* by Shane Claiborne pp. 134–5. © by Shane Claiborne. Used by permission of Zondervan. www.zondervan.com
Easter 21	Jackie Elton, Taken from Grace Pocket Liturgies, p. 101, Proost www.proost.co.uk, used by permission
Easter 25	Adapted from Harry Baker, *Broken Blessing*, Proost www.proost.co.uk, used by permission
Easter 40	Carden (ed.), *A Procession of Prayers*, p. 315. © Church Publishing Inc.
Easter 42	Simon Barrington-Ward, 'My Pilgrimage in Mission', *International Bulletin of Missionary Research*, 23/2 *(April 1999)*
Easter 45	by Chris Neal, from *His Spirit is with Us*, p. 35. BRF www.brfonline.org.uk 1995, used by permission
Easter 46	by Chris Neal, from *His Spirit is with Us*, p. 58. BRF www.brfonline.org.uk 1995, used by permission
Easter 47	by Chris Neal, from *His Spirit is with Us*, p. 95. BRF www.brfonline.org.uk 1995, used by permission

Easter 48	by Chris Neal, from *His Spirit is with Us*, p. 125. BRF www.brfonline.org.uk 1995, used by permission
Easter 49	by Chris Neal, from *His Spirit is with Us*, p. 147. BRF www.brfonline.org.uk 1995, used by permission
Easter 50	by Chris Neal, from *His Spirit is with Us*, p. 147. BRF www.brfonline.org.uk 1995, used by permission
Ordinary 1	Carden (ed.), *Morning, Noon and Night*, p. 75. © CMS
Ordinary 2	Carden (ed.), *Morning, Noon and Night*, p. 116. © CMS
Ordinary 4	Carden (ed.), A Procession of Prayers, p. 28. © Church Publishing Inc.
Ordinary 12	Taken from *The Irresistible Revolution* by Shane Claiborne p. 113. © by Shane Claiborne. Used by permission of Zondervan. www.zondervan.com
Ordinary 22	Carden (ed.), *Morning, Noon and Night*, p. 86.© CMS
Ordinary 37	Dennis O Tongoi, *Mixing with God and Money*, Bezalel Investments Ltd 2001. Cited in CMS Daily
Ordinary 38	J. W. Poole, Meditation on faithfulness © RSCM, p. Cited in CMS Daily
Ordinary 40	Jonny Baker, in *Grace Pocket Liturgies*, p. 61. Proost www.proost.co.uk, used by permission
Ordinary 67	Claire Dalpra, *Encounters on the Edge: No 38, The Cost of Community*, p. 9, used by permission and Morning, Noon and Night, © CMS
Ordinary 69	Carden (ed.), *Morning, Noon and Night*, © CMS
Ordinary 71	Carden (ed.), *Morning, Noon and Night*, © CMS
Ordinary 71	Carden (ed.), *Morning, Noon and Night*, © CMS
Ordinary 74	Mike Rose, *Grace: Pocket Liturgies*, p. 36 Proost www.proost.co.uk, used by permission
Ordinary 79	Dietrich Bonhoeffer, and Carden (ed.), *A Procession of Prayers*, p. 118. © Church Publishing Inc.
Ordinary 92	by Phil Potter, from *The Challenge of Change*, pp. 110–11, BRF www.brfonline.org.uk 2009, used by permission
Ordinary 95	Carden (ed.), *A Procession of Prayers*, p. 119. © Church Publishing Inc.
Ordinary 91	Graham Buxton, *Celebrating Life*, p. 40 and Carden (ed.), A Procession of Prayers, p. 141. © Church Publishing Inc.
Ordinary 112	Frederick Brotherton Meyer, *The Secret of Guidance*
Ordinary 114	Carden (ed.), *A Procession of Prayers*, p. 146 and Clifton Clark, *Called to Serve*
Ordinary 117	John Clarke, Evangelism That Really Works, SPCK 1995, cited in CMS Daily
Ordinary 107	Graham Kings, 'Profit and Loss', Poetry in Mission, cited in CMS Daily
Ordinary 109	Bill Bryson, *A Short History of Nearly Everything*, p. 422 © Bill Bryson 2003, Transworld Publishers
Ordinary 122	Celebrating Creation, www.ecocongregation.org, cited in CMS Daily
Ordinary 123	Buxton, *Celebrating Life*, pp. 41–2

Ordinary 124   Cathy Kirkpatrick, 'New Beginnings', The Prodigal Project, SPCK Publishing 2000, cited in CMS Daily

Ordinary 125   Titre Andre, Bula Matari and Life-Community for God's Mission in Congo, Crowther Centre Monographs 2008, © CMS

Ordinary 126   Andre, Bula Matari and Life-Community for God's Mission in Congo, Crowther Centre Monographs 2008, © CMS

Ordinary 114   Taylor, *Go Between God*, p. 150 © SCM 1972

Ordinary 128   Brian D. McLaren, 'Emerging Values', Leadership Journal, Summer 2003, cited in CMS Daily

Ordinary 129   Kirkpatrick, 'New Beginnings', The Prodigal Project, SPCK Publishing 2000, cited in CMS Daily

Ordinary 130   Sr Joan Chittister OSB, The Rule of Benedict: insights for the ages, Crossroad Publishing Co US 1992, cited in CMS Daily

Ordinary 131   David Wood.

Ordinary 136   David J. Bosch, Transforming Mission: paradigm shifts in theology of mission, Orbis 1991, cited in CMS Daily

Ordinary 142   Bosch, *Transforming Mission*, cited in CMS Daily

Ordinary 149   Andrew Wheeler, *Bombs, Ruins and Honey*, pp. 80–1

Ordinary 150   C. René Padilla, *Global Challenges that the Church Faces Today*, 2008, cited in CMS Daily

Ordinary 155   Joseph G Donders, *Cross, Hope and Glory: Daily Reflections for Lent*, CAFOD 1990, cited in CMS Daily

Ordinary 158   Carden (ed.), *Morning, Noon and Night*, p. 55. © CMS

Ordinary 162   Taylor, *Go Between God*, © SCM 1972

Ordinary 163   David Wood.

Ordinary 164   Taylor, *Go Between God*, © SCM 1972

Ordinary 167   Carden (ed.), *Morning, Noon and Night*, p. 16. © CMS

Ordinary 168   Carden (ed.), *Morning, Noon and Night*, p. 21. © CMS

Ordinary 169   Carden (ed.), *Morning, Noon and Night*, © CMS

Ordinary 172   Carden (ed.), *Morning, Noon and Night*, p. 37. © CMS

Ordinary 181   Calming the storm © USPG archives

Ordinary 182   Maria Christina Gomez cross. © Christian Aid

Ordinary 183   The Lesser Brethren, by Margaret Tarrant. © The Medici Society

Ordinary 186   Steve Bevans, *Towards a Mission Spirituality*, p. 2 used by permission

Ordinary 190   Pete Grieg, 24–7 Prayer Movement

Ordinary 191   David Wood

Ordinary 196   Ana/Brian/Kevin Draper, from Labyrinth, Outward Journey – Proost, www.Proost.co.uk), used by permission